Kayaking Alone

OUTDOOR LIVES

Kayaking Alone

Nine Hundred Miles from Idaho's Mountains to the Pacific Ocean

MIKE BARENTI

University of Nebraska Press
Lincoln and London

Chapter 3, "Henry Clay Merritt, on His 158th Birthday," is reprinted from *River Teeth: A Journal of Nonfiction Narrative* 6, no. 2 (Spring 2005) by permission of the University of Nebraska Press. © 2005 by the University of Nebraska Press.

Chapter 10, "The Swallowing Monster on Pictograph Island," originally appeared in *Interdisciplinary Studies in Literature and the Environment* 13, no. 2, (Summer 2006).

Chapter 11, "Watching Fish at Bonneville Dam," originally appeared in *Ascent* 28, no. 1, (Fall 2003).

Library of Congress Cataloging-in-Publication Data
Barenti, Mike.
Kayaking alone : nine hundred miles from Idaho's
mountains to the Pacific Ocean / Mike Barenti.
p. cm. — (Outdoor lives)
Includes bibliographical references.
ISBN 978-0-8032-1382-1 (cloth : alk. paper)
1. Kayaking—Northwest, Pacific. 2. Nature—Effect of human
beings on—Northwest, Pacific. 3. Northwest, Pacific—Description
and travel. 4. Barenti, Mike. I. Title.
GV776.N76B37 2008
797.122'4—dc22
2007023925

Set in Quadraat by Bob Reitz.
Designed by Ashley Muehlbauer.

To Juliet and Syringa

Contents

Acknowledgments

Nobody ever writes a book alone, and without the help of many, many people this book wouldn't exist. I owe my biggest thanks to my wife, Juliet. She encouraged me to take the river trip that led to this book, drove what has to be the world's longest shuttle, and supported me while I was writing the book. I think she believed in me even when I didn't believe in myself.

I also need to thank Michael Aquilino and Carter Mackley, who lent me the whitewater kayak and sea kayak I used on my trip. Even though I have a small fleet of kayaks in my basement, theirs were better suited for the demands of an extended expedition than anything I own.

A number of biologists, geologists, and other scientists provided me with information on everything from weeds to the climate of the Northwest and were then willing to read what I wrote to ensure that I got the facts right. Some of those people are named in the text, many are not. I'd especially like to thank Steve Parker, with the Yakama Nation fisheries department, and Dale Bambrick, with the National Marine Fisheries Service. Both these biologists were always willing to answer questions and spent countless hours with me making certain I understood salmon biology. If some errors have made their way into the book despite Steve and Dale's best efforts, the fault is mine not theirs.

I need to thank Kim Apperson, a biologist with the Idaho Department of Fish and Wildlife; Dan Baker, the manger of the Eagle Fish Hatchery; Janine Castro, a geomorphologist with the U.S. Fish and Wildlife Service; Nathan Mantua, a research climatologist at the University of Washington; Rich Old, a botanist and weed consultant; Betsy Rieffenberger, a hydrologist with the U.S. Forest Service; and John Williams, a Research Fisheries Biologist with NMFS, for their assistance as well. I want to thank Charles Hudson with the Columbia River Inter-Tribal Fish Commission for always having the answer or getting me in touch with someone who had the answer.

I also owe a special debt of gratitude to the staff of the Bureau of Land Management's Cottonwood, Idaho, office, especially Lynn Danly, for talking to me about weeds along the lower Salmon River; Bob Lewis, for information about the geology along that same stretch of river; and Ron Grant and LaVerne Grussing, for information about proposed hydroelectric projects on the main Salmon.

I would be remiss if I didn't thank Elmer Ward and Marlene White, not only for their friendship over these past several years but also for their willingness to answer my questions about the region's American Indians.

As for the actual writing, I would like to thank Kristin Henderson, for her encouragement and her excellent comments on my manuscript, and Joeth Zucco, with the University of Nebraska Press, for her hard work and fine editing. I want to thank all the students and faculty at Eastern Washington University's Inland Northwest Center for Writers where I earned my Master of Fine Arts in creative writing. But I owe special thanks to Professors Jonathan Johnson and Natalie Kusz. This would be a very different book without their input and support.

Finally, I'd like to thank all the people I met and talked to while I was on the water. I was always impressed by their openness, their willingness to answer questions, and their desire to help.

Kayaking Alone

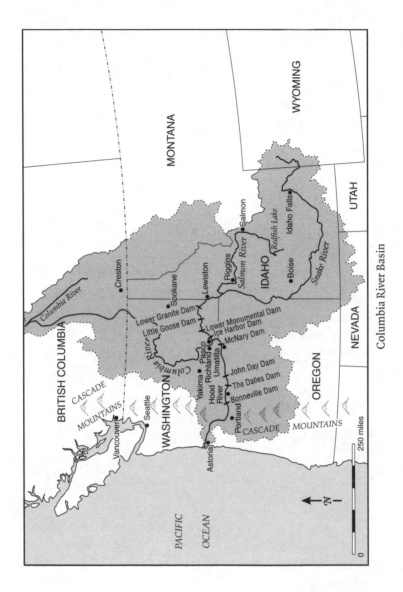

Columbia River Basin

1

Sunbeam

But exaggerated, uninformed, unrealistic, greedy expectation has
been a prescription for disappointment that the West has carried to
the corner drugstore too many times. —Wallace Stegner, *Where
the Bluebird Sings to the Lemonade Springs*

Idaho's Redfish Lake sits in the bottom of a great alpine bowl
formed by mountains—the Sawtooths, the Boulders, the White
Clouds—in a place where one mountain range melds into the
next so their names seem almost irrelevant. A creek lined with
quaking aspens and lodgepole pines meanders out of the lake's
north end then pools, creating a much smaller lake, Little Redfish, which pours itself into the Salmon River down a second
creek. In its last four or five hundred yards, rushing as if in
some great hurry, the second creek crashes over boulders polished smooth by time and flowing, pale blue water the color of
a tropical ocean, although there is no ocean nearby, and at sixty-
five hundred feet in altitude and snow possible any month of the
year, the spot is anything but tropical.

On a warm Sunday at the end of May, my fiancée, Juliet, and
I camped where that second creek meets the Salmon River. We

spent the afternoon going through all the food, clothing, and camping gear necessary for my two-month kayak trip to the Pacific Ocean to make sure I wouldn't forget anything. Afterward, I tried packing it all into my kayak and discovered there wasn't room. I told myself the packing wasn't for real, and I imagined that somehow I would make everything fit when it really counted. Of course the next morning, May 28, the water filter, the backpacking stove, the fuel bottles, the clothes, the spare two-piece paddle, the two pots that fit together like nesting dolls and would also serve as plates, and the Ramen noodles and the pasta and the instant couscous and the Pop Tarts and the oatmeal and the cashew nuts and the granola bars all took up as much space as they had the afternoon before.

The kayak provided roughly as much storage as a large backpack, and I already had saved space where I could. Instead of a tent, I had opted for a bivy sack, which is little more than a waterproof sleeping bag cover. Instead of a bulky synthetic sleeping bag that would keep me warm even if it became wet, I had opted for a lightweight down bag that compressed to about the size of a loaf of bread. I had too much food, like I always do, figuring that being cold and damp isn't so bad, but being cold and damp and hungry really sucks. I could occasionally buy more groceries when I passed one of the small towns scattered beside the Salmon, Snake, and Columbia rivers, three rivers I planned to kayak. So I decided I could leave a quarter of the food behind without any worries. I also had three thirty-three-ounce bottles of white gas, plus a twenty-two-ounce bottle I vowed to use only in an emergency, making me the kayaking equivalent of a super tanker. One large fuel bottle stayed behind, and a second probably could have, but didn't.

I went through my clothes. I had a pair of pants with zip-off legs, a couple of t-shirts, a rain jacket, assorted fleece pants and pullovers, and two sets of polypro underwear—one set to wear on the river for insulation beneath my waterproof top and waterproof pants and one set to wear around camp in the evening.

I moved my high-tech rain jacket into the leave behind pile. "You're not taking that?" Juliet asked. She grabbed the jacket and folded it into one of its own pockets clearly marked "stow pocket." Holding up the jacket, now smaller than a small box of crackers, she said, "You have room for that, don't you." It was more a statement than a question. "I bet you didn't know you could do that," she said. I hate it when the gear's smarter than I am. I tossed the fleece pants and a fleece top into the stay behind pile instead.

I shoved anything water wouldn't hurt into the stern of the kayak. Anything water might damage went into special bags, called dry bags, designed, as the name implies, to keep things dry. The bags filled the kayak's bow and stern sections, but somehow, everything fit. I pushed my head and hands through the water-tight rubber gaskets of my dry top, pulled on my life jacket, put on my helmet, slid into the kayak, hooked my legs under the kayak's thigh braces, and pulled the neoprene spray skirt over the cockpit rim to seal water out. Before she pushed the kayak into the river, Juliet kissed me and told me to be careful.

If I died on the trip—pinned upside-down against some rock, floundered in a terminal hydraulic, bailed out of the kayak and drowned during a long swim in rough water—someone, somewhere, would say I got what I deserved for kayaking alone. All the whitewater safety books say never boat alone. Many kayakers break that rule at some point, but that doesn't make it any safer. I'm certain the idea of me alone on the river worried Juliet. She and I have paddled many rivers together—we met through mutual friends while kayaking—and by the time I left on the trip she knew I was a careful boater who had some common sense when it came to whitewater. But if the situation had been reversed, I would have worried about her, even though she is a fine kayaker and capable of taking care of herself in isolated places, having once lived for a year in the Central American rain forest doing biological field work.

Juliet and I had just one discussion about safety before the trip started. My parents had sent me a walkie-talkie-sized emergency locator beacon called an EPIRB, which when activated, allows satellites to determine its position and relay that information to search and rescue teams. I had planned to leave the EPIRB behind, reasoning that it would go in the back of the kayak, out of reach, and that the biggest danger I faced was flipping, missing my roll, swimming, and becoming separated from the kayak and the EPIRB. Juliet had said she would feel better knowing I had the beacon.

Along with the EPIRB, I stashed a rope, web slings, Prussic loops, and carabineers—equipment used to free a boat if it becomes pinned on a rock—in the back of the kayak. Of course a pin kit is used to pull somebody else's kayak free and in reality was just as useless as the beacon. But I needed the ropes and slings with me in the same way Juliet needed me to take the EPIRB.

Not long after Juliet pushed me into the river, the Salmon dropped into a steep-walled canyon that closed out the world. The valley with its road, ranches, and expensive vacation homes disappeared. The river has just started its tumble toward the ocean, so it's shallow and filled with riffles instead of whitewater. The kayak constantly bounced off rocks, and I couldn't paddle without hitting river bed. An osprey resting on a half-dead conifer took to the air just before I reached its perch, flew downstream, and landed in another tree. And just before I reached that tree, it took off, flew downstream, and again perched. When it flew away the third time, the canyon had opened up enough for the bird to turn upstream. The road came back to the river, and I half expected to see Juliet pulled off on the shoulder, but she was already on her way home. I suddenly felt lonely, something I hadn't expected. The river kept pushing me downstream.

Except for a short stretch just down from Redfish Lake, the Salmon flows north from its headwaters to the town of North Fork, where the Bitterroot Mountains force it west. At Riggins, the river again turns north before looping west to meet the Snake

River. I planned to follow the Salmon 400 miles from its headwaters to the Snake, then, once on the Snake, paddle 189 miles to the confluence with the Columbia River before kayaking another 325 miles to where the Columbia meets the Pacific Ocean; roughly 900 miles in all.

In the autumn of 2000, when such a long kayak journey was only a vague notion, I had watched hundreds of salmon stranded in an eastern Washington irrigation ditch. I was there for my job as a reporter for the local newspaper, but random people pulled their cars to the side of the road and got out to gawk as well. Water diverted from the upstream reaches of the Yakima River washed through the ditch, and any not used for irrigation was returned to the main river many miles below its original diversion point. For the fish, the water carried the odor of home, and it pulled them from the main river with a force as strong as gravity. A spillway created a barrier, and the salmon crowded below it into a pool littered with pop cans and fast-food containers to hurl themselves, like fin and scale rockets, at the obstacle and continue their migration. But the spillway was impassable.

Not long after seeing those salmon, I decided that in spring I would quit my job and take a long river journey. Growing up in Virginia, I had worked briefly as a commercial fisherman and for a much longer period as a mate on a sport-fishing boat. While I rarely fish anymore, I retain a fisherman's interest in fish, meaning that anyone other than another fisherman or maybe a fisheries biologist would find my level of fascination strange. But fisherman or not, nobody living in the Northwest can completely ignore salmon. Salmon delineate the Columbia and its tributaries as clearly as any lines on a map. In 1805, camped near the Salmon River, the Shoshone Indians offered Meriwether Lewis salmon, and from that gift he deduced correctly that the Corps of Discovery had reached a Columbia tributary.

I picked the Salmon River's headwaters as my starting point not just because I had come to love the river during the time I had lived in Idaho, but also because it remains free of dams in a part of the country where dams span almost every river. Only sabotage kept the Salmon River undammed. Or maybe it wasn't sabotage but an official act. Some people claim whoever dynamited the river's only dam in the early thirties, various stories say 1931 others 1933 or 1934, worked for the state and did the demolition with Idaho's official blessing. Some people claim he acted on his own.

I started my trip at Redfish Lake, a half-day's paddle upstream from the ruined dam, not to unravel the mysteries behind the dam's destruction—they were too old and others had already attempted that with little apparent success—but because Sunbeam Dam was destroyed to save Redfish Lake's sockeye salmon, and now talk of removing dams to save salmon is constant. My plan was to navigate the same currents the lake's endangered salmon follow on their way to the ocean, making fish as much a part of my trip as kayaking.

By the time I started down the river, the Salmon should have flowed dark and sullen, pushed its way into groves of riverside trees, left its muddy stain on whatever it touched, but after a winter when half as much snow as usual had fallen, it ran clear and confined within its banks. A woman had told me the river normally reaches high water the second week of June. That spring it had peaked May 17. I rode the ice clear river through the town of Stanley past wood-sided outfitters' shops, hotels, restaurants, the houses where some of the town's hundred year-round residents live, and toward the remains of Sunbeam Dam. The valley floor turned mostly level and sometimes treeless, and for a while I could see the naked granite of the Sawtooth Mountains off to my left.

Beyond Stanley, forests of lodgepole pines ran down steep hills then spread themselves along the Salmon's rocky shore. Groundwater dripped and dropped its way into the river. Creeks added their flow. The river became deeper. It pushed harder. The kayak no longer bumped across rocks. My paddle no longer hit bottom. In a deep pool where a salmon might pause its migration home, I stopped to put on the pair of nose clips that hung by a cord from my helmet. I twisted my body to the left, held my paddle parallel to the kayak, took a deep breath, rocked my hips, and flipped. The water was as cold as melted snow.

Normally, one of the first things I do when I put on a river is snap off a roll or two, and I was especially anxious to practice that first day. My kayak was borrowed. It was German made and popular with expedition paddlers because it holds a lot of gear, but some people also claim it's hard to paddle and hard to roll. For psychological reasons, I had stayed away from the boat since winter when I had paddled it around an indoor swimming pool. I didn't want something to go wrong on a river that would destroy my confidence. So in the run-up to the trip, when I had paddled almost every day for two months, I had used my own boat and spent most of my river time surfing waves or trying to cartwheel the kayak bow over stern.

Upside down, setting up for that first roll, my pre-trip preparation seemed half-assed. My left hand always touching the boat, I swept my paddle in an arc until my kayak looked like the letter T drifting downriver, with my paddle as the base crossed by my boat. The upper body doesn't do much work rolling a kayak. Instead, the paddle acts like a stabilizer so the hips can right the boat. It's even possible to roll without a paddle. I snapped my hips. The force drove the kayak right side up. I took my helmet off, shook myself dry like a wet animal, put the helmet back, and relaxed a little. I flipped and rolled again and then again. Each time, my head came out of the water last, which is perfect form.

The kayak actually rolled better loaded than it had in the pool, but that was the only thing it did better. I worked on my forward strokes, planted the paddle in the water as close to vertical as possible and pulled it back not with my arms, but by unwinding my torso. I tried reverse strokes then the sweep strokes used to turn. A whitewater kayak is designed to turn, and a skilled kayaker flows down a river like a dancer turning graceful pirouettes, kayak and kayaker moving as one; an unskilled kayaker staggers like a baby taking its first steps, unable keep a straight line, unable to control a turn, boat and boater irreconcilably disjointed. Although I always imagine myself looking more like a dancer and less like a toddler in my kayaking, I fall somewhere between the two extremes. That first day on the Salmon though, I staggered.

The extra weight from my supplies made the kayak hard to handle. I tried to carve into eddies, my paddle acting as a fulcrum so the kayak could pivot upstream and come to rest in the calm water. Instead, I hit the rock that formed the eddy, or turned far enough below the rock there was no calm, or blasted through the calm back into the river's current, or stalled on top of the unstable line of water where the river's current, which moves downstream, met with the eddy's, which moves upstream. If I did hit an eddy cleanly, when I peeled out into the river again, I couldn't control the bow or use the water's energy to accelerate the kayak as it turned downriver. If I managed to make a good downstream turn, I couldn't keep the kayak on the right line. It always takes time getting used to a loaded kayak and nothing I went through was unusual. After some practice, I caught eddies cleaner and peeled out smoother.

But that initial awkwardness stressed my confidence at a time when I already felt uncomfortable. I wasn't paying attention to the river. So I didn't hear it grow noisier or feel its pace quicken or notice the looming horizon line until I fell off the edge and into whitewater froth. Too late to eddy out or read the water. Too late to sort rock from river, hydraulic from green water. I flipped and rolled on instinct. With half a rapid left, I paddled hard because in a kayak, when you don't know what to do, you always paddle hard. The kayak sounded a hollow plastic thud against a rock that should have stopped the boat but didn't. I almost flipped again. The kayak went straight. I wanted it to turn right. Then, as abruptly as it had all started, I was breathing hard, sliding through a calm, green pool, and looking back upstream at the rapid trying to figure out what had happened.

I faced Sunbeam next. I had seen a clear line through the rapid formed by the old dam's rubble when Juliet and I had stopped to scout the day before. But Sunbeam Dam had worried me from my first paddle stroke. The clumsy run through the first rapid only made me worry more, and not some abstract who blew up the dam or what did the dam do to the salmon worry, but a worry hard as rebar and concrete and sharp-edged blocks of dynamited granite.

A mining company built Sunbeam in 1910 and used its electricity to light the company's mine and run a mill that crushed rock so gold could be extracted. But the rock contained so little gold that the company couldn't turn a profit. It went out of business the next year. The dam, built without any passageway for salmon migrating upstream, remained. Although attempts were made in 1912 and again in 1920 to add fish ladders to the dam, nobody knows if they worked.

With no way past Sunbeam, the dam should have wiped out Redfish Lake's sockeye salmon. Sockeye are what I sometimes picture when I hear the word salmon, probably because they were the first of the five species of Pacific salmon I ever saw. In the ocean, sockeye are silver with a bluish back. In freshwater, as they prepare to spawn, they turn a deep red, redder than the reddest sunset, along their flanks, while their heads turn greener than a river's deepest pool. Sockeye feed on plankton, but at breeding time, the males grow hooked jaws reminiscent of the pincers on some evil sci-fi robot and sharp teeth line the jaws. Most sockeye spawn along sandy lakeshores, in small streams that feed into a lake, or just below lake outlets, and after hatching, the juveniles spend one or two years in that lake before migrating to the ocean. Such a life history makes it unlikely any sockeye would have spawned in the river downstream of Sunbeam, and there were no other sockeye nearby to stray into the lake to repopulate it once the dam was gone.

Still, by the 1950s, sockeye had returned to Redfish Lake. Sometimes they came in the thousands, sometimes in the hun-

dreds. Salmon biology explains how sockeye stayed alive in Redfish Lake even when they shouldn't have. Pacific salmon can live
out their entire lives in freshwater. Chinook and coho salmon
stocked years ago into the Great Lakes by fish and game depart-
ments survive by spawning in tributaries and maturing in the
lakes. Landlocked sockeye populations exist in lakes throughout
the West, including Redfish. These landlocked sockeye, called
kokanee, are much smaller than ocean-going sockeye (maybe a
foot long instead of two), but are the same species, with the same
scientific name, *Oncorhynchus nerka*. When the federal government considered listing the Redfish Lake sockeye as an endangered species, some people argued Sunbeam had killed off the
ocean-going sockeye. The resurrected sockeye were simply kokanee that had started migrating to the ocean, and since Redfish
Lake's kokanee and sockeye were really part of the same population, and there were plenty of kokanee, the sockeye didn't qualify
as endangered, they said. That hypothesis and several others ex-
plaining the sockeye's presence were looked at and rejected. The
fish were listed in 1991 despite lingering questions.

A genetic study later uncovered fish that looked like kokanee,
and never left the lake like kokanee, but that were genetically
similar to ocean-going sockeye. The scientists conducting the
study theorized that after Sunbeam was built, some sockeye
survived in the lake. These "residual sockeye," as the scientists
called them, spawned in different places and at different times
from the kokanee, so the two groups never mixed. When Sunbeam was dynamited, some of the residual sockeye's offspring
could again migrate to the ocean and back.

I don't know if each spring, for the twenty-some years Sunbeam existed, groups of juvenile sockeye smolt, pulled by the
ocean and already transforming themselves into saltwater fish,
made their way downstream, found their path blocked, and so
returned to the lake. Maybe some smolt made it past the dam to
the ocean, only to find the dam impassable when they returned as
adults. If that's the case, if some sockeye migrated to the ocean,

then genetics must have kept others tied forever to the lake, and with each generation some must have left the lake while others stayed put. This is speculation on my part, not science, but I can figure no other way succeeding generations of sockeye could know the dam had disappeared.

I like to think of the genetic variability and the force of instinct that enabled those salmon to endure. I keep that force and the complex genetics in mind whenever I hear or read about the Columbia River salmon's slide into oblivion. If sockeye could survive in Redfish Lake, then maybe salmon can persist in the Columbia and its tributaries, even though science paints a bleaker picture.

The Columbia's salmon now exist perpetually at the edge of extinction. For more than a hundred years, people have argued over their fate, faulted one group or another for their decline, and suggested doing this or that would revive the runs. In the 1930s the federal government started building large hydroelectric dams on the Columbia and its tributaries, and since then, dams have taken much of the blame for the salmon's precarious existence. The concern over dams destroying salmon runs intensified after the government built four dams on the lower Snake between Lewiston, Idaho, and the river's confluence with the Columbia. As salmon runs steadily declined and scientific evidence accumulated showing that the four Snake dams were damaging fish runs on the Salmon and other rivers, some people began talking about removing, or breaching, the dams on the lower Snake. Others, predictably, claim breaching the dams will not help salmon but will cripple the economies of Idaho, Washington, and Oregon.

People hold a variety of opinions about salmon and what to do as their numbers dwindle. Some people depend on the fish for their livelihood or their culture or both and would accept almost any plan, no matter the hardships, if salmon once again would fill the rivers. Some see the fish as symbols, either of the region or as a sort of living representation of the natural world, and they too seem willing to endure some hardship for salmon. Some people want salmon but would sacrifice nothing for them; some wouldn't care if salmon went extinct; a few probably never even think about salmon, the final group growing larger the farther they live from a river with salmon in it. Between each opinion exists another opinion multiplied off into infinity. I often use the collective pronouns "we" or "us" when I talk about salmon. In my journalist's attempt at objectivity, I try to see myself holding almost any opinion, even ones I don't agree with; I also think that all of us are responsible for the salmon's future.

Because nobody can agree on what to do about salmon, the government has sometimes concocted strange plans to maintain populations while debate continues. By the time the Redfish Lake sockeye were listed as endangered, they had almost vanished. Some years only four or eight adults returned from the ocean, some years one, some years none. So a captive breeding program began. Biologists took fish from the lake, both adults and juveniles, as brood stock for a hatchery near Boise, Idaho. Each year, four hundred eggs, carefully selected for their genetic diversity, are culled from the thousands of sockeye eggs collected at the hatchery. The salmon born from those eggs spend their lives not in a lake or river or ocean, but in concrete hatchery pens. Another four hundred sockeye are raised at a separate hatchery just in case something kills all the hatchery sockeye near Boise.

According to the federal government, the program is viewed as a "short-term safety net, pending decisions about longer-term approaches." It's not clear anybody knows what those longer-term approaches will be. Juvenile sockeye not used for the captive breeding program are released and will spawn in the lake if they survive their time in the ocean. The goal is to have two thousand sockeye return each year to Redfish and two other nearby lakes. But in the best year, only a couple hundred fish have made it back. Running the Idaho hatchery costs more than seven hundred thousand dollars a year and a group of economists recently estimated that each sockeye returning to Redfish Lake costs close to seventy-five hundred dollars apiece.

Maybe our willingness to spend so much money to preserve Redfish Lake's sockeye proves that Sunbeam Dam is part of the past. Maybe now most people would choose salmon over some business that will eventually come to an end. It's hard to say. In the late 1930s and again in the 1940s and 1950s, a company operated a gold dredge on the Yankee Fork, which joins the Salmon just past Sunbeam Dam. The huge craft had plied the river, scooping up streambed. The gold gone, the dredge now sits like a bleached shipwreck beside the Yankee Fork and mounds of what once was river bottom rest nearby in long rows like brown banks of rocky snow pushed up by a plow. The gold dredge wrecked the Yankee Fork as salmon habitat. Over time, restoration projects have improved the river's habitat, but salmon runs remain far below historic levels.

In the 1990s, an open pit gold mine that used cyanide to separate gold from rock was started near a creek feeding into the Yankee Fork. Like the mine powered by Sunbeam Dam, the new mine lost money, and three years later the owners closed it. Cyanide-tainted water from the five-hundred-million-gallon tailings pond remained, and eventually small amounts of tailings-pond water started to leak into nearby streams. People worried about what the water—tainted with mercury and cadmium, as well as cyanide—would do to the salmon that spawned in the Yankee Fork and in the main river. The mining company controlled the leaks, and various government agencies have decided to let the company drain the pond, slowly, without treating the water. Instead the river will dilute the deadly waste.

When the next mine or timber sale or who knows what else that might threaten salmon is proposed, I'm certain some people will protest, but I'm not certain economic or political expediency won't win the day. Even I might be willing to compromise for the sake of jobs and the economy, although I would like to think I wouldn't. I am certain that after the damage was done, everybody would be willing to spend hundreds of millions of dollars to try to undo it. It seems too early to relegate Sunbeam to the past.

Sunbeam's remains abut cliffs of solid granite, and this combination of suitable geology and a location close to a mine that needed electricity must have made the site irresistible to the mining company. The same granite cliffs that anchored the dam also force the road away from the river and mark the start of another small canyon. When I reached the canyon, I was still unnerved from the previous rapid and wished I could wait a day, or a week, to run the whitewater formed by the dam's rubble. But that wasn't possible. Sunbeam was right there and I had to deal with it. I paused in an eddy, took some deep breaths, and watched the water. I searched for a clean line through the rapid. Given time, anybody can learn to see river hazards, realize foam piles signal powerful hydraulics, unmoving mound waves signal pour-over rocks, rooster tails signal a rock or some other obstacle near the water's surface, but reading a river means more than just spotting hazards. It means watching how the water flows and finding lines where the currents will carry a kayak past danger.

Downstream, a section of dam jutting out from the river's left bank, or river left as a kayaker would say, forced water into a chute against the right bank. In between the green-water chute and the dam, the river tumbled through a series of dynamited granite and concrete ledges that turned the water white as the foam from a blender set on frappe. I wanted to miss the blender foam but couldn't just paddle along the right bank and slide down the chute. At Sunbeam, the river turns right, not in a gentle curve, but in a kink that straightens out almost immediately. An approach from the right would have sent me not down the chute, but across it and into the very place I wanted to avoid.

From my scouting eddy on river left, hard paddle strokes launched me across a watery seam stitched by opposing currents and into the main flow. The kayak picked up speed as the bow arced downstream. But the turn wasn't controlled. I found myself parallel with the current and headed into danger. I did a sweep stroke on the left. The kayak nosed back on course. I paddled hard to cut across the main flow. I dropped into the chute. A small eddy caught the bow and tried to turn the kayak upstream. I almost flipped but somehow stayed upright.

I have run twenty-foot waterfalls, but in the loaded kayak, a rapid that was only a class three—on a scale that rates a class one as easy and a class six as unnavigable—had the potential to create havoc. I was frustrated. I always want to be a better kayaker than I actually am, and when I don't run a rapid as cleanly as possible, I sometimes let it rattle me. I stopped to calm myself, stretch my legs, and eat lunch at the Salmon's confluence with the Yankee Fork.

While I ate, a family—father, teenage son and daughter, and a woman in her twenties I eventually assumed was a family friend—slid a raft into the river. I walked over, told them I was kayaking alone, and asked if I could float with them. "No problem," the father said. My lack of confidence startled me. I did strange things those first few days on the river. One night, I woke from a deep sleep breathing hard. I'm not claustrophobic, but right then I wanted nothing more than to escape from my sleeping bag and bivy sack. I unzipped my bag. Cool air drifted in and I started to shiver. I focused on slowing my breathing. I thought I heard a noise outside. I tried to dismiss it as imagination. I started to breathe harder, as if I were riding a bicycle up some switchbacked mountain road. The noise wouldn't go away. I threw open the bivy sack's rainfly and thrust my head outside, half expecting to see some large animal rummaging through the darkness. There was only a sky full of stars, a stand of pines that edged my meadow camp, and the sound of water spreading itself across a riffle. My breathing slowed. The dark shape of a mountain came into focus, and past that mountain was another that I couldn't see, but could imagine, and beyond that still more imagined mountains.

I can't say if I asked to join the rafters because I was worried about the whitewater downstream or because I was lonely. "Where did you put in?" the son asked as he pulled at the raft's oars not long after we started down the river.

"Up at Redfish Lake," I said.

"Where are you headed?" I had told the family I was on a multi-day trip when I had asked to float with them, so the son's question was perfectly natural. I would hear some version of his question over and over in the next two months, sometimes tiring of it, but that Monday was the first time I had heard or answered it. "The ocean," I said. The answer sounded strange in my mouth. Every now and then after that, the son would say, "The ocean, that's amazing."

"I still haven't gotten used to the idea myself," I responded once.

I had run the Salmon below the Yankee Fork confluence before and remembered some rapids hard enough to make me pay attention, but that day I found only easy whitewater. Maybe the low water explains the discrepancy. Maybe in my nervousness about the trip, I had simply imagined the rapids as bigger than they were. I used the rest of the day to get comfortable with my kayak, knowing the entire time that if I had a major wipeout, somebody would pick up the pieces. By the time I parted company with the rafters, the eddy turns and peel outs and ferries all came easier. I faced no serious rapids for the next few days and could sharpen my skills even more on fast water that presented few risks.

Feeling comfortable on the river didn't diminish my worries though. Unease crept in when I camped that evening. I stretched out in a sunny patch of grass and closed my eyes. Just before I fell asleep, something crawled onto my leg and something else onto my arm. I pulled off two ticks, tried to crush them but couldn't, then used my river knife to cut them into little pieces. I did a quick tick check and then sat on my overturned kayak. Another tick crawled through the grass and onto my leg. I chopped it into pieces too. I spread out my green plastic tarp, trying to create a tick-free zone where I could rest, and flopped myself down in the middle. I closed my eyes. But every few minutes, the sensation of something crawling up my arms or legs or through my hair, pulled me from my nap. I scanned my body and scrubbed my hands into my hair making certain I missed no spot where a tick might hide. I found nothing. Finally, I gave up trying to sleep.

I cooked pasta for dinner and made too much. I put what was left in a plastic bag so I could throw it away later. I hated wasting food. I went for a walk and not far from some beaver-gnawed aspen stumps found what would have been a better campsite if I'd had any intention of moving. I watched a few lumbering RVs and speeding cars, the last of the Memorial Day traffic, headed home on the state road that paralleled the river's far bank. A pickup truck bounced its way down the dirt road on my side of the river, and the driver waved to me. I almost wished he had stopped to chat for a few minutes.

I told myself I could end my trip any time I wanted. But I didn't want to quit. I was lonely, but not scared of being alone, cautious but not worried about drowning in some rapid. It would take time to put away the patterns and routines of everyday life and pick up those of the trip. I needed a little patience to work into my journey and I knew that. But that first night, alone with the Salmon, I wanted it to happen right away.

2

Where the Marlboro Man Might Settle

We in the United States have acquiesced to the destruction and degradation of our rivers, in part because we have insufficient knowledge of the characteristics of rivers and the effects of our actions that alter their form and process. —Luna B. Leopold, A View of the River

For the first two days of the trip, the Salmon River flowed over a bedrock bottom as it dropped from evergreen forest to sagebrush steppe. Sometimes an occasional ponderosa pine interrupted the steppe. Sometimes stands of cottonwoods knotted through with willows and red-osier dogwoods grew in a loamy spot beside the river or filled the edges of a side creek tumbling off a mountain. But often the banks were hard and rocky. Beyond the river, tan hills striped by thick bands the color of oxidized copper and rusted iron crumbled imperceptibly away to scree the same way a winter-killed elk carcass will decay away to nothing, revealing slowly, bones once covered in a veneer of hide and muscle.

Puffy white clouds dropped their shadows onto the decaying hills and the light looked like it belonged in a John Ford Western. Deer and elk and bighorn sheep, crossing and re-crossing the hills, had pounded their trails into the earth. One warm afternoon, I watched a dozen mule deer graze a patch of ground so barren I needed binoculars to see the wispy plugs of bunchgrass clinging to it. The deer looked comfortable in the way deer always look comfortable in spring. It was their fat time of year. For a few months, they would have enough to eat, and even though snow would return briefly in a few days, it wouldn't be the deep, ice-crusted, killing snow of winter.

I saw signs of people—the state road that follows the river, some hay meadows, a sign advertising lots for sale in some future ranchette subdivision—but rarely people. I was in one of the more thinly settled parts of a thinly settled region. The county I floated through, Custer, is roughly the size of Connecticut, and according to the 2000 Census, had a population of just 4,300. The next county downstream, Lemhi, is slightly smaller in area than Custer County but home to three thousand more people. And while the region is not some vast empty quarter, farms and ranches cling to its rivers like cottonwoods, long distances separate town from town and even longer distances separate city from city. Only in Oregon and Washington, west of the Cascade Mountains along Interstate 5, where rain comes with a depressing frequency, is there anything approaching sprawl. Even there, no single city boasts a population of a million. A region the size of France and England exists without a Paris or London.

My third day on the river, May 30, I passed under a two-lane bridge near the town of Challis and floated into woods so dense they obscured everything beyond the river's bank, making the world somehow shrink and expand all at once. The road disappeared. Bird songs drifted from one bank to the other. Sometimes I recognized the trill of a red-winged blackbird or saw a Lewis' woodpecker flap across the river, but mostly the birds remained deep inside cottonwood stands, unseen and unidentified. The river looped through its floodplain like a garden hose uncoiled by a lazy child, flowing gently past bare coble bars and tree-thicketed sand islands.

With its wolves and elk and bighorn sheep, and its rivers

with their salmon, and its big land area and small population, and its more designated wilderness than any other state in the Lower Forty-eight—Idaho has always struck me not as pristine, but as intact. I like the idea of intact. It implies land functioning naturally and leaves room for people in a way pristine can't. Part of the West's myth comes from the long stretches of empty space that make it look intact. There is truth behind the myth, but the land's big, open spaces also hide details that might lead to different conclusions. In the tight canopy of the Salmon's cottonwoods, where distant mountains and art-photography light disappeared, there were only details.

The thick woods came and went. In spots, cows grazed down to the river, and coming around one meander, I found a half dozen knee-deep in water. In many places, banks of light tan soil dropped like miniature cliffs, four or five feet straight into the water. In other places, the banks ended not in sharp drops but in giant riprap boulders dumped to stop the erosion. Riprap doesn't stop erosion, just moves it downstream. Over time, because of overgrazing, the building of flood-control structures, and attempts to re-route the river, the thick growth of cottonwoods, willows, dogwoods, and other plants that once held the banks in place had in many spots thinned or vanished. The changes must have started so long ago and happened so slowly that the river, with its sometimes bare and eroding banks, must now seem natural.

What I saw was not simply a matter of aesthetics. The erosion has wrecked long stretches of river where Chinook salmon once spawned and reared. It might even have changed the way the river functions. When a river tears away the edges of its channel, sometimes it will, through a process called incision, cut down into its bed until it comes to resemble a ditch bounded by high banks. Incision alters the river's ecology and hydrology. Warm water is lethal for salmon, and in a place like central Idaho, where summer highs often reach the nineties and sometimes even the hundreds, logic might dictate the rivers should turn warm enough to kill. Streamside vegetation helps moderate a river's temperature, but on a big river like the Salmon, the annual water cycle, not just vegetation, keeps it cool. In spring, running cold and high with snowmelt, the Salmon, like many other rivers, will escape its banks in places and stretch out across its floodplain. As it does, some of the river seeps into the ground and fills the water table. Later in the year, as stream levels drop, the aquifer returns this cool groundwater back to the river.

After a river becomes incised, the water table drops. It takes higher and higher flows before the river can escape its banks to reach the floodplain. Finally what was once a regular event becomes rare, and spring floods stop recharging the water table. Cool water doesn't bubble back into the river. Dry-season flow decreases, the river warms, and cold-water fish like salmon and trout disappear. All around the West, even in Idaho, it's easy to find small streams that once flowed year-round, but because of erosion and incision, are now ephemeral.

An incised river doesn't just harm fish. Cottonwoods, which get their name from their small, cotton-like seeds, always grow close to rivers. Their seeds fall like snow during late spring and early summer and need the fresh sediment left behind by spring's high water to germinate and grow. Close to a river where floods come often, cottonwoods rise in tangles, with trees of different heights and ages side by side. Farther away, where high water comes only at infrequent intervals, cottonwoods grow in single-age stands, each stand corresponding to a flood. As a river leaves its channel less frequently, fewer and fewer cottonwoods sprout. The older trees, which at the longest live two hundred years, die, and nothing replaces them. When the cottonwoods go, the beavers that eat them, the big-game animals that shelter in them, and the birds that nest in them suffer too. Many of the Salmon's tributaries are incised, but it's not clear if the main river below Challis has suffered the same fate yet. Biologists, hydrologists, and engineers have looked at the river but have reached different conclusions.

The government has proposed a program that would repair the stretch of the Salmon near Challis, but finding money for the work and landowners willing to cooperate have created delays. Before my trip I talked to a woman who had developed federally funded stream restoration projects on some of the Salmon's tributaries. Landowners wanted to protect the river, she told me, but there was also some skepticism. Not that long ago, engineers would straighten streams and riprap banks. Water then was an enemy and the goal was to prevent flooding. Now, another group from the government has come along with new ideas, claiming those past actions were all wrong. That doesn't always go over well, she said.

The woman who talked to me about the Salmon worked with Juliet. Rivers are woven into my relationship with Juliet. It's not just that we met kayaking or that we have spent many weekends paddling together. Juliet is a wildlife biologist but specializes in restoring degraded streams, so rivers are part of her job. We have books on hydrology scattered around the house and talk of rivers fills the long drives and the kitchen-table conversations about work that are part of any couple's relationship. Because she specializes in stream restoration, understands how streams move sediment and erode their banks, Juliet notices details I never could. We have kayaked down or driven beside rivers I thought were beautiful and unspoiled, and she will point out the damage. Logging might have caused erosion in the headwaters, forcing the stream to carry more gravel than normal. Road crews might have straightened the river, which often causes the river to incise as it adjusts its slope to a new, shorter course. Once, as we talked, I said, "We don't seem to treat our rivers very well."

"You're beginning to learn," she said.

As worn as some of the land along the forested stretch of the Salmon looked, it was not all ruin, and I took some comfort in that, although it may have been a false comfort. Deer sipping from the river melted back into the woods when they saw my kayak, kingfishers perched on overhanging branches searched for small fish, and great blue herons stood stately calm waiting for a meal. I listened to the birdsong and watched the wind shake the trees' leaves.

Paddling through the cottonwood forests, I pushed hard to make the mouth of the Pahsimeroi River. Idaho runs a hatchery about a mile up the Pahsimeroi. I had decided to stop there, figuring it might be a good chance not only to see salmon but also learn about hatcheries, which are where most of the Columbia's salmon come from nowadays. But on the third day of my trip, the upstream winds that blew every afternoon started around three thirty, and by four my back was sore. I stopped at a BLM campground unsure exactly how far I was from the Pahsimeroi.

I was unsure of my location because I didn't have a map for the first 180 miles of river. And I didn't have a map because I couldn't find just one that covered the entire first section of river. In her always practical way, Juliet had suggested I buy the necessary maps and string them together to create what I needed. I didn't listen, not because I have some inherent distrust of maps, but because I'm lazy and didn't want to buy and cut up all those maps, and because I figured as long as water flowed down hill, I couldn't really get lost, and because I had lived not all that far away and thought I knew the area, if not intimately, at least adequately. But I had mostly traveled past that stretch of river in a car on my way to hike some nearby trail or paddle some other, more challenging river. Driving past a place and floating through it at the pace of the river weren't the same. I always knew roughly where I was those first few days, but often not exactly where. It seemed as if the land had turned elastic and stretched so tight each stream or hill that could serve as guidepost had pulled farther from the next, distorting distances. Really though, I was seeing everything in its proper perspective for the first time, seeing how big the country was and learning how long it really took to travel through it.

After I had pulled my kayak onto the BLM campground's

concrete boat ramp, stripped out of my dry top, took off my wet neoprene kayaker's booties, which made my toes wrinkle like prunes, and put on my sandals, I learned from a man and woman that I was only a few miles from the Pahsimeroi. The man was maybe in his late thirties and muscular, with neck-length blond hair that made him look like a California surfer dude. The woman was maybe a little older and had a pronounced Southern accent. They asked where I had come from and where I was headed. I told them as the man helped me carry my kayak to a campsite. He invited me to join them for dinner that evening. I was still fighting loneliness and needed some company.

A few RVs filled the campground, but I went about unpacking my kayak, changing into shorts and a t-shirt, and rolling out my bivy sack on the tent pad as if I were alone. I didn't have the right amount of money for the campground's self-pay box so I hunted up the campground host and asked him to change some bills. He'd seen me pull in and when I told him what I was doing, he said I could camp for free.

After spending all day sitting in a kayak, I needed to stretch my legs. The campground was at the bottom of a steep hill, so there was no place to go but up. I crossed the main road that always, more or less, followed the river and hiked into a parcel of rangeland. I had no trail to follow and instead made my way the best I could. After ten or fifteen minutes of walking, I stopped to catch my breath and wipe my face with my shirttail. Wildflowers turned the steppe into an impressionist canvas: splatters of bright yellow arrow-leaf balsamroot, pink and white phlox, and purple lupine mixed with smaller dabs of deep blue larkspur and flaming red scarlet gilia, all painted against a green-gray background of big sagebrush and bluebunch wheatgrass. No trees interrupted the roll of the land and I knew if I kept climbing I would eventually see the peaks of the Lost River Range. So I kept going up.

Then I stopped. I had almost stepped on the spiked paddle of a prickly pear cactus, not a pleasant experience in sandals. I walked on, but kept my eyes to the ground. The great canvas of steppe shrunk to individual plants. I noticed the three-tipped leaves of the big sagebrush, the feltlike hair of the balsamroot's arrowhead-shaped leaves, the delicate five-petaled flowers of the phlox, and the living crust of lichens and mosses that filled the spaces between the plants. Pink pinwheels of bitterroot, the Montana state flower, clung to otherwise bare patches of rocky soil.

Native peoples throughout the region have eaten bitterroot for millennia, but it has the scientific name *Lewisia rediviva* because Meriwether Lewis first collected it in 1806 as the Corps of Discovery moved through what is now Montana. Other Northwest plants first cataloged by Lewis and Clark, "discovered" in scientific terminology, also carry the explorers' names. Syringa or mock orange, Idaho's state flower, is *Philadelphus lewisii*; ragged robin, *Clarkia pulchella*; a subspecies of wild blue flax, *Linum perenne lewisii*. Of course Lewis and Clark weren't just on a journey of biologic and geographic exploration, but of westward expansion.

The story of westward motion is, for better or worse, the story of the United States. It has shaped language: Juliet and I moved "out West," although not together; we go "back East" to visit family. It has shaped attitudes. In *Undaunted Courage*, author and historian Stephen Ambrose quotes Thomas Jefferson writing about the Europeans' superior farming techniques. "It [results] from our having such quantities of land to waste as we please. In Europe the object is to make the most of their land, labour being abundant: here it is to make the most of our labour, land being abundant." The abundant land Jefferson wrote about was to the west, and the practice of the time was to exhaust the land, then move on to new fields as if the continent stretched forever.

Settlers moved west believing that always, around the next river bend or over the next mountain range, there was more land, empty and open for the taking, and that there always would be. Of course the prairies and valleys and hills the explorers explored and the settlers settled had been inhabited for an uncounted amount of time. In a place where family connections to the land matter, American Indian voices often are ignored or drowned out in the battles over future actions, but they have much to offer and the sooner they are heard and respected, the better.

Even now, a faith in the West's inexhaustibility persists. I understand that faith. Sometimes the West seems so big that I cannot fathom the land changing in any fundamental way. That faith pushes up against another, newer belief that says the West has been tamed and in the wake of that taming, priorities should change. Maybe those who espouse this new view notice details once hidden by the seemingly unconquerable space, maybe it's just how they interpret what they notice. As a country, we are trying to see the land in its proper perspective, but what each of us sees is a little different, with views colored by our own history and needs. So we argue. I suspect we will continue to argue until some common view of the region and its priorities emerges. There's nothing wrong with that, after all, we fight over how to treat the land and manage its resources because the issues are important enough to fight over. But the only way to make progress is with civility and a willingness to listen to those we don't agree with.

I left the BLM campground early on the fourth day of my trip and reached the Pahsimeroi confluence in less than an hour. If I'd had a map, it would have shown a little black dot with the name "Ellis" printed next to the spot. Someone studying the map might assume a scattering of houses and maybe a store filled the spot. A deception. There is none of that, only a small post office, with its gravel parking lot and requisite American flag.

After I beached my kayak, I used a cable lock to secure it to the trunk of a large cottonwood, although I probably didn't need to worry about thieves. I hiked along the gravel shoulder of a narrow county road, past the post office, and into the Pahsimeroi Valley. After the lawyers and doctors drove the Marlboro Man off the open range, he might have settled comfortably in the Pahsimeroi Valley and spent the rest of his life there herding cattle. (Although I suspect his Mormon neighbors would have looked down on his smoking.) The valley is ranch country. It rests between two mountain ranges that trend roughly northwest to southeast. The tallest peaks of both are, at ten thousand feet or more, high enough to hold snow far into summer. Sliding downhill off the summer snow, the tree line comes up fast but the ragged timber stands vanish just as quickly into the sagebrush that covers so much of Idaho. Lower down, where the mountains press against the valley floor and the Pahsimeroi River meanders like a dark squiggle, irrigated fields replace the sagebrush, and scattered here and there, ranch houses and outbuildings dot irrigated pastures where horses and cows graze. The valley's lushness in a place where, except in spring, dull colors dominate, should startle, look alien and imposed. Instead, it fits into a preconditioned image of the West, and so much of the West is about perception.

I followed the road until I came to the scattered white hatchery buildings beside the dark squiggle of river. A man, who appeared to be in charge, tried to coordinate planting a large maple tree, while several others also involved gave varying opinions about where to put the tree or even if a maple was the right kind of tree to plant. When there was a break, I asked for a tour of the hatchery. The man who seemed to be in charge told me that the salmon hadn't arrived yet, so there really wasn't anything to see. "You should come back in a week or two," he said. I explained about my trip, that I couldn't come back in a week, and that I wanted to get some information about the hatchery if someone had a few minutes to talk.

The director of the tree planting turned out to be the hatchery's assistant manager, Doug Engemann. We went to his office. The phone on his large desk rang again and again, forcing him constantly to stop our conversation and talk to some person or another about supplies or work schedules or the other necessities of running a hatchery.

The whole encounter had the feel of an interview rather than a conversation. I rattled off questions, which he answered promptly between taking calls.

"Who pays for the hatchery?"

"Idaho Power as mitigation for dams built in Hells Canyon."

"What species of salmon do you raise?"

"Summer Chinook and steelhead."

"How many Chinook can the hatchery produce?"

"It has the capacity to produce a million smolt," he said. "But it takes 600 adult fish, that's an estimate, to produce that many juveniles. Only about 400 adults will come back to the entire Pahsimeroi this year. Last year, there were 467."

"Before I started the trip, someone told me that the Pahsimeroi River wasn't in the best shape," I said. "Is that right?"

"Habitat's an issue and the hatchery's working with local landowners to improve spawning habitat." The phone rang and Engemann talked to someone about what he was doing to prepare for the upcoming Chinook run. Afterward, he continued his answer. "Habitat isn't the Pahsimeroi's biggest problem. There aren't enough salmon in the river to use the available spawning habitat."

"So what's the problem?" The phone rang again. More hatchery business. After Engemann hung up, he became not evasive, but cautious. A few years earlier, a group of Idaho game department biologists had signed a letter saying science indicated that the best way to restore the state's salmon was to remove— "breaching" was the term used in the letter—the four large, federal dams on the lower Snake River in Washington. Afterward, the governor muzzled the state's biologists for a time and eventually created a new office to handle policies dealing with the state's threatened and endangered fish and wildlife species.

I told him I knew about the breaching letter and its aftermath, the political realities in Idaho, that my fiancée was a wildlife biologist, and that I didn't want to get anybody into trouble. He loosened up, but just a little. He viewed the "natural river option," a euphemism for removal of the four lower Snake Dams, as the best option for restoring Idaho's salmon, but he also said that's a political decision and not up to biologists. "Ultimately, we have to respect the electoral process and let politicians set the agenda."

Before our conversation ended, I asked, "Why is it important to save the salmon?" Those first few days of my trip, I was impressed by Idaho, the way I always am. I marveled at its wildlife, felt insignificant against its clean, open landscapes, and had begun to wonder if my focus on what had changed because of human action wasn't misplaced. Maybe the beauty that overwhelmed everything else revealed the truth. The question I asked Engemann was about much more than salmon.

His first response, to repeat the quote by the wildlife biologist Aldo Leopold, "There are some who can live without wild things, and some who cannot," seemed contrived and easy, so I asked the question again. Engemann talked about his youth and his fascination with NASA's Apollo program saying that if "we can put a man on the moon, we can save the salmon." He said that through his work with various American Indian tribes, he had learned about their connection to salmon, and that there was a moral obligation to the fish and the people who depend on them. I asked again. "I guess I view it as a form of education," he said. "Salmon aren't the only species living in an altered environment. We are too. Maybe by learning to save the salmon we are learning to save ourselves."

Before I left, I asked Engemann for the names of some of the ranchers he was working with on habitat restoration. He gave me Syd Dowton's name and told me how to get to his place. To reach the ranch, I walked back to the where I had left my kayak and then upstream for a mile or maybe two along the road that shadows the Salmon River. At the ranch, I found a no trespassing sign and cows standing on a dirt road that led to a pair of houses. Trespassing and harassing livestock weren't likely to get me a good interview. I waited.

I tried to figure out what to do next. A pale ferruginous hawk turned circles on late-morning thermals as it hunted. From Dowton's ranch along the west bank of the Salmon, the Pahsimeroi Valley's high peaks, ragged timber, and sagebrush are visible, but not its out-of-place green. I stood, for a painfully long time, in the sun, looking at those mountains and hoping somebody would come by. Finally, a battered pickup drove past, scattering cows as it went. Two dark-featured men in straw cowboy hats got out of the truck and began moving irrigation pipe.

I walked up to them, worried they wouldn't understand me and mad at myself because I had never learned Spanish. In the Northwest, the people who do so much of the work that makes the economy run—move irrigation pipe, sort potatoes, pick fruit, clean hotel rooms, and wash restaurant dishes—speak Spanish. "I'm looking for Syd Dowton," I said. One of the men took off his hat, wiped his forehead with the back of his hand, and pointed to a low, brick house about a quarter mile away. When I got to the house, I learned Dowton wasn't there. It had turned into one of those days.

I started walking, figuring I had time to cover some river before the afternoon wind came up. Just before I reached the wood-decked bridge over the Salmon marked with the no trespassing signs, a man on a dirt bike raced up to me and stopped. He asked what I was doing. "I want to talk to Syd Dowton," I said.

"And if you found this Syd Dowton, what would you talk to him about?" the man on the dirt bike asked.

I told him my name and about my kayak trip and what I wanted to talk about. When I was done I said, "I suspect I've already found Mr. Dowton." The man smiled, stuck out his hand, nodded, and said, "I'm Syd Dowton." He told me he needed to start moving cows to a new pasture up the Pahsimeroi Valley, but that if I waited at the bridge, he would talk to me as soon as he could. So I waited some more.

I heard the noise before I saw the cows or realized what was happening. The clomp of heavy hooves on hard dirt, bawling calves, and shouting overwhelmed the squawks of a squabbling pair of red-winged blackbirds. Two boys of maybe ten or twelve charged their horses around the cows, waved their hats, and whistled, trying to keep the animals from spilling off the road and into the riverside cottonwoods. Most boys their age only play cowboy. A woman worked with the boys and Dowton followed his wife and grandsons on the dirt bike. Dust drifted up into the air, highlighting the sun falling through the trees. I pressed my back against the rough bark of a large cottonwood to stay out of the way. The cows balked a little at stepping onto the bridge. One or two tried to bolt from the herd, but the family worked together, kept the cows bunched and moving forward. Soon the bridge hummed with the weight of tromping cows. They funneled off the bridge and back onto the dirt road. After the whole stomping, bawling, yelling mess had disappeared, their dust and shit remained.

Dowton came roaring back down the road and before the sound of the bike's engine had faded, he asked me, "Where are you from and what do you think about these problems we're having in the West?"

Neither question surprised me. I was there to talk to him about the problems in the West, and Idaho is the kind of place where people care if you grew up there and when your family settled. Before I moved to Idaho, I had talked to a source in Pocatello. Her family had lived in Idaho for generations, and I wanted to get a feel for someplace I'd never even visited. She explained with a story: When someone from her environmental group had testified before the state legislature, one of the first questions a lawmaker asked was how long she had lived in Idaho. She said "twenty years" and the legislator replied "I have shoes older than that."

I told Dowton I was from Virginia and that if you went just a short distance east from the house where I grew up, you'd be at the Atlantic Ocean. I talked my way around the rest of the question by saying I wanted to hear what he had to say about the West and its problems. Before I could start asking questions, Dowton wanted to know how I got to his place.

"I walked. Kayaking, walking, and hitching are my only options." Dowton shook his head in a way that me made wonder if he thought I was crazy. Dowton's family had started ranching in the area in the early 1900s, and his operation sounded typical for that part of Idaho. He ran four hundred cow-calf pairs while his son ran another three hundred pairs. During part of the year, he grazed his cattle on his land, where he grew hay for winter forage, and also turned his cows out to summer on forest service land along the East Fork of the Salmon River, a place he described as "the prettiest in the world."

Public lands grazing is controversial. Some environmental groups around the country and in Idaho want it stopped, and the rhetoric between environmentalists and ranchers is often harsh. Dowton had nothing good to say about environmentalists, a group he saw as outsiders, primarily from the East, who only cause problems. "Environmentalists don't have anything to give," he said. "People in the East are jealous of what we have out here. They're trying to force people off public land not by taking grazing permits, but by putting in so many restrictions." The restrictions will drive ranchers out of business, he said, and after that happens, the rich will come in, buy up the private land, and turn the place into their personal playground.

Dowton was fighting with the forest service. It had already forced him to cut back on the number of cows he could graze, wanted him to move them from pasture to pasture more frequently, and expected him to do more to keep them out of riparian areas. The forest service, he said, had harassed him and his family, calling at odd hours saying cows had to be moved and threatening the family with fines and the loss of grazing permits if they didn't comply. Dealing with the government had become such a hassle Dowton said he was thinking about keeping more of his stock on his own land.

Dowton might not seem exactly like Hollywood's version of a cowboy, but he's close enough. Fifty-nine at the time, he didn't look old enough to be a grandfather. He wore jeans, a western shirt, and a ball cap instead of a cowboy hat; he was close to average height, not the tall cowboy of the movies, but lean and muscular in a way that also let you know he was tough and a person you didn't want to mess with. Dowton said that a few years back, if somebody like me had shown up on his property asking questions, he probably would have thrown him off. Now he felt the need to talk so people could hear a rancher's point of view. Somewhere along the way, the cowboy went from the guy in the white hat riding to the rescue on a white horse, to the bad guy.

Even though Dowton wanted to start pulling some of his cows off public land, which some environmentalists would love to hear, he worried about the damage the cows would cause on his property. "We're probably doing some damage in the riparian areas," he said. Although the river hadn't carved the banks into steep cliffs, his property looked a little rough where it fronted the Salmon River. Adding more cows for longer periods of time would worsen the erosion, he said.

So he'd signed onto a government program that pays ranchers to fence cows out of streams. It's voluntary. No laws require the fencing. "What would you say if someone said you had to fence your land?" I asked.

"I would say it's my private property. It's one of those things very near and dear to us—property rights." Maybe it's just human nature to resist being forced to do something, even if you might otherwise do that something on your own.

"And why's it important to keep cows away from rivers?" I asked.

"Otherwise, there's erosion, which damages the land and the river," he said. The government pays part of the fencing cost, while the landowner covers the rest of the initial costs, either with cash or by working on the project, and also pays for on-going maintenance. Much of the government money comes from programs aimed at helping salmon. Dowton said he didn't think reducing erosion would have an impact on salmon numbers.

"I would just love to see the salmon back," Dowton said. He

mentioned how much he enjoyed fishing. "Nobody wants to see salmon here more than I do. But I don't think cows are the cause of the decline," he said. I asked what he thought about removing the four dams on the Snake River in eastern Washington. "No way," he said almost in a laugh. "That would affect some people's standard of living, and people always say the same thing when it comes to sacrifice. You can take the other guy's standard of living, but don't take mine," he said, then added, "I would just love to see the salmon back."

Dowton said he had to help with the cows and our conversation ended. He kick-started the bike and rode off. I didn't ask Dowton why he wanted the salmon back, didn't ask what memories he had of them, or why it was important to try to save the salmon. In the Northwest, we debate how to save the salmon, but rarely discuss if or why we should. It's just a given, and maybe that reflects the salmon's importance in regional culture. Still, the rancher struck me as straightforward and honest, and I would have learned something from his answers.

Talking to Engemann and Dowton had used up the day, and by the time I finished, the upstream winds had already started. I thought about covering some river, but worried I might not pass a good camping spot for many miles. Without a map, I had no way to check. So I hiked another mile or so back to the BLM campground where I had started that morning and found the couple I had had dinner with the night before. I asked Ken if he would drive me back to where I left my kayak so I could load it in his pickup and come back to the campground.

Ken and Kim fed me dinner again that night. Ken really was from California; Kim from Arkansas. They were both computer programmers, had moved together from San Diego to Big Timber, Montana, looking for a slower pace of life, but had eventually found themselves, even in Montana, working too much. So they sold their house, bought a trailer, and were traveling the country. They figured in a year or two they might settle down again somewhere, but didn't know where. We talked, about politics and living in the West and about how Ken and Kim had gone from being conservatives to liberals. I ate too much chili, drank enough red wine that I got a buzz, and held onto Ken and Kim's company when I put on the river again the next morning.

3

Henry Clay Merritt, on His 158th Birthday

From the start of my trip, I had considered the three rivers I planned to kayak parts of the same river, each flowing into the next to form the Columbia. If judged by discharge, the Columbia River is the fourth-largest river in North America, and along with tributaries like the Salmon and Snake, drains portions of seven states and one Canadian province. It generates more hydroelectric power than any other river system in the country; if run at maximum capacity, just the twenty-eight federal dams spread throughout its basin—which contains hundreds of dams—could light twenty-two cities the size of Portland, Oregon. It once supported somewhere between eight and sixteen million adult salmon, one of the world's most productive salmon rivers, and present-day returns seem miniscule by comparison. But those are simply facts and figures taken from books and government reports, and to uncover them, I didn't need to leave behind my home or Juliet, who was planning our wedding that summer.

I am a reporter, not just by profession but by temperament. I wanted to explore the river system that so many people, myself included, depend on, not for a story assigned by some editor, but for me. I wanted to gather my own facts. Since moving from

Virginia, coming west with opinions and ideas about the river gained indirectly, I have lived close to one tributary or another of the Columbia—first the Snake, then the Yakima, and now the Spokane—and in that closeness discovered knowledge gathered from a distance often was illusory or incorrect. We Americans have always known less than we realized about the Columbia. Even before Robert Gray sailed his ship, the Columbia Rediviva, into the river for the first time in 1792, cartographers thought they knew the Columbia, were so certain of its existence that without seeing it, they had drawn it on maps and named it the "River of the West," and without knowing its exact location, believed it part of the Northwest Passage. The Columbia carried the dreams of empire, an easy water route across the continent and a path to the riches of the Orient. After explorers, traders, and settlers had traveled the real river and found it too chaotic and dangerous, found it did not meet the expectations of an expanding and industrializing United States, we decided to alter it, investing time and concrete and billions of dollars so it could fit our desires and beliefs. Once we had finished, some people became unhappy with the new, engineered river, hoped again to see the old Columbia, and wanted to spend billions more to change at least part of it back.

So many of us who live in the region—and beyond, I suppose—want something we cannot have, a river that supplies electricity and floats goods to market and a river that is free flowing, even though one precludes the other. The Columbia's story is echoed by other rivers, the Colorado, the Missouri, the Mississippi, by almost any place people talk of tearing out dams and dikes, of reintroducing displaced species, or of restoring large tracts of land to their natural condition.

With no deadlines to meet or editors to placate, I moved at the river's pace, like a drop of water flowing from the mountains down to the ocean. To believe in a sort of kinetic understanding of stones and trees, of heavy and rooted objects, seemed strange at first, and I struggled through the early days of my trip. On June 2, 2001, two days after talking with the hatchery manager and rancher, I paused in the town of Salmon so I could visit with some locals. I had worked for a newspaper in a nearby city, a large town actually, when I first moved west, and had reported on people who lived in small farming and ranching communities like Salmon. I had eaten dinners with them, sat around kitchen tables and stood in barns with them, harvested potatoes and hayed cows with them, once even rode horseback on a cattle drive with a group of them. I almost always liked the people I met but was bothered by some of their ideas, the easy dismissal of the federal government and environmentalists, the apparent unwillingness to hear out contrary opinions, the occasional diatribes from those on the fringe about United Nations' conspiracy plots.

Salmon clusters along a state highway and the river. Beyond the cottonwood-covered riverbanks and the town's low, functional buildings, trees vanish into sagebrush, and mountains lurk in a way that creates a sense of scale and an impression of unchecked space, even though high peaks hem the valley on all sides. After checking into a hotel room, I explored the town's small commercial district, and while I did, the weather changed. The warm days of my first week on the river vanished with a wave of clouds that hid the mountains from view and a wind that hinted of the coming cold. I could almost feel the chill and damp that would wait for me back on the river.

I stopped at a diner for lunch and to warm up. The town's businesses were as functional as the buildings they occupied: grocery store, drug store, dollar store, bank. But tourist places existed as well. Some sold outdoor gear and a couple that called themselves galleries sold Western art. Near the edge of town, a few fast food restaurants had sprouted. After crossing the Continental Divide in 1805, Lewis and Clark had camped near Salmon. A booth, which has since grown into a small museum funded by a host of government agencies, stood ready to provide information about the explorers and Sacagawea, their Shoshone interpreter reportedly born nearby, to the flood of tourists expected for the expedition's bicentennial. Jobs and money come with the tourists, but sometimes so does change. Some residents worry tourism might lead to an influx of retirees and vacation-home owners from outside the region who will alter their town's character. Stories, told and retold throughout the Northwest like legends, abound of new arrivals who claimed they left some place or another, usually in California, because they couldn't stand living there, but then quickly set about trying to turn their new town into their old city because it lacked amenities left behind.

I waited for my burger and fries and read a copy of the Idaho Falls newspaper, where I had once worked. My stay coincided with a high school rodeo. Teens dressed in blue jeans, cowboy boots and hats, large silver belt buckles, and Western shirts with numbers still pinned on the back packed the restaurant's booths and tables, filled the air with noise as they and their parents relived the competition. The myth of the West and the real West coexisted easily in Salmon.

I noticed a sign near the counter: "Grizzlies Don't Serve Any Purpose in Idaho." Later, on the back of a pickup, I would see a bumper sticker that read: "Then Goldie Locks Met a Grizzly and She Didn't Live Happily Ever After." The last time anybody saw a grizzly bear for certain in that part of Idaho was sixty or seventy years ago, but some people want to reintroduce the big bruins into the nearby wilderness areas. Down the street from the diner, posted on the front window of a bar was a picture of a wolf in the middle of a red circle with a slash across it and a message below: "You can take your tree-hugging, granola-eating, politically correct, earth-worshiping, Subaru-driving, ponytailed, sandals-in-the-winter, wolf-loving butt somewhere else." Like grizzlies, wolves disappeared from central Idaho sometime in the early twentieth century, shot, trapped, and poisoned out of existence. In 1995, over the objections of those in the area, the federal government reintroduced wolves. The reintroduction, and the grizzly bear proposal modeled on that reintroduction, have exposed deep resentment toward the government and environmental groups, although that resentment existed long before anybody talked seriously of turning wolves or bears free in Idaho. Standing there in my sandals, thinking about my Subaru-driving, government wildlife biologist future wife, I decided not to go in the bar. I once interviewed writer and historian Paul Schullery about grizzly bears. He said people in the West face dramatic social change, which is always painful, and animals like bears often serve as symbols in arguments that actually turn on conflicting views about nature and man's relationship with the natural world. "It really is like they are arguing over religion," he told me. "Haven't all of us gotten advice in our life never to do that?"

The day after my walk around Salmon, the signs about wolves and bears were on my mind while I fidgeted in the backseat of a big, four-door sedan. A man named Gene drove us out beyond town to a ranch owned by his brother and his sister-in-law. Gene's wife, who had arranged the meeting but didn't want her name mentioned, rode with us. By Idaho standards, the ranch was small, 225 acres, plus the rights to graze livestock on another 248 acres of state land. Gene's brother, George, and his sister-in-law, Althea, had, in addition to ranching, worked other jobs before retiring, Althea as a nurse, George at a lumber mill in town. In Idaho, people view ranching as part of their lifestyle, and it never surprises me to meet a police officer or lawyer or teacher who also runs a few cows. Prints of a bighorn sheep and of a grizzly killing a buffalo decorated the dark wood-paneled walls of George and Althea's living room. Althea offered me coffee, and when I said I didn't drink it, offered me tea, made some special, and kept my cup filled while we talked about what amounts to Western politics, which revolves around who is doing what with the land.

Everyone in the room explained how they loved the land, enjoyed wildlife, hunting, and fishing, how they wanted to see salmon in the river, elk, deer, and wild sheep in the mountains.

But they had no use for grizzly bears, wolves, or bull trout, a fish related to salmon and now considered threatened. "Have you ever eaten a bull trout?" somebody asked. "They taste terrible."

The ability to make a living is as important as nature, Gene said. All these threatened and endangered animals have meant restrictions—on how locals use water, on where and how they graze stock, on the way logging and mining companies operate—restrictions on how people make a living and how they live, with the decisions coming from faraway bureaucrats who don't understand the community or the land the way locals do, they said. Environmentalists only want to block and obstruct to provide themselves with jobs and are no better than the bureaucrats, they all agreed.

"The people who live in the cities, in the cement world, need to come out here to see the problems those laws are causing," Althea said. "I don't know how you get everybody to see those things." Gene, a millwright and welder, talked about how he'd lost jobs when local lumber mills and mines closed, closures he blamed on environmentalists. Gene and his wife have two children, a daughter who was studying to become an engineer and a son who was in the navy. When the daughter finishes school and the son leaves the navy, there will be no jobs in Salmon for them, Gene's wife would tell me later. If children don't stay, Salmon will change, and not for the better, she said.

In a town where five real estate offices sat within a block of each other, all offering what once were working ranches for sale and subdivision, I heard worries that Salmon might turn into another Sun Valley, that tony town of movie stars and millionaires to Salmon's south, where a working person can't afford to live, or Jackson Hole, which is the same place as Sun Valley, only to the east, just the other side of the Idaho and Wyoming state line. "The cattlemen are not making it, and they're going to be gone," Althea said.

"The ranches are already being sold and subdivided," George said.

Maybe the changing already seemed inevitable. "We've lost every battle," Gene's wife said. I didn't expect the resignation. Then she asked, "How would you feel if you were in our place?"

I had no answer. It wasn't my reporter's objectivity or any agreement with their views that made me quiet. What I heard that Sunday afternoon, what I have heard so often when I talk to farmers and ranchers, is anger and frustration bolstered by fear. They feel they have no control over what happens in their lives or in their communities, which makes them scared their way of life will disappear and that they will not survive in the place they have always lived. Grazing, logging, and mining once were seen as the best uses of the federal land that makes up so much of the West, but now people are divided over how to use the land, divisions that remind me of the conflicts over the Columbia. Now, fewer cows and sheep graze public land, fewer trees are cut on national forests, and the people in the rural West, who often are tied economically and culturally to the land, must deal with that. I don't know what it's like to have my livelihood bound to the shifting values of the public, or to see my fortunes altered with each new political administration, or to have somebody tell me that what my father or grandfather did destroyed a place I love. The people who live in Salmon, and towns like it, see themselves as the ones who take care of the land. They believe that without them, the West would be subdivided into ten-acre ranchettes with no open space or room for wildlife.

That one question, how would I feel, kept me from saying what I thought: that wolves and grizzly bears and bull trout and salmon should survive but now can't, that rural Western states receive a steady flow of other people's tax money from the federal government, or that in a place where precipitation averages nine inches a year and winter seems the dominant season, life would always be hard, failures frequent, and maybe the government and environmentalists serve as convenient scapegoats. It was right that I kept my mouth shut. I understood I could never know what George and Althea and Gene and his wife knew. What I would learn by traveling into and through a place, and what they knew after living in a place, were not the same—not better or worse, I told myself, only different—and not interchangeable. I had picked movement and so would stick with it.

The next morning rain drizzled down in the valley divided by the Salmon River, and the temperature hovered just above freezing. In the mountains bordering the valley, I glimpsed traces of white on the ground and imagined peaks then hidden by low clouds, sheeted in snow so wet and heavy it bent and broke tree limbs, crushed and flattened spring wildflowers. June snow falls as a reminder. A reminder that Idaho's high valleys are not an easy place to live, a reminder that killing cold is never far away and that even the most reasonable plans can become stunted, a reminder that summer is a welcome friend who comes dressed in fine clothes for only a short visit, but that you live with winter.

I considered staying in the warm, dry hotel room to ride out the bad weather, but the trip had developed its own momentum by then. I felt anxious and hemmed in by Salmon and its buildings. I hauled gear from hotel room to kayak and prepared for a miserable day. I had left my warm neoprene paddling mitts—kayakers call them "poggies"—behind on the first day of my trip, a day when sunshine had pushed the temperatures into the unseasonable eighties, a day so beautiful it had given me the absurd notion that the weather wouldn't change and I wouldn't need the poggies to keep my hands warm. While I packed equipment and food into the nine-foot kayak, I kept thinking about how the cold river and the cold rain would numb my hands and turn them red, make them tingle, make them hurt to open or close.

The day, June 4, the eighth of the trip, was a day to get past and nothing else. The ocean remained a long way off—750 miles or so if I figured by distance, two months or so if I calculated by time—far enough away that its existence seemed more rumor than certainty, more possibility than reality. I felt all those river miles laid out ahead of me, and all that time and distance weighed on me the same way wet snow from a June storm weighs down whatever it sticks to.

I slipped the plastic kayak into a river unroiled by any rapids. The water sped me past an island overgrown with cottonwoods fresh in their springtime green, then out of Salmon. The right bank gave way to a low bluff, which gave way to a valley of pastures and hay meadows that after a while narrowed until it held only the river and the ever-present road. The river cut along the base of the mountains, and for that reason it still felt something like a rocky, young, alpine stream, even though beyond Salmon the river turned bigger, pushier, and more powerful with each mile. A rain and snow mix dripped down until dampness and cold worked their way deep into my body and forced me to dig paddle into water as much to stay warm as to make time or avoid hazards. Sometimes a car sped past on the highway. Sometimes I floated past a small house or a pasture dotted with cows. Sometimes a forest of evergreens touched the river, and in those woods, snow was just a short hike away. I thought about beaching my boat so I could walk to the snow, but did not. I realized telling the story of standing in snow on a kayak trip would impress no one. Certainly not my friends, since we had all boated in the snow before. Certainly not the people from the valley, people who expected June snow, lived with it, worked in it, and came to terms with it as best they could.

An otter, a sleek and supple distraction from the weather, porpoised to within a dozen feet of my kayak, vanished beneath the water in a trail of bubbles that followed me, surfaced again then disappeared for good, leaving me alone with the river. I found other distractions where I could: great blue herons in their rookery, mallards and mergansers, cinnamon teal and blue-winged teal, ospreys and kingfishers. Swallows surrounded me for a mile, whipped through the air and snatched insects I couldn't see off the water's surface. In some American Indian stories I have heard, swallows lead the salmon home from the ocean, and I wondered if the fish were passing below me on the way to their natal streams.

The young salmon, the smolt, transforming themselves from freshwater to saltwater fish—everything, even their very blood, changing so they could survive in their ocean home—navigated the downstream river currents with me. The animals blunted the day until even thick clouds and almost snow didn't matter. Later, I saw a bald eagle, then a golden eagle, and though I claim not to believe in signs, it was hard not to imagine the eagles meant something good.

At North Fork, a town made up of a couple of houses, a general store, a hotel, and a forest service office, the black-topped state highway paralleling the river leaves the main Salmon, takes to its north fork, and twists up into the Bitterroot Mountains. A narrow paved road, so pitted and potholed it might as well be dirt, replaces the highway and the river starts to feel wild. I wanted to put the conflict over human and political concerns behind me for a while the same way I had put the highway behind me.

Just west of North Fork, a rock ledge creates a sort of natural dam, pooling the river for a few miles. Since it was already two o'clock in the afternoon, the gentle stretch meant a decision: stop at a small forest service picnic site on river right, or keep traveling downstream, with the only assured stopping point at Spring Creek, another seventeen miles away. Rapids waited downstream, but because I didn't trust the forest service river map to show every rapid, I wasn't certain where they began. I believed I could handle all the whitewater on the Salmon, had boated much, much harder rivers, which created a built-in safety margin to compensate for paddling a loaded boat alone, but I was cold and tired—the kind of tired that comes from spending a day in bad weather—and a little hungry, all of which cut into that margin and argued for stopping. Still, it seemed early. The three redhead ducks, two drakes, and a hen that floated with me offered no suggestions.

The river has often forced people to make decisions. In August of 1805, William Clark and a handful of men scouted the Salmon below the confluence with its north fork. The Shoshone Indians already had warned Lewis and Clark that a boat could not pass down the river, but the two captains still hoped for a water route across the continent. I can imagine how they wished the Salmon would transport them to the Pacific Ocean, wished it would save them from the Bitterroots. It was, of course, not to be.

On horseback and on foot, Clark and his men followed the same stretch of river I floated, must have passed the calm pool where I drifted with the ducks, then continued their reconnaissance until reaching a spot near Spring Creek. There, on August 23, the reality of passage down the Salmon became clear to Clark. "The River from the place I left my party to this Creek is almost one continued rapid, five verry considerable rapids the passage of either with Canoes is entirely impossible, as the water is Confined between huge Rocks & the Current beeting from one against another for Some distance below." The next day Clark noted his men's disappointment, mentioned their hunger—with only chokecherries and red haws for food—and his wet bedding. Lewis and Clark made their way west on foot over the Bitterroots.

Like much of the area's history, what didn't happen seems as important as what did. Maybe those non-events remind us how wrong our beliefs about the river have been. The Salmon is the place where Lewis and Clark didn't discover an easy water route to the Pacific; the place where, in the 1870s, surveyors from the Northern Pacific Railroad failed to find a quick way west through the river's canyon and so dubbed the Salmon the "Impractical River"; the place where, in the 1930s, the government planned a 150-mile road from North Fork downstream to Riggins, but didn't finish it. The Second World War stopped construction, and the road goes only forty-six miles, most of it dirt. For years, the only practical way to bring large loads downriver was in sweepboats, barge-like craft controlled by sweep arms that resemble long oars but with blades longer than house doors, mounted bow and stern. The arms gave the boatmen the ability to maneuver left and right, but only the river propelled the boats.

Even in calm water the boats couldn't move upstream, and so at their final destinations, their captains dismantled them, sold the wood, and looked for a way back upriver. The Salmon became "The River of No Return," a name it still carries.

The Salmon River itself is sometimes described by what isn't there: the longest undammed river flowing through a single state in the continental United States. The Army Corps of Engineers had planned a series of dams starting below the river's confluence with its middle fork and stretching to just above its confluence with the Snake River. Some old maps include the dams, give their names as if construction were a certainty. Because of the area's inaccessibility—with no roads or railroads for transporting the heavy equipment and construction supplies needed to build the dams and no easy path to run the high-tension wires needed to carry the electricity generated—the dams remained a low priority. Work had not started in 1968 when the government listed the river from North Fork down to the confluence with the Snake as a wilderness study area. The 1980 legislation creating the Central Idaho Wilderness prohibited dams on 150 miles of river below North Fork. In 1988, another law banned dams from Riggins to the Snake. The Salmon River was once on the path of empire, but over time empire had passed the river by.

At the end of my decision pool, near the forest service picnic area, a fifty- to hundred-yard-wide jumble of cobble-sized stones and truck-sized boulders stretched from the river up the side of a mountain until the alluvial disaster disappeared into the trees. The stream trickling down the hillside became lost in a rockscape that looked like something left behind by a retreating glacier. My forest service river map explained how, in 1897, the reservoir for a one-man placer mining operation failed, sending water from Moose Creek sluicing down Dump Creek. Over time, the extra water had torn rock and gravel free from Dump Creek's banks and spilled it out each spring in a broad fan where the creek and river meet. Finally, in 1979, the forest service spent just under one million dollars to return Moose Creek to its original channel.

The map doesn't detail how Dump Creek cut a chasm into the mountainside that in places is a half mile wide and three hundred feet deep, or how even with the restoration work the creek might periodically rearrange its banks, ripping away rock and soil. But the banks are stabilizing. Some trees grow beside the creek, and young steelhead sometimes feed in it before migrating to the ocean. Still, as a forest service hydrologist I talked to after my trip explained, centuries will pass before Dump Creek's banks find their angle of repose and stop eroding, and even though the creek might function naturally again, it will never be quite the same.

For almost the entire time I had known Juliet, she had worked to restore a stream on private property in North Idaho that in the 1950s was turned into a ditch. Once, long before the start of my trip, I asked her what the original stream had looked like. She responded that she didn't know and in a way didn't care. Her goal wasn't to resurrect some pristine stream that once existed, but to create a new one that behaved naturally, that meandered to slow the flow of water, that flooded and filled the water table in spring so it wouldn't run dry in summer, and that remained cool enough throughout the year so bull trout could spawn and the fry mature. If the landowner wanted to grow hay or run cows near the stream, that was fine as long as it didn't alter the way the stream worked.

On the trip, I had expected to find the contradictions between the desires that produced the engineered Columbia and those that would have us return part of the river back to the way it was, on the Snake, where I would confront the four large dams that some people want removed in order to restore salmon runs. As I looked at Dump Creek, I understood I could never put human conflicts completely behind me and to try was foolish. To imagine away those conflicts is to erase consequence from decisions past and future.

I skipped the picnic area and stayed with the river. Elk grazed across sagebrush and ponderosa pine hillsides, riffles loomed, promised whitewater, then disappeared. The river braided itself around willow-covered islands formed from Dump Creek rock. The rapids never came, and I found no camping beaches. When I reached the boat ramp at the Spring Creek campground, I had no choice but to stop. I felt the river's power and heard whitewater just downstream. In a mile or two, the river would explode.

I camped for the night under a tall pine. The rain had mostly stopped by then, but the wet lingered, collected at the ends of long ponderosa needles and dropped on the ground, or on me, in heavy splats. A green plastic tarp, weighted on each corner with rocks, covered gear I wanted kept dry. I changed into dry clothes, and it took all of them to keep me warm. My bivy sack and red kayak were next to a picnic table, my camp stove and cooking pots, on the table. Dinner was what I could make by boiling water—pasta, ramen noodles, or instant couscous. I didn't care; food boredom had already set in.

I had the campground to myself that evening, and to fill time after dinner, I walked the dirt road that looped around empty campsites and the hand pump that drew water from a well so tainted with iron it was undrinkable. The campground occupies part of an old homestead settled by Jim and Mamie Hibbs sometime around 1900, after Jim had moved west from Missouri a few years earlier. The Hibbses had raised nine children there. A forest service sign dutifully points out a hundred-year-old black walnut, a tree not native to the region and obviously planted by the homesteaders. I could imagine the family gathering its nuts for food each fall. If the forest service hadn't used the spot as a campground, time already would have erased most signs of the family's life. Wild roses filled irrigation ditches the family must have dug by hand. The pink flowers were in bloom and gave the air a sweet, heavy smell.

Johnny Carrey and Cort Conley, in their history of the Salmon River, *River of No Return*, write about the Hibbses' homestead. It is a story of constant work: running a water-powered sawmill and then packing or boating the boards to nearby mines, for Jim;

washing clothes for miners and caring for livestock and children and a garden, for Mamie. After thirty years on their homestead, with most mines closed and the people who worked them leaving or gone, the Hibbses, for reasons now lost, called it quits, sold their land to a man who sold it to someone else, who sold it to someone else, who sold it to the government in 1945.

Past the Hibbses' irrigation ditches, I found a four-foot headstone of chiseled white marble protected by a chain-link fence. Henry Clay Merritt, superintendent of the Kentuck Gold Mine, born June 4, 1843, died November 2, 1884, when he fell from a supply boat headed downriver and drowned. Searchers buried Merritt near the spot where they found him, about a mile upstream from his mine. He left a wife and two children and a headstone the forest service says is the "fanciest" along the Salmon River. The Kentuck Mine closed sometime after 1918, the old mining equipment salvaged for scrap in 1941.

I did the math, figuring Merritt's age when he died, and realized it was his birthday. He was 158. I'm not prone to gestures but thought he deserved something and so picked some wild roses from the old irrigation ditches (probably against forest service regulations), returned to the grave, reached through the fence, and placed the small flowers in front of his headstone. Standing there, I wondered how the spot had looked when Merritt died, how it looked when the Hibbses had lived there, how it would look in a year, a decade, a century. Would people still work on the land, salmon still swim in the river that carried their name? Would the most important history remain what didn't happen?

4

Into the Wilderness

I am glad I shall never be young without wild country to be young
in. Of what avail are forty freedoms without a blank spot on the
map? —Aldo Leopold, A Sand County Almanac

Wilderness: Land of no uses. —Idaho bumper sticker

A convoy of pickups and SUVs pulling empty raft trailers to the
take-out for the Salmon's middle fork rattled past the forest service campground and Henry Clay Merritt's grave while I fixed
my morning breakfast of instant oatmeal. The little convoy reminded me how alone I was and that the end of my trip was a
long way off. I pulled myself a little deeper into my clothes and
held my hands close to the backpacking stove trying to fight off
the cold and wet. In those first days of the trip, the mornings always seemed oppressive, although the feeling usually went away
once I put on the river.

I was on the edge of a huge wilderness and about to reach
the stretch of river I had, before the trip started, looked forward
to the most. But that morning, June 5, the ninth day of my trip,
my paddling clothes were cold and damp, and nothing's quite as

miserable as sliding into cold, damp polypro. I stretched out my routine. I walked the empty campground before heading to the river to filter drinking water. I let the wash water I had poured into my cooking pot after breakfast stand for several minutes even though that wasn't necessary to get the pot clean. I held some of my damp polypro tight against my body trying to warm it just a little. Finally, I stripped out of my dry clothes and pulled on my paddling clothes; polypro bottoms first, then a thin shirt, and over that, a heavier shirt. I swung my arms and twisted my body back and forth trying to generate some heat before pulling on my waterproof pants and dry top. The damp paddling clothes reminded me that nothing is completely waterproof. I slipped on my wet neoprene booties, spray skirt, life jacket, helmet and then drug the forty-pound kayak loaded with sixty pounds of gear down to the river.

The day's rapids would come at me right away with almost no time for a warm-up. I took a quick look at the forest service river map, more to check distances to the Middle Fork confluence—twenty miles away—and to the Corn Creek Ranger Station—twenty-seven miles away—than for its descriptions of the downstream rapids. A river map can only give the most basic information about a rapid, and I was on my own to find the best route through each. Most of the rapids would be class three or four, which was all I really needed to know. On the river, I rushed through my warm-up of sweep and draw strokes, and before I finished I came to a small wooden bridge. The forest service had posted a sign on it that read "rapids ahead."

Just past the bridge, the river jumped off the lip of a horizon line. I worked my way downstream, moving from eddy to eddy, until I could see beyond the lip. That first rapid, Pine Creek, seethed with an unchecked energy that made it look like a videotape of the river playing on fast forward. Water frothed and foamed its way around rocks. Pressed itself into white-capped waves. Fell over boulders to form hydraulics—where the river spins back on itself in whirlpools turned sideways—powerful

enough to send a kayak flipping end over end in an endless series of cartwheels.

I needed to see the rapid in slow motion. I boat-scouted from
a small eddy where I could look for dangers and study how the
currents moved. The whitewater video slowed, and the rapid
snapped into focus. The boat-chewing hydraulic blocked the
river's left side but not its right. A smooth tongue of green water funneled straight past the rocks in the rapid's first section,
and the waves below, in the second section, were smooth and
stable. I threw myself into the river's current. The kayak turned
downstream in a smooth arc. I dropped onto the green tongue
and paddled hard, slid past the hydraulic on river left, the sharp-
edged boulder on river right, and plowed into the head-high
standing waves. I turned the kayak sideways, pressed my paddle
blade flat against the water for balance, bobbed from trough to
crest, and from each crest looked downstream for trouble. In the
runout, I caught my breath and paddled toward the next rapid.

Idaho has its share of small creeks, but what it's known for
is its big rivers with big, booming rapids. The whitewater below
Pine Creek hissed like a Dick Dale guitar lick, felt dangerous,
filled with the push and power of tons of water at work on the
kayak. But the lines were easy to read, and the treacherous spots
easy to avoid. I charged the rapids without hesitation. Each successful run brought a little more confidence, pushing the memories of the bumbling runs through Sunbeam and the other early
rapids a little farther into the past.

After ten miles or so, the river gentled for a while. An occasional truck bounced and splashed its way along a road that had
long ago turned to dirt. Cow elk and their calves grazed among
the pines. Mountains as steep as expert ski slopes and covered
with a ragged quilt of bunchgrasses met the river in a jumble
of rocks. The mountains and cliffs, the same features that give
the Salmon its beauty, shrunk views to a wedge of sky overhead,
while the river's downhill tilt created a horizon line that circum-
scribed the world ahead and behind. The way the river fit into the

land had to be felt, measured by intuition, by the distance to the next horizon line, the steepness of its banks, the force and color of its water, and the size of its tributaries.

Around noon, as the sun tried but failed to break through the clouds, the river picked up again. The Salmon's middle fork, its largest tributary, poured into the main river through a narrow gap in the mountains. Idaho rivers often are named this fork or that fork of some main river, and the Salmon's major tributaries—the East Fork, the North Fork, the Middle Fork, which actually comes in from the south, and the South Fork—follow that convention. In the Salmon basin, at its most extreme, this naming scheme has produced the East Fork of the South Fork of the Salmon River.

The Middle Fork is one of my favorite rivers. Its green waters cut a hundred-mile path through the 2.4 million–acre Frank Church–River of No Return Wilderness. The Middle Fork is part of what drew me West, a wild river flowing through a giant and mostly unpeopled landscape, and at one point I considered starting my trip to the ocean at its headwaters. That was when I still craved the idea of being alone and back before my bouts of loneliness on the river.

The idea of living alone in wild country is part of the American myth, the legacy of Henry David Thoreau and *Walden* perhaps. The myth of wilderness has somehow worked to separate the natural from the human, although I doubt that was the intent of Thoreau and the other Romantics. Still, I am as vulnerable to wild myth as anyone. As I planned my trip, I started to realize that I sought the intersection of the human and the natural, needed to understand the social, political, and ecological forces driving our conflicted desires about the Columbia and its tributaries. I needed to encounter people as much as wilderness, and so ruled out a Middle Fork beginning. Besides, I would have plenty of time in the wilderness. The main Salmon flows eighty miles through the Frank Church Wilderness, and after The Frank, through canyons that Congress never designated wilderness, but that are wild all the same.

I floated past the confluence and looked into the Middle Fork's granite canyon, trying to find the spot where I had seen a black bear on an earlier trip, as if the bear might still be there. I speculated on the possibilities lost by not starting my trip on that river. I made dozens of decisions every day, some minor, some significant, the significance of each increasing the farther I traveled from towns and paved roads. But I had no one to offer me advice or talk over the decisions with, which is one reason the trip had weighed so heavily on me those first few days. Of course there were advantages to the situation—no one to compromise with, no one to blame or say "I told you so" after a mistake, no clash of personalities, no group dynamics. Whatever my decisions, right or wrong, they were mine, and whatever happened, the river moved me downstream.

Past the Middle Fork confluence, the main again picked up energy. Flush with new water from its big tributary, the river built itself into long chains of high-standing waves punctuated by deep, churning hydraulics. I paused at the top of the first rapid and picked a line through the slalom course of waves and holes. Some hard forward strokes, a couple sweep strokes on the left, more forward strokes, and another sweep brought me safely through the whitewater.

A head-high wave, glassy green except for a breaking crest that edged it in tumbling foam, guarded the top of the next rapid. The river sucked me toward the wave. My kayak accelerated as I fell into the rapid. I gave a hard sweep on the left and spun the kayak so the bow pointed upstream. As I slid into the trough, I paddled hard. And for a few seconds, I surfed. It was an act of confidence since surfing increases the odds of flipping. I carved the boat right like a board surfer shooting the curl, then tried to cut back hard to the left. I put too much edge in the water and the wave shot me downriver, my ride over before it had really started.

When I reached a forest service boat ramp, I called it a day. The ranger station at Corn Creek seemed like the edge of the world—

there was only a concrete boat ramp, a pair of green-roofed government A-frames, a flagpole with an American flag, and a campground. The road ends at Corn Creek too, and past the ranger station, movement keeps time with the river and pack stock and changing seasons. A redheaded forest service ranger named Kelly met me after I pulled my kayak onto the ramp. She wasn't there for idle conversation. The Salmon's wilderness stretch is heavily regulated. The ranger needed to check my equipment, issue me a permit, charge me a five-dollar-a-day fee for floating the river, and make sure I knew the rules and would follow them—no soap in the water, all trash packed out, all solid human waste kept in a makeshift toilet carried in the kayak, and since I didn't have a fire pan, no open fires.

I changed into dry clothes. I had finished kayaking for the day, and headed to the office to pay and fill out the forms for my permit. A bighorn ram grazed undisturbed by people coming and going. The office was dark. Maps of Idaho hung on the walls. A VHF radio crackled in the background. A kayaker traveling alone is unusual, and Kelly asked what I was doing. I talked to her about my trip and wound up hanging out with her and a friend of hers from Salmon named Craig. Craig was waiting for friends rafting the Middle Fork to float their way to Corn Creek for a trip down the main. He said I could probably tag along if I wanted.

When I had called Juliet from the hotel in Salmon a few days earlier, I had told her I would try to find a group to run the wilderness stretch with. Both of us knew it was safer. I was still a little insecure about paddling a loaded kayak then, and also lonely. But even in my loneliness, part of me wanted to run the wilderness stretch alone. I balanced that desire against the reality that if something went wrong on the river, I might simply disappear. Nobody would know I was missing for days. My body might never be found. I recalled the stories of expeditions gone wrong that sometimes fill outdoor magazines. In many of those disasters, the victims had failed to stick to a plan developed beforehand—didn't turn back from a summit attempt at the predetermined time, didn't scout rapids all agreed needed scouting—and the impromptu change had lead to disaster and death.

After I filled out all the paperwork and paid the fees, the three of us hiked up a hillside behind the ranger station. Marmots barked high-pitched warnings as we neared their burrows. Kelly had forgotten her hand-held radio and started worrying her boss might call and become concerned or angry when she didn't answer. She thought of turning back but decided she was off duty and shouldn't have to carry a radio all the time. We kept hiking, and it felt good to use my legs. After a while we could look down on the ranger station and the river, and I got a sense of what it meant to be at the end of the road.

A burned area covered a mountain on the river's far side. Kelly said the year before, she and the other rangers had watched the fire come closer and closer and that the fire looked like it might jump the river but never did. "It was scary," Kelly said. One of us commented that the late snow that had fallen over the last few days might prevent another bad fire season, or at least delay it a bit. We kept walking. We talked, about the weather, about life in central Idaho and the politics of the region, and about ourselves. Craig's parents ran a hunting and rafting operation. He seemed content working seasonal jobs—raft guide in summer, hunting guide in fall, forest service technician in spring. Young and strong, he moved at a pace Kelly and I couldn't match, and hiked away before I ever got a sense of his future life the way I did with Kelly.

Kelly grew up in Salmon, the daughter of a forest service silviculturalist. She had left town to go to college, studied journalism for awhile, dropped out, changed her majors a couple of times, and kept drifting back to Idaho. "I want to graduate by the time I'm thirty," she said. That gave her six years.

"What's the job situation like in Salmon?" I asked.

"Salmon's a hard place to make a living. People will work two or three jobs to keep the bills paid." In the winter, when she wasn't in school, Kelly worked as a lift operator at a ski resort in Sun Valley.

"Will you come back to Salmon when you finish school?" I asked.

"I could see myself settling here, it depends. But I like it." Her reason for staying in a town four hours from anything a person might consider a city, a place where it snows in June, was that she liked living there. Not a job, not any other reason. "It would be because I'm choosing to live in Salmon," she said.

After the hike, Kelly cooked spaghetti over the A-frame's propane stove for Craig and me. It started to rain and she said I could store my gear inside and sleep on the floor. Kelly and another ranger had spent all spring piling up dead wood outside the ranger's cabin. Their wood collection was a fire hazard and against the rules and their boss planned to visit the next day. That night, they built a giant bonfire. The rain came and went, but under a canopy of pines and next to the fire, the rain didn't matter.

Three rafters, the only others in the campground, joined us. We huddled around the fire and roasted marshmallows. Somebody brought out a boombox, somebody else some beers. We talked, and I learned the wife of one of the rafters worked at the Idaho Falls newspaper where I had worked. Idaho seems so small sometimes. Often, after meeting someone new, you will find acquaintances and friends in common. Kelly and Craig, for instance, grew up with the daughter of a woman who had worked as a correspondent for the newspaper where I had worked; earlier, I had met a woman who worked with a former neighbor, and she had told me that my old neighbor had just had a baby; later, I would meet a group of rafters from Idaho Falls and of course we would find we had mutual friends.

I don't remember most of what was said around the fire, and the specifics of the conversation didn't really matter. That night, we all needed a little company. In a few weeks, after the late-spring chill faded from the mountains and the campground filled each evening with large groups of boaters, I suspect strangers wouldn't find it to be such a social place.

I went to bed after the fire burned out. Cold rain pelted the metal roof of the A-frame the forest service charged its rangers eighty dollars a month to rent. I slept dry and comfortable. Kelly made a hot breakfast for me the next morning, and I had warm and dry paddling clothes to slip into on a cold, wet day. I was grateful for the small hospitalities and happy I was about to paddle into the largest wilderness area in the continental United States.

Eight of Craig's friends in two light gray rafts, an outfitter's name stenciled on the sides, pulled onto the Corn Creek boat ramp. They had shivered through the previous night's rain and several days of snow on the Middle Fork. They stood or sat in the rafts, curled into their rain jackets with that miserable look people have when they worry they might never feel warm again. Most looked about Kelly and Craig's age, in their early twenties, and worked for a local outfitter. They were on a training trip, getting to know the two rivers where they would spend the summer rowing people who'd spent a thousand dollars or more to get away from cars and television and electricity. The trip was mostly an excuse to get on the river though.

Below Corn Creek, we drifted past two aluminum jet boats tied out on river left and a large guest lodge overlooking a great, calm eddy. When Congress authorized the Central Idaho Wilderness, it let people keep their private land interspersed with the federal land and maintain already existing structures within the wilderness. Most wilderness areas prohibit any type of motor, even chain saws, but the legislation also allowed jet boats on the main Salmon, but not the Middle Fork, and airplane access to a series of backcountry airstrips. Those compromises allowed Frank Church, who represented Idaho in the Senate back when the state's voters still sent Democrats to Congress, to get the wilderness bill passed.

Nobody now, I suspect, would accept the compromises Church accepted. Some groups would argue jet boats and small planes diminish the sense of remoteness, which they do, and that the ranches and guest lodges take away from the wilderness experience. Others would paint the wilderness as part of the federal government's "war on the West," part of a plan to deny the region its timber and mineral wealth, part of a plan to lock average people out and turn the area into a playground for the rich. Without Church's compromises, the Salmon might look very different now.

The river changed the scenery, the lodge disappeared, and the wilderness swallowed up our little flotilla of two rafts and a kayak. I paddled between the rafts, introducing myself and answering questions about my trip. The rafters had stowed my gear with theirs on the rafts, and my kayak suddenly became nimble and quick. It jumped forward when I planted my paddle and tensed my muscles. I sculpted the water with the paddle blades, tucked precisely into tiny eddies, then quickly, sometimes without even pausing in the calm, powered back into the main current. I took crazy lines through easy rapids. I surfed any wave I could surf. I let small hydraulics grab the kayak and hold it sideways until a well-timed stroke pushed the boat back into the main current. When I flipped, I rolled up laughing. I felt the river in a way I hadn't for days, and flowed with it like a drop of water or a young salmon.

I paddled through the calm pools between rapids with slow easy strokes, keeping time with the rafts' dipping oars. We all paused to watch a golden eagle hop from riverside rock to riverside rock. I assumed it was trying to get back into the air after an unsuccessful attack on a marmot, but really, I had no idea what it was doing. The group in the first raft, and I remember it as the first raft because it was always in the lead, saw a bear. I thought of the crew from the first raft as the "wild boys" although they weren't really boys. The five of them were all loud and lean and muscular, all except Craig, who seemed to me the wildest of them all, college friends and fraternity brothers. They did back flips from the raft into the freezing cold river, poured packets of protein powder into their mouths and washed it down with water, and drank beer from holes punched into the cans.

They made me laugh. To them, I was probably a novelty, some crazy guy they could talk about later. I sometimes floated with the first raft, but couldn't join those boys. A river trip when you are in your late thirties means something else, means carrying different expectations. My time as a wild boy had passed, and honestly, even when I was younger, I was never very wild.

So I spent most of my time floating with the second raft. It was quieter, which fit my mood. There were four people in the raft, two women and two men. The women, Jessica and Jo, were, in their own ways, as wild as the wild boys. They had grown up in Salmon and with the wilderness, and it seemed a part of them. That wildness made them prettier than they already were. Both were home from college for the summer. Jessica was going to work as a raft guide, while Jo, the daughter of bush pilots, was going to learn to fly.

The two men and I were the odd ones out, connected to the others not by college or hometown, but by the river. One of them was quiet and I never really got to know him. The other, Brad, was tall with curly, dark hair streaked with a bit of gray and talked a lot when he rowed. Brad was also one of the more experienced group members. He was forty-four, seven years older than me, and the trip's oldest member, its "fart," according to the wild boys. I liked him just because he saved me from that distinction. His wife lived in Boise and taught yoga, and between summer river trips, he would make five-or six-hour drives back to Boise. It was a lot of time on the road piled on top of hard, physically demanding work. In the winter, Brad managed a ropes course in Boise that was part of a counseling program for troubled kids.

Guiding is one of those jobs that sounds romantic, like being a cowboy or a boat captain, but in reality is hard work. Besides rowing heavy rafts all day, guides cook and clean for customers, set up and take down camp, lead hikes, build fires, tell stories, and solve whatever problems come along. I had to wonder why Brad didn't find an easier job closer to home, but then people will make all types of sacrifices to spend time in a place they love.

Brad had spent most of his life working in central Idaho's wilderness, not just as a raft guide, but also as a smoke jumper and hunting guide. He described his childhood in Boise as "troubled." But as a teen, he went to work in the Frank Church Wilderness for a hunting outfitter. That, he said, had changed his life. As he talked about this, the awkwardness that crops up between two people who don't know each other well but find themselves discussing a deeply personal subject flooded into our conversation.

Brad always had a story, and it always involved some adventure in the wilderness. He talked about parachuting into wildfires when we rowed past an old section of burned mountainside. When we saw a deer close to the river, he talked about spotting a cougar and her three almost-mature kittens while deer hunting. When he heard a bird sing its riverside song, he would always assign a name—rufous-sided towhee, western tanager, mountain bluebird. I'm no good at birding by ear, and he could have thrown out almost any name and I wouldn't have known the difference.

Midday, after twenty miles on the river, we stopped at a boulder-strewn beach where hot water dribbled over a mat of green algae. The crew from the first raft had already made their way up to the hot springs while the rest of us changed. We gave each other a little privacy so we could get out of our warm river clothes and into our bathing suits. I almost ran to the springs, shivering until the hundred-degree water took away the cold.

Sweepboat captains once stopped at the springs on their one-way trips downriver, and according to the river map, the captains had etched many nearby rocks with their names and the dates of their visits, although the river covered all those rocks when I was there. I could have stayed in the springs' hot water all afternoon, but the group planned to go another ten miles that day. We covered more ground than I really wanted to, but that wasn't my decision. I just followed. Of course I could have taken my gear from the raft and set off on my own. But I didn't.

Below the springs, the river turned moody. I expected rapids, but only the twist and curl of small eddies broke the river's calm. Rock walls that looked light black, if such a color exists, rimmed the river. Boulders the size of semis had tumbled from the walls to litter the bank or rest half submerged in the water. They loomed like raw, dark sculptures, unfinished versions of Easter Island's giant human faces somehow transported to Idaho and waiting only for great hammer blows to form their features. They will wait forever as the river erodes them to sand.

Brooding stands of grand fir replaced the open hills of ponderosa pine. The fir and Pacific yew and queen's cup lily and trillium might be leftovers from a time thousands of years earlier when the region's climate was wetter. Brad pointed out the campsite along Magpie Creek, in the middle of the fir forest, and warned about staying there on early-season trips. "It's too cool and wet," he said.

The sun had cut its way through the clouds a little by the time we made camp that afternoon. I wanted to go for a short hike but heard the clattering tumble of falling rocks. I guessed the wild boys were somewhere rolling the rocks down a hill, and it seemed safest to abandon the hike. Before a spaghetti dinner (even with a group I couldn't get away from eating noodles), an older man, tall and still very muscular, walked into our camp. He was on contract with the forest service building and repairing trails and was camped nearby, he said. He had heard our group pull in and came by to talk. He and Brad played the Idaho name game right away, trying to see if they knew any of the same people. The man said he had been a smokejumper and guided whitewater for years, so of course they did.

The man talked in tall tales. Most of his stories ended with him in a fight beating the crap out of someone. After he left, some of the wild boys would do their best impressions of him, each short tale ending with "so then I punched him." When the tall tale man's stories didn't end with a fight, they ended with a river-trip disaster, some carnage, and often death. They weren't the kind of stories I wanted to hear right then. When he heard about my trip, he told about a friend drowning on the lower Salmon at a rapid called Slide, said the lower was the most dangerous stretch of the Salmon, and warned me to be careful. The stories and warning put me on edge, even though Brad would later tell me that the river already had dropped enough that I wouldn't have any problems.

The next morning, the sky had turned heavy as iron again. The rain came off and on. Two rapids, Big Mallard and Elkhorn, both class fours, were just downstream. The group was quiet, slow to load rafts, and on the river, hesitant, always looking downstream, and always concerned about location. The rapids had created a nervous energy within the group and even though I didn't start out worried, the nervousness infected me. Big Mallard came and went without incident, although the group's nervousness lingered. Just before Elkhorn, Brad turned the oars over to the quiet guy. I waited while the first raft bounced its way through the rapid. The second raft slid into the whitewater, and I could tell Brad was giving the guy at the oars instructions, telling him what line to take and which oar to pull on and when.

I ran on river left, hopping from one eddy to another. The kayak slid smoothly from surging river into calm eddy. I quickly looked downstream, found the next calm spot, then powered back into the river stroking hard. I noticed water coursing over part of a slanted rock, creating something like a miniature waterfall. I decided to launch myself across the rock in a move kayakers refer to as a "boof," for the sound the kayak makes as it lands in the water. I paddled hard and angled the bow slightly to the left. Something, the shape of the rock or the way the water peeled around it, made me think some unseen hazard lurked right where I planned to land. I abandoned the boof. I stopped paddling and found myself trapped on an eddy line. I flipped.

The clashing currents spun my boat in circles, and when I reached for the surface with my paddle to roll, it had no purchase against the water. Cold. Dark. I hung upside down, tucked up tight against the kayak. I felt water trickle in around the wrist gaskets of my dry top. I felt water trickle in around the neck gasket. I didn't want to swim. I set up for anther roll. I needed air but was still trapped on the seam between river and eddy. If I tried to roll, I would only flail at the river. I had to wait and hope. I thought about pulling the kayak's spray skirt and abandoning the boat. Finally, the water felt solid again, a decent spot to roll, and I came up with a gasp.

To get my mind off the flip and near swim, I looked for surf waves, found a few, but didn't have much luck riding them. River waves come in infinite variety. Some are small, some big. Some roll smooth and glassy, others surge out of nothingness, build to a white peak, only to collapse back into nothingness again. Some come slanting off the shore at obtuse angles, ready to capsize a kayak or raft, others well up in midcurrent. Unlike ocean waves, where the water stays in one place and the wave moves, river waves stay put while the water moves. If a wave is big enough and shaped right, gravity will, with some paddling, pull the kayak down the face and keep it there.

A kayak designed to surf has a hull like a surfboard, or hard rails, so a kayaker can carve a wave. But hard rails make a kayak edgy, unstable, and prone to flipping. My kayak had a hull as round as a beer can, or soft rails, which made it forgiving because the river had less to grab, but it surfed like crap. It didn't matter. I would come up on a wave and paddle hard. The wave would hold me briefly, but as soon as I dipped an edge and tried to turn, I would go shooting off down the river, only to find another wave and try again. Each failed surf should have frustrated me but didn't. I relaxed, let go of the less-than-perfect run through Elkhorn and the morning's nervousness.

The Salmon calmed a bit and our little group bunched together. A parapet that looked like it had fallen off some medieval castle loomed over a giant eddy and sandy beach. Buckskin Bill, whose real name was Sylvan Hart and sometimes described as the last of the mountain men, believed the forest service planned to force him from his Salmon River home. The tower was part of his defense plan and was well placed. We beached our boats beneath it, easy targets for any sniper hidden behind its flat stone walls, and climbed to some pink buildings above the river. Hart had moved to the Salmon during the Depression and died in 1980. A couple from Berlin wound up opening a guest lodge on the property. "I've known them since they started and watched them build the place up," Brad told me. They used two jet boats to carry guests to a lodge on the property. "They're doing great," Brad said.

Muzzle loaders Hart had built himself, including a three-gauge rifle that looked like a shoulder-fired cannon, hung on the walls. Brad had a quick conversation with a tall blonde woman, one of the owners, before she played a video tape shot sometime in the 1970s showing Hart firing the cannon gun. He looked the part of mountain man, bearded and dressed in fringed buckskins, but he wasn't just some hermit who had settled along the Salmon River. Hart had an engineering degree, spoke several languages including Latin and Greek, and had worked for Boeing on the Norden bombsite at a factory in Kansas during World War II.

We didn't stay long. Before the tape finished, everyone headed back to the river. I bought a small bag of M&Ms, more for the novelty of buying candy in the wilderness than because I wanted them. "This is a beautiful spot," I told the German woman. "Yes," she said, "Bill picked a nice spot."

The Salmon's south fork emptied into the main river just below Buckskin Bill's. The wild boys turned up it and I followed. Johnny, a muscular guy of average height from Salmon who was, if anyone were in charge, the wild boys' leader, said migrating Chinook salmon sometimes pause in the South Fork's icy water before continuing up the warmer main river. We worked our way slowly upstream for a few hundred yards, fighting the current flowing around a small island, hoping to see dark salmon shapes in the clear water.

By some estimates, ten thousand Chinook once spawned

in the South Fork, with sport fishermen catching between two thousand and almost four thousand a season. Then, in the 1950s and early 1960s, the forest service allowed timber cutting in the watershed. The South Fork flows across the same 75-million-year-old sheet of granite that covers much of central Idaho. Over the millennia, as the granite batholith eroded away to mountain and valley and river canyon, it spread a coat of fined-grained soil across the land. In the winter of 1964–65, after road building and logging had removed the trees that kept the easily eroded granite soil in place, heavy rains fell on melting snow, the river flooded, and who knows how many tons of silt flushed into the South Fork. The floods' force, made worse by the logging, separated a large meander, where many salmon had spawned, from the river. The silt from the cleared mountainsides smothered clean gravels where salmon had spawned and filled pools where the young salmon lived before migrating to the ocean.

By the early 1970s, only a few hundred fish returned to the river, and later, when the federal government started a hatchery on the river, not because of the destructive logging but to compensate for fish killed by the four dams on the lower Snake River, the South Fork didn't have enough salmon for broodstock. Instead, biologists traveled to one of the dams, trapped Chinook that migrated through at the time South Fork salmon migrated, and used them to start the hatchery.

Over time, the South Fork has healed. A biologist with the Idaho Department of Fish and Game told me after my trip that the forest service hasn't held a timber sale in the basin since the 1960s. While water will not return to the large meander, the lack of spawning habitat is no longer a problem on the South Fork, she said. But its Chinook have not recovered, although numbers have increased in recent years because of a cyclical cooling of the Pacific Ocean. Biologists have counted between six hundred and a thousand salmon nests, or redds, since ocean conditions improved. But females will dig more than one nest, so redd counts indicate population trends, not actual salmon numbers. About a quarter to half those nests come from hatchery salmon that escape a weir placed in the river designed to capture them. It's not clear how well the hatchery fish reproduce in the wild or how many of their offspring survive and spawn, the Idaho biologist told me. When I asked her if the South Fork's wild Chinook could recover, she said that they would hold their own as long as ocean conditions remained good and precipitation average, but that drought or changing ocean conditions mean salmon numbers will again start to decline.

The wild boys and I were at most a week ahead of the Chinook migration and so saw nothing in the South Fork's cold waters. When we reached the island's upstream end, we stopped and let the current flush us back to the main river. The group spread out. I drifted between rafts but could see neither. Walls of light black rock crowded against the river. There were no rapids. The sun had come out by then and where rock met river, the rock glistened. I let the kayak drift against a canyon wall. The dark wall had absorbed the sun's energy, and I pressed my palms against it to cut the chill. The river must have worked against that rock for uncountable eons, polishing it smooth as a gemstone hanging from a pendant. My hands tingled from the heat, and I turned them over to warm the backs. I paddled until the chill returned, then again placed my hands against the canyon. Slowly, the second raft caught up to me, and my isolation ended.

Throughout the trip, Jessica and Jo had been reading *River of No Return*, going over stories of the river's old residents. After the dark canyon walls opened up, a small creek dropped into the Salmon on river left near a flat dotted with log buildings. "The Polly Bemis Ranch," they almost shouted in unison.

Then one of them, I don't remember who, started to read about Polly Bemis even though they already knew the details of her life by heart. "It began in China, September 11, 1853, when Lalu Nathoy was born of impoverished parents. Starvation forced her father to sell Lalu into slavery in order to get seed for his crops." At some point, Lalu picked up the name Polly. She had been brought to the United States, first to San Francisco then to Portland, Oregon, where a man named Hong King bought her for twenty-five hundred dollars. In 1872, he took her to a small town south of the Salmon River. She supposedly worked in a saloon owned by her master, who, as the legend goes, lost her in a poker game to Charles Bemis. Polly later denied the poker story; however, she managed her escape from forced servitude and wound up living with Bemis.

In 1890, she nursed him back to health after someone shot him in the face over a gambling dispute, and in 1894 he married her to prevent her possible deportation. Not long after that, Charles and Polly Bemis moved to the Salmon. The River of No Return describes Polly cooking, cutting firewood, gardening, caring for ducks and chickens and a cow (it's not clear what Charles did), and then at three every afternoon, stopping to fish. Charles Bemis died in 1922, and Polly left the Salmon for a while. But she missed the river, and so when she was seventy-one, she moved back to the home she and Charles had settled and lived there until just before she died in 1933.

The pictures of Polly Bemis in River of No Return show a small woman—the book describes her as being "as big as the small end of nothing, whittled to a fine point," and weighing a hundred pounds or less—with a weathered face and gray hair.

"What is it you like so much about Polly Bemis?" I asked.

"She was a strong woman," Jessica said.

"She could survive situations where many people might not," Jo said.

If the Salmon had been dammed, if slackwater had flooded over Bemis's ranch and washed away the logs of her cabin, her story might have vanished. Just as the story of Polly Bemis needed the wilderness, the wilderness needed the story of Polly Bemis.

We camped not far from the Polly Bemis ranch at a sandy spot called California Creek. By then the clouds that plagued the trip had vanished. It felt like a summer day. We went barefoot on the warm clean sand and wore just shorts and t-shirts for the first time in days. A small group of bighorn sheep wandered down the steep and crumbling hillside above the opposite river bank. A lamb raced through the bunchgrass while the adults sipped from the river. The bellies of two or three ewes bulged so clearly it looked like they would drop their lambs any day.

I watched the sheep and napped off and on while the wild boys competed in an impromptu Olympics, tossing round, polished river-rock shot puts and flat river-rock discuses for distance. Jo and Jessica joined in. Someone buried a pair of five gallon buckets and everybody pitched sand-filled pop cans at them in a game similar to horseshoes. Then a game of butt darts, where you clench a small river rock with your butt cheeks and try to drop the rock into a bull's-eye scratched into the sand, started up.

Brad brought out a Gordian Knot of ropes, showed us how to untie them, then challenged us to do the same. I gave up after a few minutes, but one of the wild boys solved the riddle. Next Brad stretched out a throw rope between two ammo boxes rafters use for waterproof storage. I took my turn on top of a box holding the yellow rope loosely in my hands. One of the wild boys stood on the other ammo box and did the same. The object of the game was to make the other person fall off their box.

"You just sat around all afternoon, but you got up to play this," one of the wild boys said. It was almost a taunt. My opponent gave a tug on the rope and I let it slide through my hands. I pulled and he did the same. Then he pulled hard. The rope again slid through my hands. The wild boy looked a little off balance after the pull and I yanked the rope, hard. But he had already loosened his grip, and I went tumbling into the sand. I chalked the loss up to age.

Between the river Olympics and a hamburger dinner, I chatted with Johnny, who was, besides the closest thing the wild boys had to a leader, the trip's official forest service permit holder. Johnny was twenty-one, an accounting major at the University of Idaho, and he told me he sometimes goes by the nickname Pup, which has something to do with an incident that earned his older brother the name Sheep Dog.

"I don't think I need to hear the details of that one," I said. "Tell me about your family. Have they been in Salmon for long?"

"My mother grew up in California, but my father's family has lived in Salmon for five generations. I have relatives who are ranchers. My father's a lawyer and a former river guide. He'll be a judge one day," Johnny said.

We didn't talk politics, but what I was digging at with my questions was ultimately political. "What do you think about the conflicts over land use in the region?" I asked.

"People have to face facts," he told me. "We just can't keep tearing the land apart like we used to; there needs to be regulation." He said he had one brother who worked for a jet boat maker in Oregon and another studying environmental law so he could work on salmon policy. "It's just kind of crazy because you live in Salmon, Idaho, but you can't catch a salmon," he said. The stretch of river through the town hadn't seen a salmon season in thirty years, and even though Johnny would pause on his rafting trips to look for salmon, he'd never caught one.

"What do you think about dam breaching?"

"I think with everything you give up, you have to weigh it carefully, but I don't have a problem with dam breaching," he said.

"Do other people in Salmon your age feel the same way?"

"Yes," he said. One person, or even one family, can't speak for a town or a region or a state of course. Central Idaho's wilderness exists, to some extent, because of bureaucrats and congressional legislation, and if people's desires changed and Congress acted, we could dam the Salmon River, cut its timber, and mine its gold. People shape the Salmon's wilderness, but the wilderness also shapes us, our desires, and our expectations of what is possible.

Johnny said he grew up on the river. "Boating on it, it's just like a spiritual thing. I think it takes a while to develop a relationship with the river—any river."

"What do you like most about guiding?" I asked.

"The best part is taking out people who have never seen the wilderness and showing them central Idaho," he said.

"And what do people like best about the wilderness?"

"The stars. They all comment on how many stars there are at night."

I stayed up late that night. Stars flared across a canopy of night sky that stretched from one side of the canyon to the other, and I let their number and brightness amaze me. The river moved like a shadow in the moonless starlight, and I could just make out the rafts tugging against the lines that held them to the beach. The noise of the river's waves cresting and breaking filled up the night as the Salmon surged its way toward the ocean.

The next morning, my final day with the group started as sunny and warm as the previous day had ended. We loaded the rafts early even though we had only eight miles to the takeout. I savored those last miles of unburdened paddling, made the most of the rapids, and even managed a couple of decent surfs. But we hit the boat ramp at Vinegar Creek before I was ready. A van and a driver from the rafting company waited. I helped Johnny and Brad and the rest of the group load gear and rafts, and when we finished, I said my good-byes.

On my own again, I expected the loneliness to come crashing back on me, but it didn't. I still had a long way to paddle, which suddenly made me happy. My trip had just started, and somehow, traveling with other people through the wilderness let me put aside most of the doubts and worries that had plagued my first days on the river. I rested on the boat ramp eating a granola bar and some fruit Johnny had left for me. The town of Riggins wasn't far downstream, but I didn't want to stop for the night in a town. I loaded gear into my kayak and started downstream to find a camping spot where I could swim in the river and then stretch out to nap on white sand under a red-trunked ponderosa pine.

5

Watching Fish in Riggins

Fisheries biologists have generally focused on populations that can be described by numbers. Biologists tend to treat the statistics as though they were independent of the ecological systems that produce them, and regard the fish as though they were under the complete control of the humans who manage them. —Jim Lichatowich, Salmon Without Rivers

People in the Northwest never have casual discussions about salmon. Because almost anything from irrigating a field, to operating a dam, to building a skyscraper might affect salmon, conflict lurks beneath any conversation on the subject, even the most superficial. For every person who sees salmon as a symbol of the wild, someone else blames them for a needless government regulation, failed farm, or lost job. A discussion about salmon is a discussion about economics, politics, biology, and philosophy.

The animals we choose to fight over tell us something about ourselves and about our society. In the Columbia and other Northwest rivers, fish called lamprey follow a life history similar to salmon. Lamprey look like eels, but their mouths are suction disks rimmed with sharp teeth. Their skeletons are made of cartilage, so as a species, they predate even the evolution of bones. Like salmon, lamprey are anadromous, meaning they are born in freshwater, migrate to the ocean to mature, then return to freshwater where they spawn and die.

Lamprey are parasites and survive in the ocean by attaching themselves to other fish, even salmon, and draining their fluids. Lamprey struggle to survive in the Columbia for many of the same reasons as salmon, and it seems the lamprey's fate is joined with that of their sometimes prey. The *New York Times* prints editorials on the need to save the Columbia's salmon, but I doubt it even knows the parasitic lamprey exist, much less worries over their fate. Salmon carry the weight of a thousand issues, focus a thousand debates, create for us a thousand problems we might otherwise ignore.

So having a discussion about salmon with a stranger isn't always an easy matter. But the day after I left Johnny and Brad and the rest of the rafters at Vinegar Creek, a chance meeting would land me in the bow of a drift boat anchored just downstream from Riggins talking to a stranger about salmon.

Beyond the Salmon's wilderness stretch, long, quiet pools separate the river's rapids from one another. Paddling the pools takes some effort, and on June 9, the thirteenth day of my trip, I had to deal not only with the still pools, but also with strong headwinds as I paddled to Riggins.

At Riggins, the river bends it course from west to north. The town started as a mining claim but has since grown into a small community along the only road connecting southern Idaho with its northern panhandle. Logging and ranching dominate the area, but in summer, Riggins is something of a whitewater town, home to a dozen or so outfitters and a jumping-off point not only for people floating various stretches of the Salmon River but also the Hells Canyon section of the Snake River.

The Little Salmon runs along the southern edge of town, and just past where the Little Salmon and the main river meet, a rapid forms. Mostly large standing waves, a submerged rock creates a powerful hydraulic hidden in the waves, and when kayaking, the rapid requires some attention to avoid a thrashing. I paddled hard into the top of the rapid, attacking it like I would any other drop. Then I stopped to gawk the way somebody might at a traffic accident in the opposite lane of the freeway. I had floated into the Salmon River's first salmon season in thirty years. Anglers stood on shore so close together they almost touched one another and filled the rafts, jet boats, and drift boats bobbing in the current. I couldn't imagine how so many fishing lines in the river at once didn't create a tangled bird's nest of monofilament somewhere underwater. I don't think I took another paddle stroke. I almost flipped.

I hadn't seen that many people in one place since my trip started. I floated past a boat ramp jammed with trucks and trailers and on toward the edge of town. I wanted to avoid the crowds but needed to go into Riggins to phone Juliet and let her know I was okay and to make arrangements for her to meet me in Lewiston, Idaho, with the sea kayak I would paddle on the next portion of the trip. So just beyond the far end of town, where the anglers thinned, I beached my kayak and walked back into Riggins.

Bars, restaurants, hotels, and gas stations stretch along the mile of highway that also serves as the town's main road. Signs taped to doors and hung in windows declared: "This business supported by salmon dollars." Other signs listed new, extended hours that would last for only another day, when salmon season ended.

I dodged cars looking for a pay phone, but when I called Juliet, she wasn't home. So I walked down to the Little Salmon River. Anglers filled the banks, had squeezed past trees, bushes, and boulders to reach the edge of a turbulent river so small one bank was just a short cast from the other. I stood on a bridge spanning the river and watched their baits swing in the current. Somewhere, invisible in the river's dark green water, Chinook salmon, some weighing maybe twenty pounds or more, pushed their way upstream. They were on the final leg of a journey that had taken them uncountable miles only to end up back at the hatchery where they had started life. Since the Chinook had entered the Columbia, roughly 575 miles downstream, the fat stored during their one to three years in the ocean had fueled their travels, because, like all salmon, they had stopped feeding after they entered freshwater. It's not clear why fish that aren't eating will strike at bait, but they will. Staring down from the bridge, I wanted to see the dark form of a salmon rocket from the shadows and inhale some angler's bait.

People often assume there are as many species of salmon as there are rivers with salmon. But only five Pacific salmon species live in North America, all members of the genus *Oncorhynchus*: Chinook, *Oncorhynchus tshawytscha*; sockeye, *O. nerka*; coho, *O. kisutch*; pink, *O. gorbuscha*; and chum salmon, *O. keta*. Two additional ocean-going species from the genus also live in North America: steelhead, *O. mykiss*, which are actually a strain of rainbow trout that migrate to the ocean and cutthroat trout, *O. clarkii*, which in coastal rivers are frequently anadromous. Unlike salmon, steelhead and cutthroat trout often survive spawning. Salmon and steelhead inhabit the entire north Pacific rim, spawning not only in North America, but also in the Russian Far East, Japan, and Korea. (Two additional species of salmon live in the western Pacific, while Atlantic salmon are in the genus *Salmo* and more closely related to brown trout than to Pacific salmon.)

Of course fish of the same species from different rivers are not exactly the same—for instance, migration and spawning timing can vary from river to river—although it takes sophisticated genetic tests to determine which river a salmon came from. Complicating matters is the fact that salmon don't always spawn in the river where they hatched. The salmon myth tells of fish surmounting any obstacle to return to their natal streams where they spawn and die. In reality, a certain number of fish, one or two percent for some species, twenty percent for others, miss their home streams and spawn in new territory. So some genetic mixing occurs. In a region where one natural disaster or another might temporarily block access to a stream or turn it inhospitable, straying ensures a few fish always survive somewhere, and that they have the ability to colonize new habitat.

For management purposes, the Columbia Basin is divided into several zones called Evolutionarily Significant Units, or ESUs in the bureaucratic lingo of endangered species. The Salmon River is part of the Snake River ESU, and the Salmon's Chinook, sockeye, and steelhead are managed together with those same species from other Snake tributaries. The Upper Columbia, Mid-Columbia, Lower Columbia, and Willamette rivers comprise the rest of the Columbia's ESUs. Not all species found within a given ESU carry the same Endangered Species Act status. In the Snake River ESU, for instance, sockeye are listed as endangered, which means they're at risk of going extinct, while Chinook are deemed threatened, which means they're at risk of becoming endangered. And the status of a given species can vary from ESU to ESU. For example, Mid-Columbia Chinook aren't even listed under the Endangered Species Act.

Chinook salmon stocks are further subdivided based on the season that adults leave the ocean. The lives of fish in each seasonal migration play out in different ways. Spring Chinook, like those from the Little Salmon, spawn in tributaries and in the headwaters of large rivers. Summer Chinook, which spawn in parts of the Salmon River system and are managed together with the river's spring Chinook, spawn slightly farther downstream in the same rivers and tributaries used by spring Chinook. Fall Chinook live in the Snake and main-stem Columbia, but not the Salmon, and spawn in the main reaches of large rivers.

Even though Chinook in the Snake and Salmon rivers are listed as threatened, the rivers' wild and hatchery fish are managed separately. In 2001 and several subsequent years, the federal, state, and tribal agencies responsible for the Columbia's salmon decided that enough Chinook would return to the hatchery near

Riggins to allow fishing. To distinguish wild salmon from hatchery salmon, hatcheries remove a small fin located near the tail called the adipose fin, and any salmon with an intact fin has to be released.

An Idaho Congresswoman once asked how salmon could be endangered when shoppers can find them in cans stocked on grocery store shelves. Because salmon range over such a wide area, and because some rivers maintain abundant populations, those affected or simply upset by the restrictions that have come with Endangered Species Act listings of the Columbia's Chinook, sockeye, chum, and steelhead argue that salmon are not endangered. They hold fast to the taxonomy of salmon. To break a species into separate populations and stocks, as the Endangered Species Act allows, is nonsense, they say. Only distinctions between species matter and the provisions that allow protection of various populations of a single species reflect only a flawed law.

Even a detailed explanation of salmon life histories cannot provide an answer about the validity of dividing a species into stocks and runs. Science can't say if healthy salmon runs in Alaska or Russia compensate for salmon lost to Idaho, Washington, or Oregon. Biologists can provide data about the biological effects of the loss, economists an estimate on economic impact, but the debate turns on opinion and politics. Still, the science is important since it underlies the various opinions and political positions people adopt. Besides, there's wonder in the repeating rhythms of salmon biology.

If the Little Salmon's Chinook hadn't come from a nearby hatchery, they would have found a cool, deep pool in the river where they planned to spawn and summered there, living for months off their fat and flesh before finally spawning. I have pushed through maple and Douglas fir saplings, scraped against the limbs of fallen cedars and cottonwoods, just to watch spring Chinook spawn. Near summer's end, both before and after my trip, I made my way to where the Yakima River leaves the Cascade Mountains' eastern slopes and flows toward the Columbia. Since the process doesn't change much with run or species, what I have seen on the Yakima differs little from what I might see along the Salmon River where wild Chinook still spawn, or what I might see on the Sacramento River in California, the Rogue River in Oregon, the Fraser in British Columbia, the Yukon in Alaska, or the Kamchatka in the Russian Far East. By late August or early September, the spring Chinook have lost the silver luster carried with them from the sea; instead, males have turned dark sided and hook snouted, females a greenish brown with hooked noses less prominent than the males'. They leave their summer pools, each female searching for a place to lay her eggs, each male searching for a female. When the female finds the spot she somehow knows by memory, or smell, or feel, she beats a nest, called a redd, into the river cobbles with her tail. Each swipe of her wide tail through the gravel pushes her upstream, but then she will pause, rise to the water's surface, and drift downstream with the current to repeat the process. In shallow water her back may break the surface. When the nest is ready, a male joins her and their bodies quiver as she releases eggs; he releases milt.

Spawning is a salmon's last act before death, and sometimes a sadness creeps in when I watch. White fungus coats the salmon's fins, and it seems their flesh falls from them even as they swim. The air smells of decay. Dead fish collect on mid-channel snags, sink to the bottom of quiet pools, wash up on gravel bars to rot away. The dead and dying salmon might feed bears, otters, minks, bald eagles, ravens, gulls, dozens of species of aquatic insects, and all types of plants growing along the river. The trees and bushes nourished by the dead salmon shade and cool the river where the young will grow after hatching, and the insects fed by the decaying salmon carcasses will in turn feed the next generation of salmon.

Hidden in their gravel redds, the salmon eggs wait for the autumnal equinox, and then they wait some more. After hatching, the salmon live for a time in the gravel as strange hybrids between egg and fish while they absorb their yolk sacks. Then they leave the gravel as fully formed fish to start their river lives.

From the start of my trip, I had always imagined I moved downstream with young salmon migrating to the ocean. But those salmon are small, maybe four to eight inches long, and often travel deep in the river to avoid predators. I wouldn't see any of my imagined traveling companions until I reached the Snake River, several days downstream from Riggins. There, I would see a beached jet boat and meet three government fisheries biologists pulling a haul seine through the river. I would stop to see what they were doing and ask if any of them knew Juliet, since they all worked for the same agency. But we would have nobody in common.

The men captured juvenile salmon with the seine, put them in a vat of anesthesia and then, with a hypodermic needle, inserted a rice-grain-sized electronic tag into their bodies. Called a PIT tag, it works like a supermarket bar code. Using a computer database, researchers couple information such as where and when a fish was tagged, its species, length, and weight to the PIT tag. When a tagged salmon passes over a reader, it gives a researcher access to all that earlier information. Readers have been installed at the various dams along the Snake and Columbia rivers, and the PIT tags let researchers track salmon on their migrations and compare the number of tagged juvenile salmon migrating to the ocean against the number of tagged adults returning to spawn. PIT tags provide survival figures and other statistics that fill the charts and graphs people use to support whatever position it is they choose in the constantly swirling fights about salmon and the river.

I asked if I could see some of the fish they had caught, and one of the men climbed into the boat and produced a clear tub with a dozen or so juvenile salmon, a mix of spring and summer Chinook, a few fall Chinook from the Snake, plus a coho or two recovering from the handling. Some looked like small trout with dark, vertical bars running down their sides. Called parr, those salmon were not ready to end their river lives. Others had the dark backs and silvery flanks of pelagic creatures. Called smolt, they were becoming their ocean selves. In the Snake and its tributaries, spring and summer Chinook typically spend their first year in the river before heading to sea on a flush of spring snowmelt while the Snake's fall Chinook migrate out just a few months after hatching. The distinctions are not universal and in other sections of the Columbia young summer Chinook behave like fall Chinook and leave the river soon after birth. Even among a single species, life histories vary.

The young of other species follow their own patterns. Coho usually spend a year in freshwater, steelhead almost always two, and sockeye usually one or two, but occasionally three. Whatever the species or run, each fish must go from parr to smolt to cross the barrier between fresh and salt water. Because the body of a fish in a river or lake is saltier than the water surrounding it, the fish constantly absorbs water and so must pass out a stream of diluted urine to keep its tissues from becoming flooded with liquid. But in the ocean, where the water is saltier than the fish, the fish always loses fluids and must drink constantly or risk dehydration. Even a smolt's blood changes to compensate for the differences between river and ocean as it heads downstream.

When the salmon leave the Columbia to begin their ocean lives, most—depending on species, run, and maybe even individual inclination—head north for British Columbia and Alaska. Some swim west along the Aleutians and reach the Bering Sea. They will mix and mingle with salmon from other rivers, and sometimes even other continents, until something calls them back to their home rivers. They will enter the Columbia. Some will stay with the main river; others turn up one tributary or another, the Klickitat maybe, or the John Day or the Snake. The Snake fish will go to the Clearwater or the Grande Ronde or the Salmon, and some of those Salmon River fish, to the Little Salmon.

I waited on the bridge above the Little Salmon for a long time, but saw no fish. I headed back to town. The day was sunny and warm. I stopped for a pistachio ice cream cone at one of those businesses with its extended hours posted in its window, then bought a few groceries at a store with one of those "salmon dollars" signs on its door. After that, I called Juliet. I struggled to hear her voice over the traffic and the pay phone's static. She told me she couldn't stand living with our dog and two cats in the one-bedroom apartment the government had provided as temporary housing after she had moved from Portland, Oregon, to eastern Washington. She had started looking for a house and hoped I didn't mind because she would probably buy one while I was still somewhere on the river. I wasn't sure I liked the idea, but there wasn't anything to do but trust her.

She wanted to know when I needed the sea kayak. I had done the math, figuring four days to cover the remaining eighty miles of the Salmon, plus another day on the Snake. But I told her to meet me upstream from Lewiston at the mouth of the Grand Ronde River in seven days, figuring if I miscalculated the travel time and showed up late, Juliet would assume something bad had happened to me and call somebody who would start a search. If I was early, the worst I would have to do is sit around and wait a couple days.

After we talked, I headed back to my kayak, figuring I might as well paddle some more that day. After walking a few minutes, I realized I had left my groceries by the phone. I ran back to the gas station where I had made the call only to find my food gone. Mad at myself for my forgetfulness, I bought more groceries before leaving Riggins. By then I had given up on paddling for the day.

Close to where the town ended, there was a small wooden building with a sign spelling out "Wapiti River Guides" in yellow letters on a blue background. A dory and an old crazy-colored kayak decorated the building's front yard and a small board with some numbers scrawled in chalk gave the river level. I remembered the warning about the lower river from the man building trails who had talked in tall tales and decided I should try to find out what waited downstream.

A blonde woman working on a computer stopped when I came in. I explained that I was floating the lower Salmon and wanted to know how long it took to reach the Snake River—pointless information since I'd told Juliet I would meet her in a week—and about the rapids downstream. It was a backwards way of doing things, and I got distracted after I noticed some pamphlets on salmon. Our conversation floated off in that direction and I forgot about the downstream rapids the way I had forgotten about my groceries.

The woman, her name was Barb, said it was great to finally have a salmon season. "It's good for the economy, but we're also worried about what people think. It's a double-edged sword. All the hatchery salmon might make people think the fish are out of trouble when that's not the case. Wild salmon aren't recovering, and I want to see wild fish," Barb said. "If you want to know more, you should really talk to my partner. He's guiding a fishing trip, but should be back in a few hours," Barb told me about a better place to camp than the narrow strip of sand pressed between river and road where I had left my boat, and we made arrangements for her partner, Gary Lane, to meet me later in the day at my camp.

I arranged my campsite and waited while three people in a drift boat anchored on the river's far side caught salmon after salmon. I thought about walking back into town to buy a fishing license, hoping I might catch a salmon myself. But asking someone who takes people fishing for a living to take you for free is rude and I didn't.

Gary Lane rowed up to my campsite in his red, yellow, and blue drift boat decorated with line paintings of a buffalo, a bear, and stenciled with the Nez Perce Indian word for Coyote, Itsiyiyi. He was tall and gray haired, wearing a black cowboy hat with an elk tooth–studded headband, no shirt, and a loin cloth. Although I hate to be judgmental, his appearance struck me as New Age and made me a little nervous. I'm always cautious, feeling someone out to see if they know salmon beyond some simplistic myth.

Lane beached his boat, and I grabbed my life jacket and scrambled onboard. He rowed us out to the head of a pool just offshore, and when he told me, I slipped the anchor into the water. Lane, his niece, and her fiancé lowered plastic lures shaped like small fish into the river and let them drift back fifteen or twenty feet before tightening their lines so the crankbaits hung in the current. It was like trolling, except the boat didn't move. I wanted to see someone catch a salmon.

After introductions, Lane and I made small talk, mostly about kayaking. "When I first started kayaking, I hardly saw anybody else on the river. In fact people thought I was crazy," he said. We talked about how kayaks had become shorter and how the sport's focus had changed somewhat from running rivers to spending all day on a roadside wave making the kayak cartwheel or spin. Of course we both admitted that we liked to play even if we still enjoyed running rivers more. Lane asked me about my trip so far, and I talked a little about the wilderness stretch and how great the people I ran it with were. Eventually we started to talk about salmon, and I saw my initial concern about Lane was misplaced. He knew salmon as symbol and as flesh, could talk the science of salmon, the economics of salmon, and the spirituality of salmon.

Lane talked a lot about the American Indians' connection to the salmon. "You don't have to be Indian to appreciate the spiritual value of salmon though," he said. He described how he had organized a welcoming festival for the salmon that year and invited members of the Nez Perce tribe to attend. The Nez Perce retain fishing rights under their treaties with the U.S. government, and tribal members frequently fish around Riggins with large dip nets and sometimes gaffs. Earlier in the day I had seen a Nez Perce man selling fish from the back of a truck to a line of customers.

In their book *Salmon and His People*, Dan Landeen and Allen

Pinkham describe how in the late 1970s and early 1980s, Idaho had tried to stop Nez Perce salmon fishing on the Rapid River, the Little Salmon tributary where the hatchery is located. The state claimed the salmon runs had shrunk so drastically that all fishing needed to end. But the Nez Perce opposed the plan, saying that not only did it violate treaties, but that they weren't responsible for the decline in salmon numbers. Nez Perce fishermen protested. There were threats of violence, and sometimes more, directed at the fishermen by local vigilantes. Finally, a federal arbitrator met with representatives from the tribe and the state. At the meeting, the state said it would continue to let the Nez Perce fish but only using dip nets without mesh bags and gaffs without hooks and that the chairman of the tribe's executive committee could catch one salmon each year. The Nez Perce said the proposal was an insult. Despite some compromises, wrangling over fishing on the Rapid River continued, with Idaho authorities arresting more than eighty tribal fishermen and charging them with a variety of game-law violations. A court ultimately threw out all the charges filed against the fishermen. Since then, Idaho has worked with the tribe managing the Rapid River fishery, sometimes even jointly closing it to fishing during years with poor salmon runs.

A late-day pink settled into the thin clouds that swept across the sky while Lane and I talked. Throughout our conversation, Lane kept a close watch on his rod tip, waiting for even the faintest hint of a strike. He had a degree in wildlife biology from Oregon State University, had worked for a time as a forest service biologist, but had traded the biologist's job for one as a river guide. "I just wanted to run rivers because it sounded adventurous." He had rowed a few dory trips on the Grand Canyon, but mostly worked the Snake and Salmon rivers. "I've been on this river for twenty-five years," he said. It was his first salmon season in all those years. "The salmon have saved our bacon for this month. Fishing season started April 27, and we've been booked solid since May 11. We've had people come from as far away as New York and New Jersey to fish. It's been a shot in the arm for our company, but not just our company. Everybody's enjoying the season," he said.

With drought and a low-water summer looming, the salmon money would let local businesses make it through what otherwise might have been a bad year. Riggins's mayor would later say that first salmon season netted his town ten million dollars in just eight weeks. "Actually, we became reliant on salmon seasons, and it would be a loss for us to lose the salmon season at this point," he would tell the Associated Press several years later. "It's the difference between finishing the year in the black or finishing the year in the red."

Even though Riggins is something of a timber and ranching town, it's recreation, especially rafting, that keeps it from becoming a ghost town, Lane said. The economic benefits from the river and salmon hadn't changed local attitudes about dam breaching, according to Lane. "It's a conservative area. You get a lot of resistance. There's a mindset that people grow up with, that you don't breach dams and you don't give up water. In the West, dams represent progress; I'd say it's progress if you can take out some dams. Everybody wants to have fish, but nobody wants to give anything up."

That year, with more salmon returning to the Columbia and its tributaries than anytime since the 1930s, it was easy to believe there was no need for tradeoffs or compromises. "The only reason we have all these fish to catch is because so many were put in the rivers from hatcheries," Lane said. The numbers seemed impressive. Around 416,000 spring Chinook and another 76,000 summer Chinook made their way up the Columbia, many headed for Idaho. Of course, some estimates contend that in the late 1800s, the Salmon River alone produced about a million of the Columbia's 2.5 to 3 million spring and summer Chinook.

Simple numbers don't explain what has happened to the Columbia's salmon. At one time all the river's returning salmon started their lives in the gravel of a stream. Now most, seventy to eighty percent by some estimates, start their lives in a hatchery. Without hatcheries pumping out fish, there wouldn't be a salmon season, might not be any salmon at all, Lane said. "But I would much rather have wild fish spread over the entire river system."

"What's wrong with having hatcheries produce all the salmon?" I asked. Rod tip held to the side of the boat, lure still wiggling in the current, Lane seemed for a moment intent on his fishing and didn't answer right away. But then he said, "We're so caught up in ourselves that we don't show enough respect for other life forms or for other people. A hatchery salmon isn't the same as one spawned in the wild. We're always throwing things out of whack and then trying to balance things out," he said.

The clouds had faded to gun-metal gray and the light had turned dim. It was time to go. I wouldn't see anybody catch a salmon. Lane rowed us downstream through two rapids that I would paddle the next morning. Barb waited for us at a boat ramp in a battered yellow and white Suburban with a sticker on its rear bumper that read: "Frankly my dear, I don't want a dam." As we drove back toward Riggins, Lane peeled aluminum foil from the filet of a Chinook he had caught and smoked himself earlier in the season. I dug into it like a starving man. Barb asked if I wanted to take the salmon with me, but I didn't have room to store it, and even if I did, could never have eaten it all before it went bad. Instead, I took a few more greedy bites before they drove off.

In the highway pullout where Lane and Barb dropped me off, a man and a woman took turns photographing the salmon they had caught that day. It was the people I had seen in the drift boat across the river. They held the fish in front of them the way anglers do when they pose for a camera. The fish, still silver-sided and green-backed, weighed maybe fifteen pounds and the couple was justifiably proud of their catch.

At my river camp, I thought of it as mine for the night anyway, there was a man fishing. He cast his bait, a cluster of fish eggs I think, into the river and let the current sweep it downstream. After it had drifted a minute or two, he reeled back in and cast again. After I made certain my food and gear was safely stowed away, I asked the question people always ask fishermen. He said no, he hadn't had any luck, but that it didn't bother him. "Wouldn't the bank fishing be better closer to the mouth of the Little Salmon, or on the Little Salmon?" I asked.

"Probably, but I'd rather not catch anything than deal with all the people," he said. The man asked what I was doing, and I told him. Telling somebody you are headed to the ocean by kayak when you are almost six hundred miles from the ocean usually brings more questions. That's how I slipped into conversation with him. I can't remember if at some point we introduced ourselves, but I do remember he told me where he lived, and even though I can't recall the city's name, I remember he had traveled a long way to fish.

"Do you do much fishing?" he asked.

"I like to fish, but I don't go much anymore. I'm not sure why, maybe just a change in priorities," I said. He seemed to understand. But I went on to tell him that growing up back East, fishing had been my obsession, that I had worked as a commercial fisherman and as a mate on charter fishing boats, had put some money in the bank with those jobs and won a tournament or two, that I had fished mostly for marlin and tuna, and that in those days the only thing that really mattered to me was the catching, even if I let the fish go instead of killing them. I told him that as I got older, the catching became less important, although I still liked to catch fish when I went fishing. "Now, I'll even watch fish," I said.

"That need to always catch something is a phase everybody goes through. Over time you grow out of it, or should grow out of it anyway. It's natural," he told me. We talked until dusk came and went, until it became too dark to fish, until the man who didn't care if he caught a fish, left without catching one.

6

Dragonflies and the Plant Migration

One of the penalties of an ecological education is that one lives alone in a world of wounds. Much of the damage inflicted on land is quite invisible to laymen. An ecologist must either harden his shell and make believe that the consequences of science are none of his business, or he must be the doctor who sees the marks of death in a community that believes itself well and does not want to be told otherwise. —Aldo Leopold, Round River

I was in a funk. My conversations from the previous night with Lane and the fisherman tumbled with me as I went through my morning routine. I was about to leave the Salmon River, the mountains, and the whitewater, and start my trip down the windswept reservoirs of the Snake and then the Columbia. Already, I missed the mountains, felt they were behind me, although they were not. Alpine forests had again dissolved into loose stands of ponderosa pines. Soon the red-trunked trees with rough bark that smelled faintly of vanilla would fade into a landscape of bunchgrasses where for miles, nothing taller than low shrubs grow.

Even time was about to change. Just downstream from camp, at a narrow rapid called Time Zone, where the river roils itself into a mass of standing waves, an hour would appear when I passed from the Mountain Time Zone into the Pacific Time Zone. I would cross some type of line in that rapid that went beyond just time zones.

The day started warm and slightly overcast, but as I went through my morning routine, the clouds continued to thicken and I knew a front was coming. The weather was about to change back to cold and wet. I could usually filter drinking water, fix the oatmeal that I ate every morning, clean the pot, and pack my boat in an hour. But on the morning of June 10, the fourteenth day of the trip, nothing went right. My stove didn't work. I took it apart and carefully cleaned the pinhole opening where the spray of fuel ignited like the engine of a fighter jet in afterburner. The cleaning wasn't a major chore, just a hassle that didn't help my mood.

Then I had problems loading my kayak, which made me suspect that even after the winnowing of gear at Redfish Lake, I had overpacked. I arranged and rearranged. I added my trip journal and rain jacket to the stern dry bag and shifted packages of Ramen noodles and bags of pasta. I shoved my bivy sack in and moved the pots. Even after I filled the dry bag, the shifting and adjusting went on. Adding the water filter meant moving a fuel bottle. Adding the EPIRB meant moving another fuel bottle. It took an extra half hour not only to squeeze in all the gear, but balance the kayak so it wouldn't list to one side going down the river. By the time I finished, I wanted to scream and kick the boat.

I bounced my way through Time Zone without incident. Before I used up the hour gained by the time change, the warm weather was gone, replaced by wind, clouds, and a cold rain. A highway shadowed the river's right side and the slosh of car tires against wet asphalt mingled with the splash of moving water. The river moved between cliff walls and an open valley, between the nothingness of rock and the smell of alfalfa. Low hills edged the valley, and while I knew the hills rose into mountains, the clouds and rain obscured my views. I had only the river. Hidden by the water, young salmon moved downstream with me on their way to the ocean while adult salmon moved upstream on their way home.

I passed kayakers in their short, flat-hulled play boats stacked into a roadside eddy. One at a time, they would ferry across the current to take their turn in the white pile of a breaking wave. Some rode the foam sideways trying hard not to flip. Others pulled off spins and cartwheels that made the rest of us shout. And after each finished, they worked themselves back into the eddy for another ride. I hung at the end of the line. "Why don't you go in?" the paddler in front of me suggested. "Not today. I'm paddling a loaded boat." I watched a few more rides before peeling out downstream.

The rapids vanished for a while but that close to its terminus, the Salmon is a big river, and its flatwater held the same potential energy as a coiled rattlesnake. Around lunchtime I came across four men and two women loading rafts with gear. I hadn't envisioned the trip as a dangerous adventure, but the tall-tale man's comments from a few days earlier had put me on edge. I wound up paddling with the group even though a man with a North Carolina accent loading the rafts said none of the lower's rapids were too hard when the water was low like it was then.

I never really joined the group. I paddled with them. I camped with them. I ate their food. But I remember little about those six people. They were pleasant, fed me fajitas for dinner, French toast for breakfast, four were students at the University of Idaho in Moscow, and the other two ran the school's outdoor gear rental shop, and that's all.

We floated together below White Bird Creek, where the highway and river parted company for good, and into a narrow canyon beyond the reach of cars. We camped that night on a small beach with sand so full of burrs and dried cow patties I couldn't go barefoot the way I had at other spots. After dinner and a beer, before I drifted to my bivy, the clouds peeled back to reveal a million stars in the line of sky visible between the canyon walls.

The clouds stayed away during the night, and when I woke up, the sun already was over the canyon walls bringing a promise of warmth for the day. That promise had drawn strange creatures out of the water: dragonfly nymphs. Brown-bodied, predatory, and dangerous in appearance, with crab-like legs and pincer-like lower jaws, they reminded me of miniature monsters from a bad 1950s horror movie.

Some nymphs already had split their shells in their struggle to transform themselves. Fully formed dragonflies rested on rocks, free of their aquatic lives, but not quite ready to fly with their new wings. Bulbous-headed and bulging-eyed, creatures at once both beautiful and monstrous, their bodies still hadn't taken on the glossy hue of burnished metal they would wear as true adults. As soon as they could fly, the dragonflies left the river.

I don't know what species I saw that day, but most river-rearing dragonflies are strong fliers that travel many miles throughout their lives. A biological need, a memory not of place but of water, would eventually draw them back to a river to breed after several weeks. Dragonflies don't return to the exact spot where they were born. Instead river dragonflies return to rivers and pond dragonflies to ponds. The strategy allows each generation to spread their genes, to avoid the disasters that come with shifting rivers or drying lakes, and also to join distant lakes or distant streams together.

During breakfast, nymphs continued to crawl from the river. Dragonflies continued to buzz away, taking their memory of water with them. I had found a half nymph, half dragonfly on my bivy sack that morning, and it was still there after breakfast. I went through my morning routine of packing but saved my bivy until last just to give the insect a chance to finish emerging from its shell. The dragonfly had died in transition from aquatic to aerial, trapped by its old body, with only its new wings and head exposed.

Watching the dragonflies was a chance to see change move at a pace I could understand. Water erodes rock and carries moun-

tains to the sea, rivers shift, plants and animals evolve, even continents move, but it happens so slowly we ignore it. People often
see nature as static, but it's not, and watching the dragonflies
that morning was like watching a time-lapse movie of everything
around me. If I had not felt the need to move downriver, to make
certain I would meet Juliet when we had arranged, I might have
stayed on that beach all day.

I placed the half dragonfly on a rock in the futile hope it was
still alive. I knew better. I pressed and shoved and squeezed all
the gear, and then myself, into the kayak. The river promised rapids, and I practiced my strokes to warm up. The first whitewater
came as glassy rollers, and I bobbed from trough to crest without
a worry while Green Canyon began to squeeze the Salmon tight.
The water's pace quickened as it pushed past walls of basalt until
some unseen rock or ledge piled it into surging liquid mounds
and finally white-capped waves. I turned my kayak upstream and
paddled hard with windmill strokes to catch a wave even though
it was hopeless. My kayak never surfed well, and full of gear it became too sluggish for anything except running rapids. But it was
important just to try. I flowed with the water as it surged down
the river.

Nothing moves in a straight line on a river. Even as gravity
pulls it to the ocean, water swirls in hydraulics, pauses in pools,
and is drawn upstream in eddies. Watching those greasy sheets
of green water, I knew I would come back to the lower Salmon
one day in a kayak designed to play and with a raft hauling my
gear. I would work my way onto a wave. Paddle hard. Feel gravity
start to pull my boat toward the trough. Feel the river rush under
the hull even as the kayak stops. Feel the balance between the
moving water and the wave, between change and stability. Everything along the river must come to terms with those same forces.
It's on a wave that I can sometimes understand a river, compre-
hend its power, understand how, given time, it can remake the
land, cut its way through rock or rearrange its banks and bed,
how the river is always the same and always changing.

We floated through a few more rapids and I tried to surf a few more waves before the canyon released the river. At Pine Bar, the group from Moscow beached their rafts. Their trip was over. I didn't stay to help them haul gear or load rafts onto trailers. I went on my way, and it didn't bother me.

Below Pine Bar, I bounced my way down a few small rapids before the water turned flat and smooth. On a calm river, when the light is right, as it was that day, and the sun reflects off the water in a certain way, as it did that day, a river can look as solid as polished stone. I floated down a river turned rock for a time, until the light shifted and a breeze rippled the surface, and the Salmon turned back to liquid.

The lower Salmon's riverbanks were once molten lava. As it dried, the lava formed itself into spiral fans and multisided columns. Somewhere around 200 million years ago, back when dinosaurs roamed the land and dragonflies buzzed like hawks through the sky, western Idaho was the edge of the continent. The lower Salmon and its dried lava canyons didn't exist. If geologists have correctly read fossils found in rock that was once seafloor but is now mountainside, North America fell into deep ocean not far from Riggins. Around that same time, a series of islands had formed somewhere in the Pacific Ocean. By about 150 million years ago, North America was moving slowly west, maybe an inch or two a year. As geologists David Alt and Donald Hyndman note in *Roadside Geology of Idaho*, one or two inches a year add up over time: a mile after thirty-two thousand years, more than a thousand miles after fifty million years. By the time those fifty million years had passed and those thousand miles were traveled, the Pacific islands and the western edge of Idaho had met, and the coastline had moved west.

The coastal Idaho that disappeared after the collision 100 million years ago is what we have worked so hard to undo in the last hundred years. The dams and locks built on the Columbia and the Snake rivers have re-created what geology took away, made Idaho once again part of the Pacific Rim, turned Lewiston, a landlocked town built beside the once-shallow Snake River, into a seaport where wheat and logs and paper and potash start their journeys to Japan and Korea.

I often think of the three rivers I paddled, the Salmon, Snake, and Columbia, as one river. Even before I left the Salmon, I thought of them that way. A Swainson's hawk will summer on eastern Washington's sagebrush steppe, winter on Argentina's pampas, and between those two places fly over the bunchgrass hills of the Salmon River country only twice a year, yet somehow connect all the land it travels across just as a salmon brings the mountains to the sea, carries the ocean back to the mountains, or a dragonfly connects river to prairie and one river to another. I don't want the Columbia River we created to impress me, but I am impressed—by its long reach, by the way its dams and their reservoirs and the tugs pushing barges up and down the river-turned-reservoirs make shifting continents and oozing lava seem irrelevant.

The lava came seventeen million years ago, after the Pacific islands had crashed into North America, and for eleven million years it poured out across parts of Idaho, Washington, and Oregon, again moving the coastline west. It obliterated everything. It engulfed trees and animals, blocked rivers, left whatever had existed under a half mile or more of rock, rock that would eventually line the lower Salmon, the lower Snake, and much of the Columbia. Six million years ago the lava stopped. The Seven Devils Mountains rose, ice age glaciers came and went, the Salmon River cut its canyons—Green, Cougar, Snow Hole, and Blue—through the hardened basalt. Where the river could not erode a section of rock, or a boulder partially blocked its channel, a rapid formed.

I had the river to myself for a while in Cougar, the lower river's second canyon. I wanted to find a beach I could call my own that afternoon, strip naked, and swim. Instead, I encountered six catarafts strung out on the river. As I moved from raft to raft, I learned the eight rafters were from Idaho Falls, and of course we knew a few of the same people. The whitewater community is an even smaller place than Idaho. Kayaking in Wyoming once, I met two men from New Zealand. I knew one person in that entire country, a woman I had paddled with some when I lived back East. The two Kiwis knew her.

By the time I reached the front of the catarafts, I had been invited to dinner, and it somehow seemed rude to turn down the invitation. Besides, Snow Hole, the rapid that gave the third canyon its name, and supposedly one of the hardest on that stretch of river, wasn't far downstream. Running with a group would be smart. I spent the night not on a solitary beach but with people I didn't know who lived in a town where I had once lived and still had friends.

I felt the pull between being alone and being with other people, between my confidence in my own paddling ability and a belief in the safety of numbers. Maybe because I wanted to be alone that night but wasn't, or maybe because I was tired, which made me lazy, I gambled that I could get away with sleeping out in just my bag. But I miscalculated. Not long after dinner, black clouds filled the sky, the temperature dropped, and a rain that wouldn't end anytime soon started. I dug my bivy sack from my boat and searched for a level spot among the armchair-sized rocks littering the beach. Everything got wet. I tossed and turned in the dampness, and it was still raining off and on the next morning. I put my wet gear back in storage bags designed to keep things dry, put on wet clothes designed to keep me dry, and started down the river.

The river dumped into its third canyon just before Snow Hole Rapid. A western tanager flitted along a rock shelf halfway down the canyon wall. The small bird with its bright red and yellow head, black wings, and yellow body conjured other river trips: spring days with my friends from Idaho Falls boating the Fall River, a Snake tributary that flows west out of Yellowstone National Park and through eastern Idaho's potato fields; summer afternoons with Juliet on the White Salmon, a Columbia tributary that flows south off the glaciers that cap a dormant Washington volcano and then through a narrow gorge where yellow monkey flowers cling to canyon walls. I forgot about my damp and fitful sleep the night before.

Somehow, I had gotten ahead of the rafters. I eddied out on river left above Snow Hole Rapid to wait. Safe behind some boulders, I looked downstream and read the drop. Jumbled rocks had accumulated below vertical cliffs and spilled out into the river, partially damming it. Water pooled before rolling past a mobile home–sized boulder that split the mid-river current into a pair of distinct chutes. A twisting path of smooth water weaved itself through the chain of rocks that spanned the left chute. A few well-timed strokes and I could run it without much worry. Mess up though, and things might turn ugly. I ferried across the river and scouted the right chute. A few rocks broke the surface but created little danger. I was tempted to run the drop and keep heading downriver but waited for the rafters instead. I didn't want them to worry if they couldn't spot me below the rapid.

As soon as the rafters showed, I fired myself into the rapid and ran river left, the harder side, with no troubles. Below Snow Hole, one of the rafters laughed and said the rapid didn't seem that hard. I agreed and after that we parted company. My worries about the river's dangers had not been misplaced though. After my trip, I learned that at the high water levels typical in early June, waves powerful enough to surf a jet boat form along the lower Salmon and a wave higher than a two-story house makes the river's last rapid almost unrunnable. I had seen or boated much of the Salmon River and thought I knew at least a little about it. But the lower had been a mystery. I sometimes wonder what would have happened if it hadn't been a low-water spring. I hope somebody would have told me about the giant waves and impassible rapid. I still get nervous just thinking about my ignorance and the possibilities.

Beyond Snow Hole, the river looped itself around a high hill coated with new spring grass to form a five-mile-long meander.

If the river flowed in a straight line, it could have covered the distance between the meander's start and finish in less than a mile. Eventually, the Salmon will slice its way through that mile of rock and leave the meander as a disconnected lake or a dry coulee. Who knows how long that will take. Part way round the meander some small stone huts, the homes of Chinese miners who once searched the land for gold, appear above the water. After that a rapid called China, a big hydraulic where some of the miners supposedly drowned, stretches three-quarters of the way across the river but with easy passage on the left. Finally, near the end of the meander, the canyon releases the river for a while and the whitewater becomes nothing more than riffles.

Free of the canyon walls, the horizon opened up. It wasn't gentle country. It looked like somebody had taken a backhoe, ripped apart a giant parking lot, and stacked the broken black asphalt into high ridges. The rain had turned intermittent by then, and the day shifted between dark squalls and sunlight. Long streamers trailed below wind-blown clouds like deadly tentacles hanging from a Portuguese man-of-war jellyfish. Light and shadow and rain made viewing the torn hills almost tactile, as if I could feel each rough fold, sharp ridge, and talus-covered slope rub against my skin just by looking. I watched a golden eagle hunt beyond the river, soaring on whatever updrafts it could find among the afternoon winds, drifted past a grove of black locust trees, an Eastern species probably planted beside the river by a vanished pioneer, and startled a badger snuffling along the riverbank.

I was close to the Snake, close to the end of one river, the start of another. I wanted one more night with the Salmon. Alone. Twenty-five miles from anything but a cattle ranch, the river fell into Blue Canyon, its last, and in that canyon I found a small beach where I stopped for the night, my sixteenth on the river. A patch of native blanket flowers (a gardener would know them as brown-eyed Susans) grew where the beach and canyon wall met, although some flood will eventually wash the flowers away.

Coyote tracks followed the water's edge. I paused from laying out clothes to dry and stringing a green plastic tarp between some boulders to examine the tracks. At the upstream edge of my beach, where the sand gave way to rock and water, a fish dimpled the surface of a pool. A smallmouth bass. Transplanted in the 1920s from the East and Midwest to the Yakima River, the Columbia tributary where I had once lived, the bronze-backed smallmouth have spread from the Yakima to the Columbia and many of its other tributaries. The fish told of change.

The sun stayed out long enough to dry my gear, and I managed to stash it just before the rain, and then the hail, came. I spent the rest of the afternoon comfortable beneath the tarp riding out the weather. My gear was dry. I was dry. On a long river trip, that's happiness.

Once the storm passed, I felt the need to go not so much for a hike as a walk, to think about the miles traveled and the miles left to go. The studio apartment–sized beach didn't offer much walking room. The canyon wall was steep but not so steep I couldn't hike up it, and I soon found an animal trail to follow. It was cold, the way Idaho is so often in spring. I had bundled myself into my clothes for warmth, but after awhile unzipped my rain jacket and took off my fleece hat. I unconsciously named the plants clinging to the cliff side as I hiked—bluebunch wheatgrass, yarrow, lupine, prickly pear cactus, and wild parsleys—and wondered what plants were missing.

The firs and pines of the mountains were memory, and I wouldn't see a true forest again until the Columbia reached the Cascade Mountains. The dry country held a beauty different from the forests. In the arid reaches of the Columbia's massive basin, it is the open space, the distant mountains, the red-streaked sunsets that first capture the imagination. In that dry land, plants seem an afterthought, spread here and there in random bunches with only open ground between. There are shrubs, there are grasses, sometimes there are trees. Who needs to know more than that?

It's easy to believe in such a world until spring. For a few weeks, between the frozen white of winter and the dry brown of summer, the land becomes a smear of blooming colors. Look closely then, and only plants will matter. Even after the flowers fade, when mountain and sky again dominate, the land will feel different from before. Plants will no longer seem an afterthought. It's like hearing an orchestra perform Beethoven's Ninth Symphony, complete with a choir singing the "Ode to Joy" in German; listening to the music after that, maybe played on a piano, without all the strings, brass, woodwinds, and singers just doesn't sound right, even though it's all the same notes.

Before I came West, I understood almost nothing about the land, not how mountains and valleys define place and not how place defines life. The mountains—the Cascades, the Blues, the Seven Devils, the Lemhis, the Lost Rivers—steal water from the storms, which in winter come spinning off the Pacific Ocean like arching commas of clouds, leaving the valleys only a promise of moisture. Usually. Just enough snow, just enough rain, makes it past the thieving mountains to keep the valleys from becoming true desert, although people often refer to them as deserts. I hadn't known this anymore than I had known the names of the plants that grew among the mountains and valleys.

In a way, I had been embarrassed that I could look over a field of flowers and not know what I saw. In a country of high mountains lifted from the bottom of ancient oceans and black-rock deserts spewed from deep inside the earth, in a country where nothing looked familiar, I had needed something to call by name. For the same reasons meeting neighbors makes a new house a home, I decided I should learn to identify wildflowers, shrubs, and trees. I had expected nothing more to come from it than from a casual friendship. Names, however, are the bedrock of memory.

On weekend hikes during those first springs, my pack weighted with books full of Kodachrome meadows and darkroom forests, I spent as much time looking at the ground and books as absorbing the big sky for which I'd come West. Those hikes were my first attempts at substituting knowledge for long family connection to place and of understanding the region where I live, and it's what eventually launched me on the river trip down the Salmon to the ocean.

Identifying plants in the field confounds even botanists at times. For instance, many wild parsleys look maddeningly alike, and there are, in the West, eighty species of just one type of parsley, the *Lomatiums*. In a land where plants weren't the first thing to capture my imagination, it turned out there were simply too many to learn. I resigned myself early on to the fact that I would never know some of them. I cheated at my task after moving to eastern Washington and meeting Juliet. As a wildlife biologist, she knows almost as much about plants as animals. After all, what animal, including humans, can survive without plants? And since it's much easier to ask a person who knows the answer than to look it up, I bombarded her with constant questions on our hikes, or more accurately the same question constantly. She fell in love with me anyway.

"What's this?" I would ask pointing to one plant, then another and another. "Oregon sunshine," she would respond. Or maybe "shooting star." Or "pallid evening primrose." Juliet didn't know every name, which left books as guides. Identifying a plant involves more than matching an object to a picture, so we would sit on the ground to inspect some flower neither of us knew, look at its leaves, its stalk, its petals, enter a small world that consisted only of the plant and maybe buzzing insects, or scurrying lizards, or coyote tracks, or dried winter elk scat, just to discover a few words that would serve as label. It was, I thought, merely an exercise of attaching printed names to living objects. I didn't realize everything a name implies. Hidden in the language of plants, in sepals and petals, in flowers that are raceme or umbel, in leaves that are alternate or opposite, in the telling of one plant from another, is a memory of place.

We are captives of our senses, especially of what we see. We will look at land and judge it ugly or beautiful or harsh, and based on that judgment decide the land's value and condition. The night I had spent with the Idaho Falls rafters, that wet night when I'd wanted to be alone but wasn't, we had camped at a spot called White House Bar, although the white cabin that supplied the name was long gone. Before we had eaten and before the rain had come, I had gone for a hike up the hillside behind our camp. I wanted to take in the river country I had already judged as beautiful. Cow pies covered the ground. Chukars, partridge-like birds originally from Asia and introduced to provide sport for hunters, gave their two-note calls from somewhere high up the canyon. A brittle, broom straw–thin grass called cheatgrass grew over a dry depression that once held water miners had used to blast gold from the earth. Ubiquitous in the West, cheatgrass is a plant of Jordanian deserts and Asian steppes. The horses of Genghis Khan might have filled their bellies with cheat, but since those days it has spread farther than any Mongol horde, now grows in Iceland, Australia, New Zealand, Canada, and across a hundred million acres of the Mountain West, including many of the lower Salmon's hillsides.

Beyond the dry depression, a mass of green plants the size of small shrubs, each on the verge of blooming, filled the hillside. I wore shorts and sandals and felt small stings up and down my legs and on my feet with every plant I passed. A wreath of sharp spikes grew below each bud ready to erupt into flower. Yellow starthistle is a kind of knapweed. Like cheatgrass, it is a Eurasian plant and a weed.

I learned about weeds on a hike with Juliet along a creek whose waters, after moving from creek to river to another river, eventually drain into the Columbia. On an April Sunday, the aspens and cottonwoods springtime green, we headed toward a lone ponderosa pine growing far above the creek. We found the bones of a bighorn sheep along the way, and as we walked, I heard the names of other plants. "Knapweed" or "tumble mustard" or "Dalmatian toadflax." I learned a new question to ask with the identity of those plants. "Is it native?" They were weeds. At its simplest, a weed is any plant out of place, making a rose bush in a wheat field a weed. The plants Juliet showed me growing wild were out of place in an ecological sense. Sometimes known as "invasives," they came mostly from other continents, often Asia, but also Europe, and sometimes even from other parts of North America, and were introduced either accidentally or on purpose, mostly within the last hundred years or so. Not all alien plants cause problems, but some like cheatgrass and yellow starthistle do. Away from their original environments, from the animals and insects that graze on them, from the rodents that eat their seeds, and from the other plants that compete with them, they are free to spread across acre after acre, displacing native plants as they do.

After giving up my hike through the thorny weeds that evening at White House Bar, I noticed a small plant with leaves that radiated out in a semicircle from a central point and a spike of purple flowers. A lupine. Lupines, relatives of peas and soybeans, are poisonous to livestock, and maybe for that reason they seem to survive in disturbed and altered spots where other native plants don't grow. But only that one lupine grew among the cheatgrass and yellow starthistle. I realized it was the only native plant I could find. I saw no balsamroots, with their arrow-shaped leaves and yellow flowers that look like oversized daisies; no prairie smoke, relatives to the rose with nodding pink flowers that grow in groups of three and turn to smoke-like streamers after releasing their seeds; no penstemons, with their five-petaled flowers, two on top, three on the bottom, that always make me think of someone sticking out their tongue.

I wasn't certain which plants once grew beside the Salmon and which did not. All I knew was that it was different when bunchgrass and wildflowers stretched to infinity. The plants were what I had instead of memory, an imperfect memory at best. Through them, through their names, I could almost see what once grew in place of the weeds. Along the Salmon, there are no signs to identify the plants, nothing that says which plants are native and which are weeds. I had only the knowledge gathered before the trip and carried down the river to show me how the land had changed. What bothers me, scares might be a better word, is that I would have understood none of this if I'd let plants remain an afterthought, hadn't learned to tell one from another. Something unknowable is lost as the land becomes less diverse, simpler than it once was, and we become poorer too, as if we decided to limit an orchestra to only a few instruments, or worse, replaced the instruments with new ones that can't quite hit the same notes. Looking at that hillside full of weeds along the Salmon seemed no different than hearing Beethoven played on a kazoo. I wanted to hear the whole damn orchestra.

Had I traveled the lower Salmon fifteen years earlier, I wouldn't have noticed the yellow starthistle. First seen in Idaho in the 1950s, and along the lower Salmon River in the mid-1970s, it grows throughout almost all the canyons now, some places widely scattered, some places in thick stands. The land around the river is always changing, and yet from a human perspective it seems to remain the same. A plant, MacFarlane's four o'clock, *Mirabilis macfarlanei* is its scientific name, grows in a few places along the Salmon and Snake rivers. A threatened species, I know its flowers—colored an improbable mix of rose and purple—and broad green leaves only from pictures. It has retreated to a few patches of suitable habitat for all the usual reasons: overgrazing by livestock, trampling by livestock and careless hikers, and weeds. Other four o'clock species tend to grow in warmer climates, and the MacFarlanes makes botanists suspect that once the land around the lower Salmon, with its varied terrain and elevation, served as a plant migration corridor. Migrating plants: it's a strange thought and must have been a slow process.

As the planet cooled and warmed, glaciers came and went, some plants found refuge in small islands of suitable habitat around the Salmon until conditions became more favorable and they could again spread. I wonder now, with all the strange new plants, if species that have survived so many changes will survive whatever changes come next. What is happening now is subtle. As cheatgrass and yellow starthistle mature, they become impossible for animals like elk, deer, and bighorn sheep to eat, forcing them to move more frequently in search of food. Some rodents, like the Great Basin pocket mouse, Merriam's shrew, and maybe the western jumping mouse become less common as weeds spread. Who knows what the loss of those rodents means for the golden eagles, the migrating Swainson's hawks, the summering red-tailed hawks, and wintering rough-legged hawks.

Cheatgrass also changes the fire cycle, bringing blazes every two or three years to ecosystems where fire once came only infrequently. With more fire, native plants not adapted to the faster fire cycle die out. "Cheatgrass brings fire and fire brings cheatgrass," a range ecologist once told me. We have somehow shifted the balance between change and continuity, somehow altered land and place in ways we do not yet understand.

My last night on the Salmon, as I hiked above the camp where I would spend the night alone, I saw the usual weeds, but not as many weeds as usual—just some scattered cheatgrass and yellow starthistle, which hadn't taken over that stretch of canyon yet, but one day might. For a moment, I imagined the land as it must have been, imagined it that way because it seemed important, the right thing to do, like placing flowers on a wilderness grave even though you have no connection to the person buried there. Then I put away that image of the land, put away what I had learned, put away what I knew about the plants and what they told of change, and looked again.

The river's dark water flowed past the even darker canyon walls, an eagle rode the day's last thermals, and the orange-blossom fragrance of white-flowered syringas growing in a draw scented the breeze. It was late, time to go if I wanted to make it back to camp while there was still some light, if I didn't want to hike through cactus in the dark. I tried to commit the place to memory, tried to hold on to the way it looked and smelled and felt that spring day. I wondered then, once I had finished my trip to the ocean, once I had seen and learned whatever it was I would see and learn, once I had paddled the Snake and the Columbia, what else I would have to put away so I could look at the land and the river.

7

Into the Breach

By the time the Clearwater River joins it at Lewiston, Idaho, the Snake River has traveled roughly 900 miles of its 1,036-mile course. The longest Columbia tributary, the Snake starts high in the Rocky Mountains of Wyoming. It flows south out of Yellowstone National Park, passes the Tetons, and goes through Jackson Hole before it turns west and crosses into Idaho, where it carves across the southern portion of the state like the curved blade of a scimitar, tumbling, along the way, over falls higher than Niagara. Dam after dam captures then releases the river. Sometimes the Snake pulses with whitewater, sometimes it dries to little more than a trickle. Its water irrigates wheat, alfalfa, and the state's famous potatoes; spins the turbines that generate electricity for the irrigation pumps that water the potatoes; for the machinery that turns the potatoes into French fries; and more recently, for the state's high-tech microchip factories.

Eventually, the river turns north and forms the border between Idaho and Oregon. Just before the river enters a gorge deeper than the Grand Canyon, three dams built by a private power company block salmon, especially fall Chinook, from miles of spawning habitat. To make up for the loss, the power company that built and runs the dams pays for the hatcheries near Riggins and on the Pahsimeroi River. Below the dams, as the river prepares to leave its deepest canyon, the Salmon empties into it, and not long after that, the Snake becomes the border between Idaho and Washington. At Lewiston the Snake abandons Idaho, turns west, and flows more or less in that direction through Washington until it joins the Columbia 140 miles later.

Four dams built and run by the U.S. Army Corps of Engineers block the Snake in its final miles. Those four dams might be the most controversial in the country, viewed as the bringers of progress and prosperity by some people, of destruction by others. The dams and their reservoirs made Lewiston a seaport. Along the Clearwater, upstream from the Snake confluence, cargo containers sit stacked one atop the other and tall silver grain elevators line the river's north bank. Barges pushed by tugs will carry the grain elevators' wheat and the containers' cargo, along with dozens of other commodities, downstream. Much of it will end up in Portland, Oregon, where it will be loaded onto ships headed for Asia.

Where the Snake and Clearwater rivers meet, the Corps of Engineers has built a high levee to keep the dammed waters from inundating Lewiston. On top of the levee, there is a metal sculpture celebrating rivers commissioned by the Corps of Engineers. Although it was white stone when I first saw it, the sculpture is now the color of polished bronze. At its front, a beautiful woman in a simple buckskin dress kneels. Rivers cascade from her hands into rocky pools. Her long hair billows back to form mountain ridges; the mountains' flanks roll off her dress. Along the sculpture's sides, bass-relief eagles soar among the peaks or rest in trees; grizzly bears, black bears, wolves, and cougars stalk; bighorn sheep and mountain goats rest on rock outcrops while below, a bull elk with oversized antlers bugles. A great blue heron fishes where a pool of burnished water empties into the metal river that borders the sculpture's base. Beavers build a dam, salmon leap, and a massive sturgeon lurks.

The sculptured is titled *Tsceminicum*, which a plaque says is the Nez Perce word for "meeting of the waters" and the traditional name for the Snake-Clearwater confluence. The sculpture, according to the plaque, "interprets Indian mythology with its symbolic earth mother at the headwaters of these rivers. Presented are the native wildlife of the area presided over by the Coyote—most important figure in Nez Perce legends." Nearby, the Corps of Engineers displays information about Lewis and Clark's journey west. A dugout canoe, a scaled-down replica of the ones the explores used to travel the Clearwater, Snake, and Columbia rests beside a small stone marker that says Lewis and Clark camped at the confluence on October 10, 1805. The spot is now under water backed up by a Corps of Engineers' dam.

On June 14, the eighteenth day of my trip, I was headed to Lewiston. It was my last day in the whitewater kayak, the last morning I would spend shoving food and gear into every available space of the kayak. I wouldn't miss it. I had arrived two days early at my rendezvous point with Juliet. Fortunately, I had managed to find a working pay phone so I could call her and arranged for us to meet farther downstream and a day earlier. There was no fee to camp at the government-run boat launch that had been our planned meeting point, but it wasn't the kind of place I wanted to spend any extra time. The ground was so hard I couldn't even pound in the single stake it took to secure my bivy sack, and the place smelled from the family of skunks that lived nearby. I was glad to be moving on.

I faced the river's final rapids that day. Long pools separated one rapid from the next, and there wasn't much to the rapids, just some splashy waves. In the morning, I floated past a band of bighorn sheep grazing the river on the Idaho side. A radio-collared ewe left her lamb, charged down from a ridge, and followed me for a quarter of a mile. It was the last time I would see wild sheep.

Giant aluminum jet boats carried a constant flow of tourists upstream into Hells Canyon on sightseeing trips. I felt like a skateboarder on a freeway, always worried that one of the speeding boats would flatten me. Around lunchtime, a headwind started and the day became a grind. Finally, near Asotin, Washington, the Snake's energy faded, the water came to a standstill, and the river became a reservoir. There would be no more whitewater.

It takes constant effort—small correction strokes at bow or stern—to make a whitewater kayak go in a straight line, and on flatwater, where the river doesn't push and straight is the fastest way between two points, paddling becomes a form of torture. I was exhausted by the time Juliet met me with my pickup truck. We loaded my kayak and found a hotel room in town.

Lewiston is built on what was part of a 7.5 million–acre reservation retained by the Nez Perce in a treaty signed by the tribe and the federal government in 1855. Eight years later, after whites discovered gold along the Clearwater River, the government, in what I'm told the Nez Perce still refer to as the "Steal Treaty," shrunk the reservation to just a tenth of its original size. Lewiston became Idaho's first capital, but after a year, the territorial government moved south to Boise. Lewiston now is an industrial town where the smell of a pulp mill located along the Clearwater sometimes turns oppressive and newer industrial structures share the downtown with historic buildings.

The place made me claustrophobic. When I drove through the low, brick buildings of its small downtown, I rolled my shoulders inward as if that would make me take up less space. Part of my discomfort came because, after eighteen days on the river, driving again felt a little strange. Part of my discomfort came because Lewiston presented no horizon, and after the river, I was used to space. The levee bordering town hid the Snake and Clearwater from view. Only the two-thousand-foot canyon walls that reached up from the Clearwater and the Snake's north bank were visible. The Corps of Engineers had turned the levee's crest into a paved trail, and people spent their evenings biking, walking, and inline skating on it. From the top of the levee I could look out on the river. When I was up there, I felt more relaxed.

My time in town was like suspended animation. I wasn't on the river, but the river was all I could think about. Juliet had brought a book of navigation charts that covered every mile of the Snake and Columbia from Lewiston to the ocean, and for two days I studied the charts the way I might study a textbook before the final exam in some subject I had to pass. I bought a pair of dividers and measured out miles on the charts, as if current diligence could make up for the first days of my trip when I traveled without a map. I filled the charts with numbers and notations. I marked potential campsites. I would face four dams—Lower Granite, Little Goose, Lower Monumental, and Ice Harbor—on the Snake, and four more—McNary, John Day, The Dalles, and Bonneville—on the Columbia. I noted the location of each dam, and of its spillway, powerhouse, and navigation lock.

On the Snake and Columbia rivers, the tugs pushing barges, the cruise boats made to look like old-time sternwheelers, and the occasional motor or sailboats get around each dam using a lock, which is like a concrete channel sealed tight by doors that allow the manipulation of the water level inside. Draining a lock lowers vessels headed downstream to the level of the river below a dam. Flooding a lock lifts vessels headed upstream to the level of the river above a dam. The Corps of Engineers controls when the locks open and what kinds of vessels can use the locks. For the rest of my time on the river, I would not have complete control over my trip.

Juliet and I slept late each morning. I took a hot shower when I woke up and another before bed. We went out to eat, and I enjoyed the break from noodles and oatmeal. We talked. I asked about wedding plans and who had or hadn't responded to invitations.

"Don't you want to hear about the house?" Juliet asked.

"Sure," I said, but kept flipping through charts as she talked.

"It's two stories with hardwood floors and an unfinished

basement. And it's close to a park and has a fenced yard for the dog," she said.

"I hope it doesn't need too much work. I'm not good at stuff like that," I said.

"It's an older house, but it's in pretty good shape. Nothing needs to be done right away." I wasn't sure I liked the sound of that.

"Tell me about the trip," she said.

"It's been great," but I couldn't sift the details and events to find the few that stood out. Talking about a trip in progress wasn't an easy thing. Finally, I mentioned the snow, the whitewater, and the group I had run the wilderness stretch with.

Each day, after sleeping late and showering and eating a big breakfast, Juliet and I drove out of town and up the Clearwater River toward the mountains. One day we visited a place that had a captive wolf pack, one day a hatchery. Built by the U.S. Army Corps of Engineers in 1969 on a peninsula where the Clearwater and its north fork come together and managed by the U.S. Fish and Wildlife Service, the hatchery compensates for Dworshak Dam. Dworshak is tall, monolithic, imposing, impounding a deep reservoir surrounded by blunt-topped, tree-covered ridges. When the corps dammed the North Fork of the Clearwater, it didn't build a fish ladder, which is something like a watery stairway twisting up from the river and over a dam that allows migrating fish to pass upstream. Without a fish ladder at Dworshak, the North Fork's salmon and steelhead vanished; instead the hatchery is supposed to produce what the river no longer can. The hatchery originally produced steelhead and rainbow trout. Then in the 1980s, as part of a plan to compensate for salmon lost to the lower Snake's dams, the hatchery began producing spring Chinook as well.

"This place is packed," I said as I searched for an empty space in the parking lot.

"Kayak," Juliet said pointing out a pickup in the staff lot with a whitewater boat on top. It's a game we play when we travel, always looking for kayaks. "It must be kids' fishing day," she said. Children and parents toted balloons and fishing rods and clear plastic bags filled with a rainbow trout or two caught in the hatchery's trout pond.

The hatchery looked industrial. Asphalt surrounded its single-story olive buildings. Pumps and compressors hummed, pushing water through the silver pipes that crisscrossed the asphalt. Inside, stacks of trays where fish eggs incubate sat on the other side of glass windows. Nearby, the oversized, sink-like nursery tanks where the young fish stay until they grow to two inches gurgled. Outside, mesh nets kept hungry birds from the concrete raceways where salmon and steelhead parr grow before they are released into the river. In other raceways, mature Chinook salmon swam slow circles around their concrete pens. They had already lost the metallic silver shine of the ocean but hadn't turned the brownish red of spawning season. White fungus coated one fish; another floated dead. That afternoon, back in Lewiston, Juliet and I strolled along the levee. We sat on a bench near the confluence sculpture. Sometimes silver fish dimpled the water's surface. It didn't occur to me that they were steelhead smolt migrating to the ocean.

The last thing I did before I left the hotel in Lewiston was call my dad back in Virginia. It was Sunday, June 17, and I wanted to wish him a happy Father's Day and let him know I was all right. After I hung up, Juliet and I drove to the river. I had spent the previous evening doing laundry, shopping for groceries, and taking food out of the cardboard boxes it had come in and putting it in waterproof zip-lock bags. At the river, Juliet helped me pack my gear into the seventeen-foot sea kayak I would paddle for the rest of the trip. I expected hot, dry weather so I swapped my down sleeping bag for a lighter one and left my polypro underwear, along with my dry top, splash pants, neoprene booties, and helmet with Juliet. I kept the t-shirts, the pants with the zip-off legs, a fleece pullover, a fleece vest, the high-tech rain jacket I had wanted to leave behind

that first day back in the Idaho mountains, and the EPIRB locator beacon. I left the throw rope, rescue slings, and carabineers
behind. The sea kayak's large, waterproof hatches covering large,
waterproof compartments made fitting all the gear and supplies
inside easy. I slid the two halves of the breakdown paddle under
the bungee cords that crisscrossed the kayak's red stern deck and
a full water bottle under the bow bungee cords.

When I hit the beginning of the Snake's first dam pool, I had
worried that even in a sea kayak, the rest of my trip would be
a miserable slog. Unlike a whitewater kayak, which is made to
turn, a sea kayak goes fast in a straight line, and paddling it in
the river's stilled water felt like riding in a speedboat. I fell into
the meditative right-left-right-left rhythm of paddling, heard the
sploosh as the paddle blade entered the water, noted the solid
pressure of water trapped on the blade, felt the tension in my
muscles when I pulled the paddle through the water, and saw the
drip of river water falling back to itself in tiny drops as the paddle
swung forward for the next stroke. The sea kayak sliced through
the river, leaving a small wake outlined by dimpled swirls to mark
its path. Lewiston and Idaho fell behind me.

Boats skimmed across the river around Lewiston—jet boats
filled with anglers, boats pulling water skiers, powerboats just
cruising back and forth—and I had that skateboard on a freeway feeling again. But the farther I traveled, the fewer boats I
saw until they all but disappeared. Seagulls bobbed in the water.
Oil-black crows and long-tailed magpies floated above the river.
Small, silver fish occasionally dimpled the water's surface. Carp
sometimes rolled, gulping air like oversized goldfish in a giant
fish bowl. In places, the gray tops of long-dead trees reached
above the water's surface. A building along the river became an
oddity. Only scattered docks for loading barges, occasional storage tanks, and grain elevators interrupted the shoreline. It was
good I had left my loneliness back on the Salmon.

The lower Snake is remote in a way that's hard to grasp. The villages where Lewis and Clark found food and hospitality are gone.

The small farming towns that once dotted the river disappeared when the dams were built. It somehow felt as distant from civilization as any spot along the Salmon River. The lower Snake is the West as we have always imagined it—rugged, arid, unpopulated, infrequently visited, and beautiful in its remoteness.

A state highway follows the Snake for a few miles on river left. A narrow county road follows for roughly thirty-five miles on river right. A set of railroad tracks stay with the river from Lewiston to the Columbia. Only barges pushed through the water by tugs, the rare car crunching along the road, or short trains a dozen cars long clackity-clicking over the tracks reminded me of a world beyond the river, even though each barge, each dammed-up river mile should have told me how the Snake serves the needs of those who live beyond its canyon, including me. Besides providing a cheap shipping route to the ocean, the lower Snake's dams generate roughly five percent of the region's electricity. The electricity goes to homes and businesses around the Northwest and sometimes to places as far away as California.

Basalt walls that sometimes rise higher than a thousand feet confine both sides of the Snake. In some places, the canyon walls fall almost straight into the river. In other places small flats border the river. The cliffs don't form a solid wall but are textured by small ridges jutting out at various angles and broken by creeks that have cut deep gashes into the land.

A paddle from Lewiston, Wawawai Canyon breaks the cliffs along the Snake's north bank. Sometimes wide enough to hold a ranch, the canyon and its creek of the same name drop from the rolling Palouse wheat country to the river, ending at a muddy bay the shape of a poorly drawn triangle. Before the Snake was dammed, a small town existed at the canyon's end. Now there are only the picnic shelters, bathrooms, tent pads, and irrigated lawns of a park built by the Army Corps of Engineers and run by Whitman County. I only knew about the town because of a sign beside a paved walking trail.

Two men fished the bay the evening I camped there. They

caught one sunfish after another, none much bigger than a large man's hand. The first fish I ever caught was a brightly colored sunfish, and they are a staple of first fishing trips everywhere, especially in the South. Like smallmouth bass and shad, which were introduced from the East, and carp, which were introduced from Europe and Asia, sunfish were introduced into the Columbia in the 1890s, probably from the Midwest.

After I ate, I wound up talking to the men for a while. Both were botanists. One was from Florida. The other, Rich Old, was a consultant who sometimes did weed identification work at Washington State University. Old was tall, maybe in his forties, and spoke with the clipped rhythms of a Westerner. He lived in Pullman, seventeen miles away, but his father had been born in Wawawai in 1912, before the dams—"in a house right over there," Old said, pointing into the main river. Carp rolled constantly while we talked. I asked if the government had helped relocate people displaced by the dams. "If you call saying 'here's your money, now get the hell out,' relocation," he said. Nobody had proposed high levees to save their homes, and many residents of the small, lower river communities opposed the Snake dams before they were built. So did fisheries biologists; conservationists; some fishermen, who predicted the dams would destroy Idaho's salmon runs; fiscal conservatives, who didn't like the idea of the federal government spending tax dollars on construction projects that benefited only a few people; and businessmen from Boise and the Puget Sound area who feared a dammed Snake River would bring economic development to Lewiston at their expense.

As Keith C. Petersen writes in his book, *River of Life, Channel of Death*, even in Lewiston, which had the most to gain from the dams, and where people had lobbied almost a century for dams that would allow river navigation, and where business and civic leaders wanted a seaport and the water route to Asia that Lewis and Clark hadn't found, support for the Snake's dams wasn't absolute. Now, in Lewiston and the small Palouse farm towns, support for the dams seems unshakable.

"People were opposed to the dams then because it seemed like the government was shoving them down people's throats; just like they're opposed to dam breaching now because it seems like the government is shoving that down their throats," Old said. "The same people that were opposed to the dams back then probably have 'Save Our Dams' bumper stickers on their cars now, as if the dams are theirs."

I once heard a congressman dismissively describe an ad in the *New York Times* supporting dam breaching. His comments about the ad made it clear that the readers of that newspaper should have no say in what happens to the Snake River dams. The dams, of course, belong to everybody. The federal government paid for them with taxpayers' money, although electricity users throughout the Northwest—people in both large cities like Seattle and Portland and small towns like Colfax and Pomeroy—are repaying the federal government for construction costs. And taxpayers throughout the country not only financed construction of the river's navigation system, but continue to fund much of its ongoing operation and maintenance costs.

Advocates for the status quo often will claim that those who live in the wrong place or moved to the region at the wrong time or have the wrong job or belong to the wrong political party should have no say in the Snake River's future. They will pare away those they believe should have a say until finally, only comments from those who share their views are legitimate. I have heard the same limiting arguments made when listening to people fight about cutting timber, building mines, and controlling predators.

Old attributed the shift in attitude by locals toward the dams to time. "Before the dams, people swam, fished, and enjoyed the river. The river was the way it was," he said. "Now people swim, fish, and enjoy themselves." His bobber jerked underwater, and he snapped his rod tip up to set the hook on another bluegill. "I mean we're having fun now. And this is the way we know the river. After a while, people forget," he said.

Besides childhood memories, the park's plants reminded Old

that Wawawai was once a settled town. He spoke in Latin names.
I constantly asked for common names. He pointed out *Robinia
pseudoacacia*, or black locust, often planted as shelter around
homes and farmsteads; *Ailanthus altissima*, or tree of heaven,
an Asian tree thought to bring good luck and planted to mark
weddings and births; *Saponaria officinalis*, or soapwort, a showy
European flower planted as an ornamental and because, when
crushed, it produces a rich greenish lather a person can wash
with. When I asked Old what the town and river had looked like
before the dams, he said simply and quietly, "It was beautiful."

At some point, Old asked me how I would get past Lower Granite Dam, which was just three miles downstream. "I don't know," I
said. By then, I knew it would be difficult. A park employee had told
me that a few weeks earlier, the Corps of Engineers had refused
to let a man headed downstream in what the employee described
as a glorified rowboat lock through at Lower Granite or help him
around in any other way. The man had paid the park manager a lot
of money to drive him past some of the dams, the employee said.
I knew I wouldn't pay anybody to drive me around the dams on
principle. Besides, I didn't have much money with me.

After hearing the story, I had called the Corps of Engineers'
Walla Walla, Washington, office from a phone in the garage attached to the park manager's house, which doubled as the park's
office. I had tried hard not to yell at the woman from the corps, but
I was desperate, and if I had thought yelling would have helped
get me around Lower Granite, I would have yelled. The woman
explained how unsafe a kayak, or for that matter any other boat
without a motor, was in the dam's navigation lock. I never really believed her danger argument, and she never explained why
a lock was dangerous. Not only wouldn't the corps let me use
the locks at any of its dams, it wouldn't drive me around the
dams. "According to the law, the corps is supposed to provide
river navigation," I said. The woman again told me I had to find
my own way around. "But according to the law, . . ." I said as
if repetition would somehow open the locks' giant metal gates.

"Could someone in a ten-foot aluminum johnboat pushed along by a five-horsepower engine use the locks?" I asked. "Yes," she said. I tried to explain how a kayak was safer than a small skiff, as if logic might win the argument for me. "Non-motorized vessels are not allowed in the locks," she repeated. I went back to the "but according to the law . . ." approach. It didn't work the first time I said it; it didn't work any better the last time. I hung up not knowing what would happen the next morning.

On June 19, the twenty-third day of the trip, I ate my oatmeal from the same pot I had cooked it in and readied myself to do whatever it was I needed to do to get around the dam. I knew that if for some reason the corps said I couldn't cross its property, if it wouldn't even let me portage on foot, I was finished. I quickly packed away my gear, climbed in the kayak, grabbed my paddle, and stretched the spray skirt over the cockpit. An older man walking around the park with a younger woman came over and asked if I wanted a push into the bay and I said "sure." Once in the water, he asked where I had come from and where I was going. My destination sounded as unlikely on the Snake as it had on the Salmon. The man and his daughter were visiting, from Texas I think, and he told me he had helped build Dworshak Dam. "I'm sorry about that," he said. I said he had nothing to apologize for. "Everybody needs a decent job, and if you hadn't done the work, somebody else would have."

Silver smolt splashed across the reservoir in the last mile or two before the dam. It looked like rain. By then I could see Lower Granite, and I searched for a place to beach the kayak. The best I could do was land on its boulder–strewn face. I hauled the boat onto the rocks, took off my spray skirt, and scrambled to the top of the dam ready to confront a government bureaucracy. I hoped I would make it past Lower Granite.

Lower Granite was the last dam built on the Snake or Columbia. Others were planned, most notably a Corps of Engineers' project on the Snake near Asotin, Washington, but none were started. Lower Granite marks the end of an era. Something changed between the time the government started the first dam on the Columbia and when it finished Lower Granite. Even before its completion in 1975, people, fisheries biologists in particular, tried to stop the dam, but the momentum to build proved unstoppable.

Originally, the Corps of Engineers had opposed the Snake dams, arguing economics didn't justify the effort or expense. But dam supporters lobbied incessantly. In 1936, after forty-six years of claiming otherwise, the Corps recommended a series of dams, with navigation locks, for the Snake, but only after completion of four large dams planned for the Columbia. In 1945, Congress authorized construction of dams on the lower Snake, but a congressional authorization doesn't mean much. A big project needs money, and in *River of Life, Channel of Death,* Petersen describes how the head of the Inland Empire Waterways Association, Herbert West, and other dam supporters, battled for another ten years. They again fought fiscal conservatives; fisheries biologists, commercial fishermen, and sportsmen worried what the dams would do to the river's salmon; and railroads worried a navigable river would steal their business. Finally, in 1955, Washington senator Warren Magnuson slipped a million dollars for work on Ice Harbor Dam into an appropriations bill. Not enough money to bring a veto—President Eisenhower had opposed the project for fiscal reasons—the bill's passage had ensured construction of Ice Harbor, and construction of Ice Harbor had ensured construction of the lower Snake's three other dams.

In a way, certainty dammed the Snake River. "One reads the newsletters and correspondence of the IEWA and is struck by the firmness of its resolve, by its absolute conviction that its cause was just. Herb West never doubted his eventual victory," Petersen writes. The fisheries biologists on the other hand had a "mentality of failure." And that, Petersen writes, doomed them. "To wage successful battle with true believers like Herbert West, one must also be a true believer."

The Snake dams look nothing like Dworshak. The spillways, powerhouses, and locks are concrete, but a portion of each is earth fill, and when people talk about dam breaching on the Snake, what they mean is removing the fill and leaving the concrete. Even though the concrete structures would remain, they would be useless. No water would flow through powerhouse turbines, no barges would pass through the locks.

Calls to tear down the dams didn't come right away, and didn't come from some giant environmental group or a prominent biologist. A Mennonite music teacher from Boise named Reed Burkholder first suggested dam breaching. In an interview with *Tri-City Herald* reporter Mike Lee published in 2000, Burkholder describes what motivated him after he moved back to Boise in the late 1980s. "I'd never had an environmental thought in my life. But when I heard about four dams that screwed up one of the most exciting things about my childhood, . . . I was incensed and outraged . . . I still am," he told Lee. "I wanted to know what happened to the salmon runs in my absence. I went to college in 1965 and we were fishing for salmon all over this freaking Salmon River country. Then I turn my back, live a normal life, get married, have a couple of kids, and I come back to my home state and said 'what's happened to the salmon?'" Burkholder first proposed taking out the dams at a public meeting in 1992. "Environmental groups were not at all interested," Burkholder told Lee. "Deaf ears. It just went right past these guys." So Burkholder started giving slide shows and speeches, Lee writes. People started to listen, and by 1995, the Corps of Engineers made dam breaching an option for restoring Snake River salmon.

The lower Snake's dams have captured much of the public's attention, but other dams in the Columbia Basin also cause problems for salmon. Large dams without fish ladders, on the Snake above Hells Canyon and on the upper Columbia, combined with smaller, ladderless dams on lesser tributaries, now keep salmon from reaching more than half the habitat once available for spawning. While plans call for removing a few of the small dams, nobody mentions tearing out the big impassible dams. Even talk of adding fish ladders is rare.

The argument for breaching the lower Snake dams while ignoring other dams throughout the Columbia Basin goes like this: just as the Snake and its tributaries produced more salmon than any other river feeding the Columbia, the Salmon River and its tributaries produced more salmon than any river feeding the Snake. And while the Snake and its tributaries behind those impassible Hells Canyon dams have been severely altered by human activity, many of the Salmon's tributaries flow through the federally protected Frank Church, Selway, and Gospel Hump wilderness areas or through national forests, so they remain in relatively good condition. With the four lower Snake dams gone, the reasoning goes, salmon runs in those protected rivers would increase enough to boost the overall number of Columbia salmon in a way improving runs on other rivers couldn't.

Sometimes one group or another will point to Redfish Lake and Sunbeam Dam as an example both of the benefits of dam breaching and the harm caused by the lower Snake's dams. But Redfish Lake's sockeye cannot provide a simple narrative for what has happened. The lake's post-Sunbeam sockeye runs peaked at a little less than five thousand fish in 1955, when the salmon already crossed two large dams on the Columbia during their migration. By 1960, when the sockeye crossed three dams, the run had dropped to seventy-five fish, and a year later, when the first lower Snake dam came online, only eleven fish returned. While this has happened, a run of sockeye on the upper Columbia has managed to stay off the endangered species list even though some of the fish cross nine dams on their migrations.

By the time I took my trip, the government had shelved dam breaching, but the idea hasn't gone away. Certainty built the dams, and certainty might just as easily tear them down. But it is doubt that now defines feelings toward the dams. While virtually every politician in the region and beyond claims to support saving salmon, few advocate dam breaching. When Seattle's city council did, city councils and county commissions across eastern Washington responded with their own resolutions to boycott all things Seattle. Although the economic effects of such boycotts would have been negligible, Seattle's mayor apologized for the city's resolution.

Support for breaching ebbs and flows. Polls conducted in Idaho by Boise State University found a roughly even split for several years between those who favored breaching and those who opposed it. But after 2001, when California suffered blackouts and regional electricity prices jumped, support for breaching fell, while support for keeping the dams rose. The shift seems to match a 1995 Boise State University poll where seventy percent of Idahoans expressed interest in improving salmon and steelhead runs, but only twenty percent said they wanted to spend more than five dollars a month to do it.

Some might dismiss the poll results as somehow unique to Idaho, reflecting the conservative views of those from one of the red states, in the recent language of political analysis, and not indicative of regional opinion. Despite their reputations as sodden, latte-drinking liberal bastions, much of Washington and Oregon is as red as Idaho. The Cascade Mountains cut the region in half, not only ecologically, with a dry East Side and a wet West Side, but also politically, with a rural, conservative East Side and an urban, more liberal West Side.

The poll results also reflect an uncertainty that stretches far beyond the region and appears in many places. The battle over dam breaching isn't just about the fate of four dams in eastern Washington, but also about how people view the natural world, about whether we regularly modify the world around us to suit our needs regardless of consequences, or if at some point we start to modify our actions to fit the world around us. The conflict between the desires that dammed the Columbia and Snake and those that stopped dam construction after Lower Granite have not yet sorted themselves out.

When I tried to convince the woman from the Corps of Engineers that I should be allowed through Lower Granite's lock, I had, in my frustration and worry, said dam breaching suddenly sounded like a really good idea. It wasn't the brightest comment, and I worried it might come back to bite me as I searched the dam looking for someone who could tell me how to get around it.

Steelhead smolt swam back and forth in front of the dam, always moving but going nowhere. A great blue heron stood patiently on shore. A young army officer in camouflage passed me off to someone else, until eventually, I found myself talking to a man from the corps' public affairs office. He had a pack of cigarettes tucked into the breast pocket of his white shirt, and when he introduced himself, he shook my hand too long and too vigorously like a bad salesman trying to sell me something I didn't need.

"I had an e-mail saying you might be coming through and that you might be mad," he said. I didn't make small talk and asked right away about using the navigation lock. "Absolutely not," he said. It wasn't safe for a kayak. "The lock moves forty-six million gallons of water," he told me, as if that figure should impress me, as if flowing water were some type of novelty. The Snake once held some notorious rapids, and the history of navigation before the dams is one of sternwheelers grounded on river bars and sunk by hidden rocks and snags.

I tried all the arguments I had tried over the phone the night before. They didn't work any better. The public affairs man again mentioned the "forty-six million gallons of water" the lock moves. I still wasn't impressed. I asked if someone could drive me around in a truck. "No truck," he said. "It would set a precedent."

The man told me the corps had had "the policy for years," even though Juliet called and received a faxed memo of the policy

banning canoes and kayaks dated that May. Later, the lock operator at another dam would tell me that until the May memo, the
corps never had any formal policy. "It was up to the lockmaster," he would say. "I've sent plenty of Boy Scouts on canoe trips
through, and there was never any danger."

Arguing with the man from the corps at Lower Granite, I understood how completely we had changed the river by damming
it. On the Salmon, when I faced rapids, I had to decide: could
I run them safely. I never portaged, but if I had, I would have
expected no help, and, most likely, received none. If rapids still
filled the Snake, I would have faced the same decision at each
and would be on my own to find a way past. Because of the dams,
because the Corps of Engineers controls the river, opens and
closes the locks, manages the land along the river and around
the dams, I needed its help. The dams changed how I looked at
the river. On the lower Snake I found a series of linked reservoirs
that moved not to the natural rhythms of a river, but a river managed by bureaucrats and engineers to float tugs and barges and
make the electricity that I use every day.

The corps' public affairs man gave me my options for getting around the dam: portage myself, pay someone to drive me
around, or wait and try to ride through the lock on another boat.
Under the corps' rules, I could lock through while riding in a
motorboat with my kayak tied to it. There was no dock below the
dam, which meant not only would I need to find a willing boat
owner, I would have to climb from a boat back into my kayak, a
mid-river procedure promising more danger than going through
the lock on my own.

Hauling kayak and gear over the dam would kill most of the
day and leave me too tired to paddle afterwards. So I waited. I ate
lunch. I walked around the dam. I watched the schools of steelhead smolt going nowhere. I ate some more. The day grew hot,
and I started to sweat even when I didn't move. To save water
in that drought year, the corps had limited the number of times
it would open the navigation locks for non-commercial traffic.

When the time for the next lock opening came, there was no boat. I would portage.

I drug the kayak up the dam face. I unloaded my gear. I took a drink of water, loaded as much gear as I could carry into storage bags, and started to walk. I crossed the paved road that runs along the top of the dam and headed toward the river down a half-mile-long dirt road. With each step, little puffs of dirt shot out from under my sandals and coated my feet. Before I headed back for more gear, I rinsed my feet in the river. A thin layer of caked and dried mud coated my feet by the time I made it to the top of the dam to pick up a second load of equipment.

I sat down, wiped my face with my shirt, and took a drink, then grabbed more gear and headed back to the river. The straps of my sandals cut into my feet and by the time I reached the river, dropped off the second load of gear, and hiked back to the upstream side of the dam, small, red sores rimmed by dark circles of dirt had appeared on both ankles. I sat down, took another drink, then used the rest of the water to rinse the sores clean before covering them with duct tape.

All my gear was around the dam. But I still had to deal with the kayak. I picked it up and threw it on my shoulder the way I would a whitewater boat. I made it the hundred yards to the dirt road before the kayak hit the ground with a thud. Seventeen feet long and weighing more than fifty pounds, the kayak was too heavy and unwieldy to carry on my shoulder. I thought about dragging it, and if it had been mine instead of borrowed from a friend, I would have.

Finally, I snatched the kayak off the ground, rested it on my shoulder, then rolled it onto my head. I made it another hundred yards with the kayak balanced that way before the boat pitched forward, blocking my view of the road. I stopped, leveled the boat, and got my bearings before moving on. I stumbled on a rock and almost fell. My shirt was wet with sweat. I was breathing hard. I stopped. I had no more water, so couldn't even take a drink. Once my breathing slowed, I again balanced the kayak on my head and started to walk. After a half-dozen pauses on the half-mile portage, I reached the river. The entire portage had taken almost two hours. Before I repacked the kayak, I found my filter, filled a water bottle with filtered river water, and then drank the entire bottle. Back on the river, I turned around, looked at the dam, and raised my middle finger. I'm sure nobody saw, but it made me feel better.

I camped that night on river left in a dusty grove of black locusts, the dam still visible. The shade felt good and I rested in the trees until the day cooled. Signs tacked to trees by the corps reminded me to pick up my trash. I was suddenly like so many other people around the West, both dependant on the federal government—I used the cheap electricity from the federal dams and my future wife worked for the government—and angry at it for the way its policies affected my life.

At dinnertime, I waded across silt-covered rocks until the river reached my knees. I wanted to get past the shallows, where little balls of algae bobbed, before filtering fresh drinking and cooking water. I sat next to the river on an old chair that looked like it had been stolen from a school auditorium and ate my Ramen noodles. A tug, the *Hurricane*, pushed four barges, one full of cargo containers, two that I guessed were filled with wheat, and another loaded with who knows what down the river. Someone had painted a pair of orange and black hurricane warning flags on the tug's white deckhouse, somehow giving the tug its own personality. The *Hurricane*'s radar antenna spun, and I wondered if the echoing microwaves showed the skipper anything he couldn't see for himself from the wheelhouse: the way the river bent or how its canyon narrowed or widened slightly maybe, or the channel markers the corps had placed to help with navigation, or other traffic moving on the river.

After the tug passed, the river slid away from the shoreline like an outgoing tide, moved not by the pull of sun and moon, but by human need. Peak power use was over for the day; the river shut down for the night. It ebbed and flowed not in twelve-hour cycles but to the demand of washing machines and air conditioners and electric lights. I cleaned my pots and laid out my bivy and prepared myself for another day on the dammed river and another day after that.

8

Locking through with Smolt

You mean the white people are taking fish out of the river and putting them on the land and taking logs off the land and putting them
in the river? —Comment by Nathan "Eight Ball" Jim, Warm
Springs Tribal Elder, as related by a Yakama Nation fisheries
biologist

Not even rivers are eternal. Near Lower Monumental, the third
of the lower Snake's four dams, the dried bed of an ancient river
breaches the canyon wall on river left. Bunchgrass and shrubs
fleck the coulee, and while it doesn't look so different from
many of the others that tumble into the river, the coulee is a reminder that nothing is static. Millions of years ago, the Snake
flowed west across what is now Idaho and Oregon and drained
into the Columbia River somewhere downstream from its present confluence. Then, around two million years ago, about the
time modern salmon first evolved, a series of volcanic eruptions
in western Idaho clogged the Snake's ancient channel, forcing
the river into roughly its present course.

The Salmon River existed before the Snake's course shifted,
and all that water had to reach the ocean somehow. In places

around the lower Snake, trapped between layers of basalt, geologists sometimes find deposits of smooth river cobbles. Those worn and rounded rocks suggest a long-vanished river that emptied into the Columbia once washed across the area now drained by the lower Snake. Geologists suspect it was the ancestral Salmon, and that the coulee near the dam formed after the modern Snake intersected with the ancient river's channel.

Since Lewiston, the Snake had seemed static. There was no noticeable current. I had expected wind but paddled greasy smooth reservoirs instead. And each windless day felt like a reprieve. My goal, always, was the next dam—after Lower Granite, Little Goose, after Little Goose, Lower Monumental—but sometimes the miles passed away so slowly. Below Lower Granite, I started playing mental games to fill each day's space. But the mental games always involved physical action. Sometimes I would paddle hard for five minutes then slip into an easy pace for five more minutes before again upping the tempo. I might do half a dozen hard-easy intervals and kill an hour before assuming a pace I could hold all day. Besides breaking the monotony, the intervals strengthened me for the upstream gales I anticipated on the Columbia.

When the river meandered, I attempted to travel in as straight a line as possible, and with unnerving frequency crossed and recrossed the navigation channel, which was somewhat risky because of barge traffic and the river's size. At least the noisy tugs and their tows moved slowly, at maybe six knots, and even when I didn't see them, I heard them, and could change course to get out of their way.

When I had nothing else to do, I swerved left or right, sped up or slowed down, trying to hit carp with my paddle or run them down with my kayak. Tails and dorsal fins poked above the water, and a slow spread of concentric ripples betrayed the presence of an endless supply of seemingly easy targets. It was mindless activity that left a meandering wake, and I suspect that in pursuing it, I gained back all those miles saved straightening river bends. I never hit a carp. They sank away from the kayak like green-brown submarines avoiding a depth-charge-laden destroyer.

Despite my unevenly paced, carp-chasing course, I covered the roughly forty miles between Lower Granite and the second dam, Little Goose, in two days. I reached it on the summer solstice in time to make the afternoon lock opening. I hoped a boat I could travel through with might show up, but none came. The day was hot. I didn't have the energy for a long portage, so I decided to deal with Little Goose the next morning. I paddled a mile back upstream to a boat ramp built by the Corps of Engineers and camped.

I settled into the gravel turnout of the ramp the best I could. It was a busy place. A half dozen or so people in a big, new RV and a pickup with a bumper sticker that read, "I Love that Dammed Snake River" had taken up residence at the boat ramp while they fished for smallmouth bass. I heard someone complain, "There are so many smolt right now, I think the bass are full from eating them."

Another man, not with the larger group, sat in a web lawn chair in the shade of his old RV smoking one cigarette after another, throwing each still-smoldering butt into dry cheatgrass. I expected something to catch on fire. He saw me unloading gear from the kayak and asked where I was headed.

"The ocean," I told him and stopped to chat. The man, his name was Earl, had come to the river for bass too, but waited on a friend with a new boat so they could take it out the next morning. Retired from a job at a tin can plant in Walla Walla, Earl said he had time to wait. He was sixty-nine and had lived in the area all his life, fished the river all his life, and remembered it from before the dams. "The old Snake, people didn't run it much in boats—this was before jet boats—and before you could get on the river you had to learn it. The river was shallow with lots of rocks," he said.

"What was the fishing like before the dams?" I asked.

"Back in them days, if you were a fisherman, you were a trout fisherman. The Snake didn't have trout, but the bass fishing was good, with some big ones. The sturgeon fishing was good then too," he said. He told me about a nine footer he'd caught in Hells Canyon a few years back. All sturgeon caught anywhere on the Snake must be released. "God, that's a lot of fish to turn loose," he said, and threw his smoldering cigarette into the dry grass. Besides bass, Earl said he fished for steelhead on the Snake during fall and into winter and had caught a salmon that spring, but in the past, when he wanted to salmon fish, he went to Alaska.

"Do you think it was worth trading a free-flowing river for the dams?"

Earl lit another cigarette before he answered. "For me, I don't think it was a good trade, but for the general public—yes. There are a lot of benefits to the dams. They provide jobs. Barging is good. Before the dams, wheat had to move by trucks, and the trucks messed up the roads. For an old dyed-in-the-wool fisherman though, it didn't do much good." Despite his nostalgia, Earl opposed dam breaching, an idea pushed by a group he labeled "do-gooders." Earl blamed the salmon declines on the terns and sea lions that live downriver, and on overfishing. It was the usual list, and I didn't argue with him about its validity.

"Is it worth spending billions of dollars on hatcheries and dam modifications just to try to keep salmon in the river? I mean Canada and Alaska have plenty of salmon. We both know that," I said.

"What do we do with the salmon? The Indians catch all the salmon so they can have a big powwow or whatever," he said. "Anyone who wants salmon can go to Alaska." Sometime during his answer he tossed his cigarette into the grass and lit another. "This is extinct, that's extinct—who gives a shit. It's a changing world, there are lots of things that went by the wayside and nobody cared. We need to get on with life and what animals go extinct, we can do without."

Earl mentioned the many meetings held around Washington,

Oregon, and Idaho where people gave their opinions about keeping or breaching the Snake's dams. He said that at one, a woman, a do-gooder, got up and stated that in order to save salmon, the dams had to go. Someone asked if she'd ever seen the Snake and she answered "no." I don't know if Earl was at the meeting or heard about her comments second- or third-hand, don't even know if the story is true. But people believe the story and retell it as if it were fact.

I'm certain Earl thought of me as some do-gooder, but we talked for a while anyway. We traded fish stories and discussed bird dogs, which Earl had raised and trained all his life. I never mentioned that I'm a terrible wing shot. Finally, Earl excused himself and said it was time to make dinner. I was hungry too and set about fixing pasta. As I waded out to where the river was mostly free of floating algae so I could filter water for cooking and drinking, someone from the new RV crowd said I was welcome to their water. The offer was nice, but I said no thanks. I liked standing in the cool river. Just before I went to sleep, a pack of coyotes filled the air with yips. I could overhear a woman say, "We've been serenaded each night."

A ripping sound, like somebody tearing old sheets into rags, yanked me from midnight sleep. Wind. It shook the side of my bivy sack. It made the dried grass beyond the boat ramp's gravel turnout hum. I propped myself on one elbow and listened. I told myself the wind would die out by morning and tried to sleep. But the wind invaded my dreams, and I was in a foul mood by the time I woke. I faced a long portage followed by a long paddle into a hard headwind.

I was already in my kayak, pulling the spray skirt over the cockpit when Earl came down to the boat ramp. His friend, the one with the new bass boat, had offered to drive me around the dam. I had told Earl about my problems with the Corps of Engineers the day before, and he had seemed sympathetic, but I hadn't expected help. Sometime during the trip I had decided I wouldn't ask for help but also wouldn't turn it down when offered. I was glad for the offer, and my mood lightened a little. I bounced past Little Goose on a gravel road, my kayak shoved inside a trailered boat pulled by a dark pickup. Below the dam, I shook hands with Earl and thanked his friend. I had escaped a portage, but Lower Monumental waited two days away, if the wind dropped.

An endless procession of white-capped waves marched up-river while hard gusts cut smooth streaks through the ranks. The wind blew twenty knots or so, hard enough that I didn't want to be on the river. I didn't realize then how puny that wind was. In a week twenty knots would seem close to calm. That day it felt ferocious. So when I reached a state park at the confluence of the Snake and Palouse rivers a little after one o'clock, the decision to stop was easy. The park was an oasis of irrigated green in a drying landscape. The campground was a long haul up a steep hill, but the manager said I could camp on a small island in the mouth of the Palouse. He told me I had to wait until most visitors left for the day since the island officially was closed to overnight stays. I napped. I swam. I had a burger and fries from the park's snack bar. I napped some more. I called Juliet, but she wasn't around. When the people, who had come mostly to swim, went home, I slipped into my kayak and paddled across the lagoon that separated the island from the rest of the park.

I was grateful for the secluded spot. On the Snake, I was frequently relegated to Corps of Engineers campgrounds and often pitched my bivy beside RVers and noisy car campers. I was happy to get away from them for a night. Because of the dams, the Snake had flooded out past its old banks, and was wider than a natural river. But the dam pools were not really lakes. The river reminded me of a fjord or some other strip of water constrained by high cliffs. No beaches formed along the river's margins, and I longed for the Salmon's perfect sand. Flat spots suitable for camping were hard to find. When I did find one, prickly cheatgrass and thorny yellow starthistle often blanketed it. A low shrub that looked something like a miniature black locust tree, but thankfully without the sharp spines, crowded the shoreline. Rich Old, the botanist I had met at Wawawai had said the shrubs, Amorpha fruticosa or bastard indigo, were native to Midwestern states and planted by the Corps of Engineers to prevent erosion. They had turned weedy and were spreading up and down the Snake's side canyons, displacing native plants as they went.

I beached my kayak against some cattails that edged the lagoon and pitched my bivy sack in a shallow dip that hid me from view. Even though the manager said he would tell the ranger who patrolled at night that I was on the island, I thought it best to stay out of view. Around dusk, I slipped back to my kayak to get my camp stove and food so I could make dinner. A beaver stood on its hind legs, flat tail pressed against the ground for balance, chewing cattail stalks. When it saw me, it slipped into the lagoon and vanished under the water with a loud slap of its tail.

I didn't want to disturb the beavers, so I walked across the island and ate looking over the Palouse River. The wind had dropped out by then and the calm water reflected the high walls of the deep canyon like a mirror. After dinner, I walked back to the kayak to put away my stove and cooking pots. A beaver cruised offshore, just its head above water, and at my approach, it smashed the surface of the lagoon with its tail and dove. I heard another slap, and then another as two more beavers disappeared under the water. I went to sleep that night to the sound of beavers gnawing trees and cattails and doing whatever other business it is that beavers do at night.

A Palouse Indian story tells how a giant beaver created the Palouse River's canyon as it tried to escape from four giant brothers hunting it. The story's language is poetic and metaphoric, but also geologically accurate and underlies the violence that created what is now such a peaceful spot. According to geologists, starting about sixteen thousand years ago and ending around twelve thousand years ago, as the last Ice Age ended, a melting ice sheet released torrents of water from a lake that once covered what's now western Montana. The lake held more water than Lake Erie and Lake Ontario combined, and when the ice dam that blocked its outlet collapsed, great floods careened across eastern Washington at fifty miles per hour in an act of simultaneous destruction and creation. There may have been a hundred floods, and the biggest flowed at a rate equal to about ten times the combined flow of all the world's present rivers.

The Bretz Floods, named for the geologist who proved they had occurred, washed away rolling hills of fertile soil, stripped the earth down to scablands of eroded rock, and changed the course of rivers. In the floods' rushes to the ocean, they poured into the Snake and Columbia rivers. They left gravel bars as high as city buildings. They carved a great gorge for the Columbia River to flow through and left Oregon's Willamette Valley with the fertile soil—taken from eastern Washington—that would bring pioneers trekking west on the Oregon Trail. They shifted the Palouse River east, creating in the process a two-hundred-foot-high waterfall and a deep basalt canyon between the river's new mouth and the waterfall.

Part of the same massive ice sheet responsible for the Bretz Floods also covered the upper third of the Columbia Basin. But salmon survived in the ice-free sections of the river and in its tributaries. They survived the Bretz Floods, and along with straying salmon from other unglaciated rivers south and north of the ice sheet, slowly spread to streams once smothered by glaciers. By the time Lewis and Clark traveled the Columbia, it was one of the world's great salmon rivers, with somewhere between eight and sixteen million salmon and steelhead headed upriver each year, many destined for the Snake.

Now the Columbia and its tributaries produce hydropower, and any salmon and steelhead run approaching two million is considered huge. The relationship between dams and salmon looks simple: as the number of dams increased, the number of salmon decreased. So eliminating the lower Snake's dams should provide clear benefits. Of course it's never that simple.

The story of the Columbia's failing salmon runs reaches back beyond the construction of its first dams. In 1811 and again in the late 1820s, salmon became scarce on the main Columbia above the Snake, according to some journals written at the time. Whatever caused those failed runs, the salmon quickly recovered, and commercial salmon fishing became a major industry. In 1883, the Columbia's canneries handled forty-three million pounds of Chinook, a record at the time. Chinook harvests dropped to around twenty-four million pounds after that and remained stable for three decades. In his book *Salmon Without Rivers*, fisheries biologist Jim Lichatowich writes, "The stable harvests over the thirty years from 1889 to 1920 created a numerical illusion that apparently fooled even experienced biologists."

The same rich, oily flesh that sustains spring and summer Chinook on their upstream migrations also made the canneries desire them over any other salmon. But during the thirty years of what looked like stable harvests, the fishermen caught, and the canneries packed, fewer and fewer spring and summer Chinook. Each year, more fall Chinook filled cans that otherwise would have gone empty. Lichatowich notes that in 1878, most Chinook caught were spring and summer run. By 1919, most were fall run.

Besides Chinook, other species of the Columbia's salmon were under increasing fishing pressure. And along with the overfishing, logging and mining destroyed salmon spawning habitat, irrigation projects dried up streams and sucked young salmon from rivers and left them dying in fields, and small dams built without fish ladders made tributaries inaccessible to returning adults. Then in 1933, a private utility completed the first dam on the main-stem Columbia near Wenatchee, Washington. By 1938, the federal government had completed its first dam on the main river; by 1941, its second. Plans called for dozens more. Dam supporters claimed fish ladders would allow the river's salmon to continue to thrive, although the second federal dam, Grand Coulee, was built without the ladders. With the completion of that dam, an important stretch of spawning habitat vanished.

Biologists suspected the Columbia's salmon could survive a dam or two, but predicted that if every planned dam was built, even if they had fish ladders, the salmon would be doomed. After the dam-building era had ended, the biologists' predictions looked uncannily accurate. The Columbia's salmon populations crashed and stayed low for twenty-five years, and many of its runs wound up on the endangered species list. Most people blamed the dams.

The problem with the big dams isn't so much what they do to adult fish migrating home from the ocean, but what they do to the young fish heading to sea. Smolt on the Snake and Columbia pass a dam in one of four ways. Some go over the spillway. Some go through the turbines. Some go through a bypass system, which herds them away from the turbines and into a water park ride of pipes that eventually shoots them into the river downstream of the dam. All the methods kill fish; turbines the most, spillways the least.

Finally, at three dams on the Snake and one on the Columbia, some of the smolt diverted through the bypass system end up on barges or trucks that haul them downstream past the last dam. The Corps of Engineers estimates ninety-eight percent of the transported smolt survive the trip downriver. But the percentage of barged and trucked smolt that make it to adulthood and return to the Columbia varies greatly. Sometimes, especially during droughts, they return at noticeably higher rates than fish left to migrate in the river. Sometimes they return at only marginally higher rates. (The differences are often within the statistical margin of error.) Sometimes barged smolt do worse than fish left in the river. And many fish left to migrate in the river die.

Initially, most smolt—eighty-four percent of the Chinook and eighty-nine percent of the steelhead forced to navigate all eight dams between Idaho and the ocean—died, according to research by biologists from the National Marine Fisheries Service, or NMFS. In drought years, almost none survived. Over time, engineers modified the dams, and now NMFS claims Chinook smolt have a roughly fifty-fifty chance of making it through all eight dams. Nobody knows how many smolt survived before the dams, or even what's normal on a free-flowing river, said John Williams, one of the paper's authors. Smolt die on any river, he said. Diseases kill them; birds and fish eat them. On a free-flowing river, those deaths are hard to quantify. The dams make it possible to count PIT-tagged salmon migrating to and from the ocean and to estimate survival rates in a way almost impossible on an undammed river.

Direct deaths at any one dam—being crushed by the turbines or from the lethal concentration of gases sometimes created by the spillways for instance—are low. There are other hypotheses about how dams kill young salmon, and at least some scientists disagree with all of them. The dams have widened the Snake and Columbia rivers, slowing the current in the process, which has probably tripled the time it takes for smolt from Idaho to reach the ocean. The longer journey may leave the small salmon more vulnerable to predators, rising water temperatures, or diseases. Depending on which biologist you talk to and what study you read, the connection between a slower downstream migration and increased mortality is either clear or nonexistent or somewhere in between.

Some research suggests many smolt die after they have passed the last dam, but that it's the dams that really killed them. Most of the survival studies have measured how many young salmon die between the first dam on the Snake and the last on the Columbia. But the fish have another 145 river miles to travel between the last dam and the ocean. Some researchers hypothesize that smolt battered and damaged by spillways and bypass systems and turbines simply don't die until after the last dam. Other researchers suspect that because of the slowed migration, smolt use up stored fat as they move downstream until they run out of energy somewhere beyond the last dam, and others claim that dam-delayed migration somehow delivers the young salmon into the Columbia's estuary at the wrong time. Delayed mortality, the phenomenon all those hypotheses try to explain, has been controversial.

Terns and cormorants and a variety of fish eat the smolt swimming the river's last miles and would even if there were no dams. In the ocean, seals, sea lions, killer whales, and salmon sharks feed on the maturing salmon; sports fishermen catch them with rod and reel; commercial fishermen with nets and trolled baits. Trying to tease out what the dams killed and what something else killed becomes difficult.

Not surprisingly, some scientists have discounted most dam-caused delayed mortality in the same way they discount the effects of the dams on salmon in general. They note that salmon have vanished, or are struggling to survive, even in rivers without dams. Some instead point to predators, some to overfishing, some to damaged spawning habitat, and almost all to the ocean. Salmon abundance fluctuates somewhat from year to year, as anyone would expect, and greatly in twenty- to thirty-year cycles. The argument goes that natural cycles influence salmon population trends more than almost any human activity, and ocean temperature influences those natural cycles more than anything else.

Many people are familiar with El Niño, a periodic, short-term warming of the Pacific Ocean, and La Niña, the equally short-term cooling that follows. But Pacific Ocean temperatures also fluctuate in patterns that last for decades. In the 1980s, fisheries biologists noticed not only that salmon numbers in Washington, Oregon, California, and Alaska would increase and remain high for twenty or thirty years and then drop and remain low for twenty or thirty years, but also that when Alaska had good salmon runs, Washington, Oregon, and California had poor runs and vice versa.

More research revealed that since the mid-1800s, the eastern Pacific has cooled about three degrees Fahrenheit for two or three decades, then warmed about three degrees Fahrenheit for another twenty or thirty years, before again cooling. The size of salmon runs fluctuates with the shifts in ocean temperature. For a variety of reasons, runs in Washington, Oregon, and California increase when the ocean cools, while runs in Alaska increase when the ocean warms.

The temperature shifts influence the amount and types of plankton in the ocean, and since plankton is the base of the food chain, the amount and types of plankton determine how much food is available for everything from krill to whales to salmon. With the right ocean conditions, the number of salmon that survive jumps exponentially, a jump removing dams could never match, according to those who argue breaching would make little difference in the size of salmon runs.

The last warming cycle coincided with completion of the last Snake dam and the collapse of the river's salmon stocks. Eventually, in the 1990s, several scientists, including University of Washington climatologist Nathan Mantua, became confident enough in the pattern of shifts, a pattern now called the Pacific Decadal Oscillation, or PDO, to predict that the ocean was about to cool. In a field where change usually happened in the distant past or will happen in the distant future, their prediction was risky.

Around 1998, the eastern Pacific's waters cooled, and as predicted, the number of adult salmon coming back to the Columbia went up. By the time I traveled the river, returns had increased from near extinction to numbers not seen since before the first big dams were built. Tens of thousands of Chinook headed up the Snake River. The biologists who said ocean conditions, not dams, were responsible for the disappearing salmon seemed vindicated.

But just as some scientists have rejected the idea that increased migration times or dam-caused delayed mortality can account for the decrease in salmon, others argue that the shifting ocean temperatures do not account completely for the drastic population declines seen on the Columbia and Snake. Those scientists will agree that the ocean is important, more important than any other single variable perhaps, but to back up claims that it's not just the ocean, they might point out that when irrigation water management along the Yakima River changed, its spring Chinook runs rebounded during a time of poor ocean conditions, or that when the salmon runs in Alaska dip, they don't approach extinction. The biologists who work in Idaho for instance, the ones who travel streams and spend their days counting salmon and redds, will almost always say that they see more good habitat than fish to fill it, which indicates that something beyond ocean conditions or habitat destruction is keeping salmon populations low.

A study published in 2003 by a group of NMFS biologists in the journal *Ecological Applications* warned that a cooling ocean wasn't enough to prevent extirpation of some of the Columbia's salmon runs. The study states, "Overall our results suggest that the declines seen over the last twenty years are not solely due to a temporary period of poor ocean conditions, but are more likely to be a more long-term phenomenon."

After my trip, I doubted my own opinions and conclusions about dams and salmon. For whatever reason, it wasn't enough for me that from the time I hit the beginning of the first dam pool near Asotin, until the time I crossed the last of the Columbia's dams, it felt like I was kayaking a series of interconnected lakes, not a river. In many places, muddy shallows extended from the shoreline far into the dam pools. A bed of clean cobbles was unusual. Carp and other warm-water fish like bass clogged the rivers just as weeds clogged their banks. Salmon seemed out of place and common sense would say dams carried at least some of the blame.

But I wanted something to add a sort of certainty to my observations. I studied graphs that showed how dams altered the basic processes that make a river a river: slowed the current, reduced peak flows, changed the timing of when the Snake and Columbia flowed full or low, and altered how the rivers move sediment. I read through scientific papers about salmon and dams. I talked to biologists I knew and to biologists I didn't know. One likened the debate over dams to a "scientific food fight," with competing theories whizzing back and forth. One said, "I don't think science has very much to do with what's going on. People hate change. The reason we're doing all this research is to keep things from changing." Another, who doubts breaching the Snake's dams will do much to restore salmon said, "The people who compile those lists of the most stressful jobs, the ones that always include police and firefighters, they should add dissident scientist."

A former girlfriend who had spent her career working for various public advocacy groups once called me a consensus seeker. It wasn't a compliment. As a couple, we could have argued over the direction of the sunrise, so I try not to worry about comments made during a long-over relationship. But her basic point is true: I lack the convictions of a true believer. I am, instead, skeptical about almost everything. Maybe working as a reporter has made me this way; maybe my skepticism made me a reporter.

In what I read and what I heard, I searched for a simple answer for what happened to the salmon and an easy place to put the blame. And with those two things, I might take a stand. Of course if simple answers existed, an army of scientists wouldn't spend millions of dollars each year producing reams of studies.

Almost everyone in the Northwest pledges they're on the salmon's side, although they may then go on to propose some plan that will make life for the salmon more difficult. When I worked for the newspaper in Yakima, I covered a congressional field hearing, one of those events where senators and representatives swoop in from DC, put on a dog and pony show for the local constituents, but actually accomplish very little. The hearing was about salmon and the Snake River dams, and people had traveled a long way to attend despite its dubious value. I questioned two men who had driven over together from Lewiston that morning to sit in a Pasco, Washington, community college auditorium. They were older, retired, both with gray hair and gray beards, both union men from a state where unions now retain little influence. "We can have both dams and salmon," they both told me. "But what if we can't?" I asked. There was a pause before one of them answered, "Then the salmon will have to go." The other man agreed.

In a December 2002 edition of the magazine *Wheat Life*, which is published by the Washington Association of Wheat Growers, Earl Roberge writes that we can have both dams and salmon, but that if for some reason we cannot, the salmon should be allowed to vanish. "It is not a desirable choice and pray God it never happens, but if the salmon were to become extinct in the Snake, the sky wouldn't fall and life would go on with no noticeable disruption." Later, in the same article he writes, "Extinction of a species as noble as the Snake River salmon is not a popular choice, but were the fact forced upon us—and remember it definitely is a possibility—we would still survive." He goes on to argue that if the dams disappeared, everyone in the region would suffer.

Besides holding a worldview equating dams with progress, those who want the Snake's dams left in place often have powerful economic incentives for taking the positions they do, and they will argue economics justifies keeping the dams. Breaching, they say, will devastate the region's economy, resulting in lost family farms, shuttered businesses, and vanishing communities.

Breaching advocates also argue economics, using the language of dollars and cents to bolster a position often held for emotional or personal reasons. They say conservation and alternative energy sources will compensate for lost electricity, rail lines for lost river navigation, and that with the dams gone, fishermen, whitewater boaters, and tourists will flock to the river. They say the region will ultimately end up with more jobs and a more vibrant economy than when the dams blocked the Snake. But even if somebody could prove their economics unequivocally wrong, many would still support dam breaching.

One of the pleasures of being a reporter is that I get to doubt whatever any person or group says. After reading through the various economic studies each side in the breaching debate uses to support their positions, I suspect that even with all the statistics and models, nobody can really predict what would happen if the Snake's dams are removed. Breaching would hurt some people economically and help others, just as building the dams hurt some people and helped others, and regardless of whether the dams stay or go, the economy will change and some people will profit and others will suffer. I think both the claims of economic disaster and of economic renaissance are exaggerations, but it's that inability to assure an outcome that makes us so uncomfortable.

While many of us are personally unwilling to make huge economic sacrifices for the salmon, like spending more in a year on salmon restoration programs than we do on cable television, we also seem unwilling to reduce salmon to a mere commodity, pork bellies with fins perhaps, that can be traded away when something more valuable comes along. So just as breaching advocates use economics to bolster positions that are not based on economics, supporters of the status quo use science in an effort to show dams don't hurt salmon, or hurt them very little, to bolster positions that have nothing to with the science. They play up studies that cast doubt on the damage caused by dams and try to discredit the science and the scientists who disagree with their position. But even if science could unequivocally prove dams were responsible for the salmon's decline, some people would oppose breaching.

The debate over dam breaching is not a debate about science any more than it is a debate about economics. It exists instead at the spot where science, economics, and the environment intersect with politics, culture, and emotion. It is the same spot where so many issues now facing us exist. Dam breaching forces us to examine our priorities. If salmon had taken precedent when planning the region's hydro-system began, nobody would have built the Snake's dams. If salmon were to take precedent now, the Snake's dams most likely would vanish. Dam breaching makes

us ask questions science cannot answer, makes us consider what
we will want from the river in ten years, a hundred years, or a
thousand years, and forces us to try to predict how a world that is
never static will change over time.

Dam breaching forces us to deal with the uncertainties always
left by science. When I talked to John Williams, the biologist at
NMFS who studied smolt mortality on the Snake and Columbia
rivers, he said that in 1990, people would say, "We know where
the smolt are dying. They're all dying before they get to Lower
Granite." Since then, research has shown that isn't the case.
Now people claim the smolt are dying in the estuary from delayed mortality, he said.

I think it's fair to ask if we would really gain anything from
another twenty or thirty years of study.

Most biologists have taken a kind of middle ground in the debate about dams and salmon: acknowledge the role of natural
cycles, habitat damage caused by human activity, and past overfishing. They say breaching the Snake's dams will not guarantee
renewed salmon runs, but also that as long as the dams remain,
recovery is unlikely, and the risk of the salmon's extirpation from
the Snake River and its tributaries will remain high. Science, it
seems, has left me to deal with my uncertainty on my own.

The river should have washed away my uncertainty as I paddled it
and camped beside it, but it couldn't. The dams didn't bring sud-
den and violent transformation like the Bretz Floods, but a slow
and creeping change, a drawn-out deluge that hasn't ended. And
while that slow flood has altered the river drastically, something
about the Snake seems unchanging and constant, even though I
know better.

When I woke up at my island campsite, the beavers were still
going about their beaver business. I made oatmeal for breakfast
then packed up quickly and was on the river before people again
filled the park. By the time I stopped for lunch, the day had turned
overcast and humid in a way that gave it an almost tropical feel

completely out of place for the dry eastern Washington steppe. While I ate my midday meal of granola bars, cashew nuts, and strawberry Pop Tarts, all washed down with filtered river water, I worked through my charts calculating the distance to Lower Monumental Dam.

Beyond the bastard indigo along the riverbank, a lone tree, half dead, stood surrounded by brown grass. I was close enough so that even with the naked eye, I could see a pair of kestrels had nested on a leafless branch, but not so close I could make out details—the male's blue wings or the female's brown-striped tail feathers—with my small binoculars. The little falcons worked in shifts feeding their young. One adult minded the nest while the other hunted. Sickled wings carried the hunter away above dry grass but never out of nest-tree sight. Tail pointed toward the ground, wings flapping wildly like a giant hummingbird's, the kestrel hovered for an instant, moved on, hovered again and moved on, before finally stooping to snatch a vole, a mouse, a small bird, or a large grasshopper. The hunting kestrel then returned to feed the young while the other bird flew off to hunt. It was perpetual motion. Hunting and feeding. I watched the birds long after I had finished lunch, but finally, it was time to move on. The kestrels stayed to their work; I went around a bend in the river.

I reached Lower Monumental that afternoon. A tug nosed into the lock pushing four green barges with the Tidewater company logo stenciled on their sides in high, white letters. I walked over in time to watch. The lockmaster stood in a glass room and controlled the tug's steady descent into the lock. When the tug stopped sinking, the lock's doors opened, a light turned green, and the tug pushed its tow downriver.

When the lockmaster left the control room, I went over to talk to him. I didn't plan idle conversation. "So is the corps still not letting kayaks in the locks?" I asked. He looked me over before he started talking.

"I saw you paddle up," he said. "If you'd asked, I'd have let you go through with the tug." A tug and four barges pretty much fills the roughly 666-foot by 86-foot lock. "It didn't look like there was any extra room, even for a kayak," I said. I just wanted to get around the dam. "Being in the lock alone seems a lot safer than being in there with a tug and barges," I told him.

The lockmaster told me he thought the corps' new policy about the locks didn't make much sense. In his twenty-plus years working at the dams, he'd sent plenty of canoes and kayaks through without any problems, he said. The lockmaster offered to drive me around the dam, or, he said, I could lock through with a smolt barge due in a couple of hours. Of course I wanted to go with the barge.

I had seen the tugs, each pushing a single, red-hulled barge, moving up and down the river since Lower Granite Dam. In a normal year, river managers leave at least some smolt in the river to migrate on their own, but because of the drought, and a decision that all of the river's water was needed to generate electricity, the corps and NMFS had decided to transport as many smolt as possible. Transporting fish has gone on so long, and so many fish are barged or trucked, that engineers and biologists talk about it as if it's normal. I've never gotten used to the idea, and even during a drought, when the practice provides a clear benefit, I find it troubling.

It's not the cost or the normally dubious effectiveness that makes me uncomfortable. Taking salmon from the river and loading them into trucks and barges just seems wrong. It's an admission that the river has become hostile to salmon. We might as well raise all the Columbia's salmon in captivity the way we already do with the Redfish Lake sockeye.

I waited for the barge. I walked around the dam and watched a young couple catch one steelhead smolt after another. Washington fishing regulations treat the fish as rainbow trout, and the couple put each steelhead caught on a stringer.

When the tug and barge finally arrived, I climbed into my kayak and waited a little more as the skipper maneuvered into the lock. Then I paddled in and took hold of the tug's port side. I had argued with the corps and doubted its safety concerns, but paddling into the lock, I worried that maybe the corps was right. The space was frightening, confining, and dark. The water-tight gates closed behind me, and I waited for a sucking current to pull me forward as the lock drained.

A grill smoked on the tug's stern deck and a heavyset crewman came outside to flip steaks. I wanted to forget that my dinner would be noodles. "How far are you going?" the crewman asked. "The ocean," I said, and he gave me a thumbs-up before going back into the tug's cabin. Jets of water shot from the barge as pumps moved water from river to barge, barge to river, all to keep thousands of salmon and steelhead alive. A sheen of fish oil spread across the lock and its odor mingled with the smell of steaks cooking over hot charcoal.

The descent into the lock was almost imperceptible. There was no sucking current. Water dripped down the scum of green algae clinging to the lock as its walls grew higher and higher. The air felt cool and damp, like I had walked into a deep basement on a hot summer day. After ten minutes or so, the downstream doors opened and a light turned green. I paddled back into the day's heat ahead of the tug so its prop wash wouldn't blow me away.

I cleared the lock and the tug's path and waited. The tug threw boils of whitewater as her skipper maneuvered toward shore to pick up a load of small salmon to haul downstream, as if the fish were any other cargo, no different from wheat or woodchips. I saw the coulee that had once held an ancient Salmon River, a reminder that the Salmon and Snake where part of the same river, but also a reminder that the Snake had not always followed its present course, and that it would not always exist.

Three years after I ended my trip, NMFS, which manages Pacific salmon, said the Snake's dams had become an indisputable part of the environment, permanent fixtures, and they would not come down. It was as if some bureaucrat somewhere believed a government document could stop shifting continental plates or flowing lava. As we debate the future of the Snake and its dams, I think we should remember that not even the river is forever. One way or another, the dams are doomed. Technology will eventually make them obsolete or they will reach the end of their engineered life span and become too expensive to maintain or geology will destroy them or human desire, perhaps the strongest force of all, will do them in.

I stopped for the night at a corps campground just downstream from Lower Monumental and set my sights on Ice Harbor, the Snake's last dam. I figured I would be there in less than two days. I woke the next morning to rain and a wind that in my naiveté seemed troublesome. I knew nothing of wind then, and made twenty miles that day, a distance that would soon become a luxury. I crossed Ice Harbor the following afternoon, June 25, my twenty-ninth day on the river, thanks to a fisherman who tied my kayak to the roof of his car and drove me around. I camped not far from the mouth of the Snake. Downstream, the Columbia, the great "River of the West" waited.

9

River of Empire

The exclusive right of taking fish in the streams running through and bordering said reservation is hereby secured to said Indians, as also the right of taking fish at all other usual and accustomed stations in common with citizens of the United States. —Treaty of June 9, 1855

By the time the Snake and Columbia rivers merge near Pasco, Washington, the Columbia has already traveled roughly 875 miles of its 1,200-mile course. By then, the river stretches more than two miles from bank to bank in some spots; although a half-day's paddle downstream, it narrows to less than half that distance. The Columbia starts in British Columbia at the outlet to a large lake nestled between two ranges of the Rocky Mountains. In its first miles, the great river is little more than a mountain stream and by late summer shallow enough to wade across in some places.

From its headwaters, the Columbia flows north for two hundred miles, then turns for the United States. By the time it crosses the border, the Columbia is a major river already saddled with several dams. In the United States, the river coils itself into a big bend, but still moves generally south. Other dams block its course: Grand Coulee—which destroyed a run of summer Chinook known as "June hogs" that sometimes weighed a hundred pounds—Chief Joseph, and Wells, Rocky Reach, Rock Island, Wanapum, and Priest Rapids, all owned and operated by public utility districts.

After Priest Rapids, the river runs unencumbered for fifty miles. The Hanford Reach is the longest free-flowing, non-tidal stretch of the Columbia left in the United States. It remained that way only because the government built the reactors that produced plutonium for thousands of nuclear bombs beside the river there. Now, the cold war over, radioactive sludge stews in leaky tanks while groundwater flushes decaying elements with names like americium and strontium toward gravels where the river's healthiest run of fall Chinook spawn.

The Snake joins the Columbia near Pasco at a wide spot just below the Hanford Reach. Downstream, at Wallula Gap, the river narrows, then a few miles later, twists to the west, and after a few more miles, becomes the border between Washington and Oregon. Two hundred twenty-five miles later, near Portland, where tides influence the river, it again grows wide and turns north, before bending west, as it must, to meet the Pacific Ocean.

I reached the confluence of the Snake and Columbia on an oily calm morning that gave no hint of the waiting wind. I worried over wind on the Columbia the same way I had worried over rapids on the Salmon River. Even before my trip, I knew I would come to hate the wind. I had anticipated it daily on the Snake, but it had mostly stayed away. On the Columbia, where in summer forty-knot gales drive the river into a mass of giant waves with such predictability that they draw windsurfers from around the world, I expected no reprieve.

I stopped at a state park located at the confluence before leaving the Snake for good. Named after Sacagawea, the park was another irrigated oasis of fresh grass and picnic tables shaded by green maple and locust trees. The park's small interpretive center gives the history of the fur trade, the area's Native people, and America's westward expansion. Just outside the center, a plaque states Lewis and Clark stopped at the confluence for two days in the fall of 1805. Clark traveled about ten miles up the Columbia during that brief stay and his journal entries describe the clarity of the Columbia's water and a number of villages along the river, each filled with scaffolds of drying salmon.

Before my trip, I had read historian Stephen Ambrose's book about Lewis and Clark, *Undaunted Courage*, watched Ken Burns's Lewis and Clark documentary, and read parts of Lewis and Clark's journals. The expedition's bicentennial was approaching and between Lewiston and the ocean, I traveled the same route as the Corps of Discovery. I stopped at the park as much because Lewis and Clark had stopped there as for any other reason.

The Lewis and Clark expedition often is painted as a heroic journey, an American *Odyssey*, some writer or another has called it. In the epic, the Corps of Discovery treks west across a vast, untrammeled expanse of land. Following orders from President Thomas Jefferson, they maintain good relations with the Indians they meet along the way. Sacagawea and Clark's slave York participate fully in the expedition. When the group finally reaches the Pacific Ocean, they vote on where to spend the winter, and at a time when African Americans, women, and Indians were disenfranchised, York and Sacagawea take part. The story is democratic and multicultural and lets us imagine a history without the Civil War or Indian wars, without Jim Crow or manifest destiny. Of course whatever potential for alternative history the saga might suggest, it wasn't realized.

An arrogance toward the Indian peoples who fed and sheltered and guided them comes through in some of the Lewis and Clark writings. In those journal entries, and in a Jeffersonian Indian policy that envisioned incorporating American Indians into the body politic of the United States only after they had shed their Indian ways, are the seeds of all the broken promises that followed. Instead of Homeric epic, maybe we should tell the story of Lewis and Clark as Greek tragedy.

The expedition wasn't simply the exercise in science, diplomacy, and democracy we would like to imagine. As Ambrose writes in *Undaunted Courage*, Lewis handed out medals with the image of Jefferson on them and trade goods not just because he wanted friendship, but also to bring the Indians into the U.S. trading system and to cut the British out of the fur trade with Asia. Along with the United States and Great Britain, Russia and Spain laid claim to some of the Pacific Northwest as well. The possibility of empire always flowed with the Columbia's water.

Eventually, the United States and Great Britain struggled for dominance in the Northwest. It was an imperial struggle and, like all imperial struggles, ignored those already living in the region slated for conquest and colonization, ignored their existing political institutions, their lives, and their hopes for the future. The British implemented a kind of scorched earth policy, attempting to strip the land of its fur-bearing mammals, to keep the Americans at bay. But it didn't work, and the British eventually retreated north of the Forty-ninth parallel.

With the British gone, only the region's Native peoples blocked widespread U.S. settlement. In 1855, Washington territorial governor Isaac Stevens negotiated treaties with leaders from the Nez Perce, Walla Walla, Yakama, Palouse, Umatilla, Cayuse, Klickitat, and others. At the Walla Walla treaty grounds, Stevens cajoled and then threatened the Indians, telling the gathered leaders "You will wade in your own blood" if the treaties go unsigned. Eventually, three treaties were signed, one for the Nez Perce, and two that confederated a number of related but independent tribes and bands into the Umatilla and Yakama. Another treaty, negotiated that same year, confederated several other groups into the Warm Springs. The treaties let the United States stretch from Atlantic to Pacific, let settlers homestead, railroad men lay tracks, and businessmen build towns and cities. The Indians ceded millions of acres of their homelands in exchange for permanent reservations, schools, hospitals, blacksmith and gunsmith shops, and the promise of peace with the whites.

The park at the confluence of the Snake and Columbia seemed dedicated more to the Lewis and Clark journey as epic than any other view of the trip, but that may simply have been the way I interpreted the displays and plaques as I walked the park's irrigated lawns. In the cool of the windless morning, I dallied at the park, figuring that in the calm I could cover any distance I set my mind to that day. Before leaving, I studied my charts and settled on a long, diagonal course that would take me across the Columbia's main channel to its far bank. The river was smooth as polished glass, and I had the impression of speed when I started to paddle. My chosen route put me in the path of a tourist boat built to look like an old sternwheeler. I considered changing direction to pass off the boat's stern. But I believed I had the time and distance to hold my course. Halfway through the crossing, somebody left the boat's wheelhouse, looked in my direction, then went back inside. A minute or two later, the same thing happened, and I caught the glint of sun on binocular lenses. I noticed then how the boat's bow showed the same portion of starboard and port as it had when I started the crossing. That should have screamed collision.

I should have shifted my course and passed off the boat's stern. Instead, I paddled harder. Each blade, left then right, hit the water once every second, for a minute. Sweat dampened my ball cap and dripped into my eyes. After two minutes my arms felt like somebody had tied fifty-pound weights to them. After three minutes my chest strained against my life jacket. Nothing had changed. I still didn't shift course. Someone came out from the wheelhouse and didn't go back inside. I don't know if the channel turned, if the boat changed course to avoid me, or if I simply outran it, but eventually I started to see more of the port bow and realized the boat wouldn't crush me. I relaxed and slowed my pace.

I ate lunch on a lump of basalt cut off from the shore by a foot-wide channel. Plugs of bunchgrass dotted the ground and a small, spindly tree of some sort grew from a high spot, making the lump look like a child's drawing of a tropical island. The tourist boat had turned up the Snake toward Lewiston. I tried to put the possibility of a collision out of mind. I needed to readjust my sense of proportion to match the big river and promised myself I would be more cautious crossing the channel.

The day turned hot after lunch. I moved through the heat toward Wallula Gap, where high basalt walls choked the Columbia. When the Bretz Floods reached that narrow gap, it forced a pause as so much liquid squeezed through such a small space. A lake that backed up to Lewiston formed for a few days during each flood as water pushed its way, at fifty miles an hour or more, through the gap. Moving with so much force, the floodwaters chiseled rock below the gap into strange shapes, and I found myself in a landscape dotted with black hoodoo pillars of water-carved basalt. Even confined by cliffs, the Columbia was wider than any of the other rivers I had paddled.

Clouds filtered past all day, at first high, thin, and white. But they thickened and darkened, and by afternoon it looked like rain. The wind came with the clouds, a slight freshening that over time built itself into a thirty-knot storm. Waves grew with the wind until they rolled over the river like foaming ocean swells. It was the first real wind of the trip, but not what I expected. Instead of the blasting head gale and crashing head sea I had prepared myself for, I faced a tailwind and following sea.

A particularly big wave, foaming crest and deep trough, caught my kayak and surfed me down the river for a few seconds. Another wave rolled under the kayak and I paddled hard until the boat matched its speed. Then the paddle became a rudder that kept the kayak on track while I surfed. The theme song from *Hawaii Five-O* buzzed somewhere in the back of my brain.

I started to lose the wave and took two quick strokes to keep pace, but the wave collapsed. The kayak made a hard right turn.

A strong sweep stroke put me back on course. I imagined that I saved energy surfing my way downstream, but in reality, I'm certain it exhausted me in a way paddling flatwater wouldn't have. I caught wave after wave. It wasn't as much fun as surfing whitewater, but it was close enough.

After a month on the river, I had settled into the trip. I felt I could handle any problem that might come up, which made me comfortable. Motion defined my life. Almost anything I did required some type of movement on my part. I paddled twenty miles a day. To go anyplace off the river, I walked. Even getting drinking and cooking water usually meant a few minutes of hand pumping my filter. None of it was a burden. Maybe the knowledge that I would eventually stop moving allowed me to savor my kinetic life in a way I couldn't if I were a perpetual nomad. Maybe my comfort stemmed from much simpler sources. I had everything I needed—enough food to eat, a stove and fuel to cook it with, a filter for purifying drinking water, a bivy sack and sleeping bag for shelter. I moved to no schedule. I stopped when I wanted, traveled when I wanted. I needed nothing else.

My first evening on the Columbia, I nosed the kayak toward a patch of sand in a small cove sheltered from wind and waves by a scattering of low islands. A great blue heron stood motionless. Another, all flapping wings and dangling legs, flushed when I paddled too close. A hen mallard quack, quack, quacked her concern after I beached my kayak. A fringe of pink-flowered milkweed marked the change from sandy river bar to brown cheatgrass uplands. I set up my bivy and bag on the sand and hung my spray skirt and lifejacket to dry on a dead tree. I put my camp stove on a level patch of ground and dug out the water filter, cooking pots, and Ramen noodles from the kayak.

While I ate, the wind dropped and the rain started. At first a drizzle, but then harder. Mosquitoes swarmed. It was still hot, but I bundled myself into my rain jacket and a pair of long pants, cinched closed at the ankles with drawstrings, seeking protection from the mosquitoes. My hands, feet, and face were still exposed. I stomped and swatted, sometimes leaving a crushed bug and a bloody smear. Small, red welts started to appear on my hands and feet. I thought about using some DEET, but I've never liked the idea of putting something on my skin that can melt plastic.

A herd of deer grazed along the uplands, and a pair of bucks, their antlers little more than velvet spikes, stepped through the milkweed border onto the sand. Cautious, heads turning, black noses high, they nuzzled the air for strange scents. I sat perfectly still. They must have seen and smelled the kayak and camping gear, but I was downwind and they never looked my direction. A mosquito landed on my face. I stayed motionless. Another landed on my foot, drank its fill, and flew off. The deer crept to the river and lowered their heads. Small ripples spread from their muzzles as they drank. They backed away from the water, and one turned my direction, froze, sniffed, and then bolted. The other followed. When I moved around the beach in the fading evening light, stowing gear and readying for bed, I was careful not to step on any of the deer tracks, as if destroying them would destroy my memory of the deer.

The rain came harder after dark, and I fell asleep to its steady pounding. I was up early the next morning. The night's rain had turned to a lackluster drizzle, and I tried to keep dry as best I could while packing away wet gear. When I went to put on my spray skirt, I found earwigs clinging to it. When I picked up my life jacket, I found earwigs inside its neoprene hand warmer.

Even though they're harmless, something about earwigs gives me the creeps. Maybe it's the two prongs on their tail that look like a scorpion's stinger, or the name, which makes me picture the shiny, black bugs making a home for themselves in my ears. I found a stick and dug them out of the lifejacket's hand warmer. I washed the spray skirt over and over in the river. I pulled out my headlamp and shined it into every crevice of the kayak cockpit, making sure no bugs had stowed away. It took thirty minutes, but I was earwig free and on the river.

There was a slight tailwind, just enough to ripple the water, and I moved quickly down the river. I crossed McNary Dam with the help of the lockmaster, who broke the rules and drove me around in a pickup. By the time I reached the town of Umatilla, Oregon, a mile and a half below the dam, the sun had burned its way through the clouds. On a billboard, Umatilla declares itself the walleye capital of the world, but it didn't look like the capital of anything to me. Its low buildings almost sag. The town has an Indian name, but isn't on a reservation, and a visitor is as likely to hear one of the thousands of farmworkers, who toil in the surrounding vineyards, apple and cherry orchards, watermelon patches, and potato fields, speak Spanish as any other language. The interstate, the Umatilla River, and the Columbia River border the town. Just to the south, protected by high fences, barbed wire, and I'm sure men with guns, rows of bunkers used by the army to store nerve gas surround a chemical weapons incinerator. Signs along the interstate wait ready to flash warnings if any gas leaks from the bunkers or incinerator.

I was in Umatilla to meet with representatives from the Umatilla tribe, which goes by the official name of the Confederated Tribes of the Umatilla Indian Reservation. The Umatillas had restored salmon to the river that bears the tribe's name. I wanted to know how they did it, and hoped that in learning how one group brought salmon back from extinction in one river, I might learn something larger. I arranged the meeting in May, a few weeks before my trip started. I had talked on the phone to a pleasant and patient woman named Deb Croswell, who handled public relations for the Umatillas. I explained my trip and said that I wanted to talk to somebody about salmon and the river when I reached the town of Umatilla. It must have sounded like a strange request, since I asked for a meeting, wanted someone to drive an hour or so from tribal headquarters near Pendleton to meet with me, but couldn't give a date or time. We agreed that once I started my trip and had a better estimate of my schedule, I would phone again. The day before I reached the Columbia, I called Croswell from a pay phone, and to my surprise she remembered me and scheduled a meeting. When we talked that second time, I figured it would take two days to reach Umatilla, but gave myself an extra day just in case.

I wound up with a day to kill in town. I spent my first night next to the freeway at an overly well-lighted campground built at the top of a rise overlooking the town's marina. The whiz of cars and semis drowned out the sounds of my neighbors, who were working a construction job for the summer and camped in a sprawling complex of tents. I managed to dry out my bivy, but some late afternoon squalls blew through and stayed well into evening. It rained hard enough that some water seeped in near my feet. I decided to get a hotel room the next night.

After checking in, I did laundry and grocery shopped. I had jotted down a shopping list in a yellow Rite in the Rain notebook. I crossed off each item—Ramen noodles, oatmeal, pasta (two bags), cheese, olive oil, nuts (peanuts and cashews), dried fruit (pineapple), zip-lock bags (large), bread, peanut butter, breakfast bars, Pop Tarts (strawberry), and Band-Aids—as I added it to my cart. Back at the hotel, I showered, shaved, then spent the rest of the afternoon napping on a soft bed while the television and air conditioner droned. When I was awake, I snacked on the fresh cherries the man who owned the hotel had given me when I checked in. That night, I ate out.

The next morning, I showered again, the last I would take for many days, gathered up clean clothes and groceries, and hiked the half mile back to the marina. I had finished loading supplies into the kayak when a white minivan with government plates pulled into the parking lot. A dark-haired woman, professionally but casually dressed, stepped out from the driver's side. I introduced myself to Deb Croswell, and she introduced me to Antone Minthorn, who at the time was the tribal chairman. He was tall, barrel chested, and wore his graying black hair in a pair of braids that fell across the chest of his red shirt. A pair of suspenders held up his jeans.

The three of us sat down at a picnic table and made small talk for a few minutes before they began to explain the Umatilla Basin Project. On my trip, it became easy to slide into a belief that salmon had no future, that nothing anybody could do would keep them returning to the Columbia and its tributaries. But the Umatillas had brought salmon back to a river where they had been absent for almost seventy years, and I hoped that meant I was wrong.

The area around the Columbia is a semidesert of sagebrush and bunchgrasses perpetually a missed rainstorm away from drought. But the soil is rich, and with enough water, almost any crop will grow. All along the river, and beyond, irrigated orchards, vineyards, hay meadows, and fields of hops, asparagus, and potatoes break the steppe into alternating patches of green and brown.

In the early 1900s, the Bureau of Reclamation built an irrigation project that dried up part of the Umatilla River for much of the year, making it impossible for salmon to migrate. "They wiped them out, they wiped the salmon out," Minthorn said of the irrigation project. The tribe decided the situation violated its treaty with the United States. Even though the federal government over time had passed laws that allowed non-Indians to own land and settle on reservations, tried to terminate various tribes, and relocated tribal members to cities, the Indians have survived and the treaties remain binding. The treaties signed by the four Columbia River treaty tribes—the Nez Perce, Umatillas, Warm Springs, and Yakamas—are almost identical to one another, and along with guaranteeing a reservation, hospitals, schools, and the like, they maintain the Indians' right to fish at "usual and accustomed places." The dried-up river violated the tribe's treaty-protected fishing rights, and Minthorn said the Umatillas saw two options for dealing with the matter: litigation or negotiation. Northwest Indians had used the courts before to protect their fishing rights.

In the 1960s, Indians, most notably Richard Sohappy and Da-

vid Sohappy Sr., intentionally broke state law by gillnetting on
the Columbia River during a closed season. Oregon took them
to court. The federal government stepped in on behalf of the Columbia River treaty tribes and the Sohappys. In 1974, a federal
judge ruled that Indian fisherman had a right to half the "har-
vestable fish," which in practical terms works out to a small portion of any run, although the precise percentage varies based on
the number of returning salmon. Because of Judge George Boldt
and Judge Robert C. Belloni's decisions, the four Columbia River
tribes became co-managers of the Columbia Basin's salmon and
now work with Oregon, Washington, Idaho, and the federal government to determine fishing seasons and harvest limits.

"The difference between today and 1855 or 1940 is that the
tribes have sovereignty and practice sovereignty. We were like a
ghetto in a big city nobody cared about. Now if the treaties aren't
honored, we can do something about it," Minthorn said. But the
Umatillas decided against court, at least until they tried other options. The tribe sat down and worked out a deal that kept water
in the river by replacing the irrigation water farmers and ranchers took from the Umatilla with an equal amount of water from
the Columbia. With a deal that put water back in the river, the
Umatillas then started on the equally hard task of bringing wild
salmon to a river where salmon had gone extinct.

After talking for awhile, the three of us climbed into the van and
Croswell drove us to a small irrigation dam on the Umatilla River.
At Three Mile Dam, salmon moved like apparitions through a
holding pen's murky green water. Dark shadows appeared then
vanished; invisible tails twisted water into swirls. The salmon
became flesh and scale and fin only after Brian Zimmerman, a
fisheries biologist for the tribe, pulled them, one at a time, from
the pen. Anesthetized with carbon dioxide, Zimmerman slid a
male Chinook onto a silver steel table so he could measure it.
The broad, powerful tail that had for two years propelled it across
countless ocean miles didn't move. Its body was deep and mus-

cular, its back as green as the Pacific, its flanks and belly, a bright silver. Black spots freckled its back, and I guessed it weighed fifteen pounds or maybe a little less. There's always that tendency to overestimate a fish's weight. "They're beautiful," Minthorn said to no one in particular. So far that year, forty-six hundred spring Chinook had migrated up the Umatilla River, and another four hundred were expected. Later, fall Chinook, coho, and steelhead would make their way upriver well into autumn.

Zimmerman measured each salmon from the pen, noted its length, girth, and sex. Normally, after examination at Three Mile Dam, fish go back in the river, but by midsummer, even with the water exchange and even in the best of water years, the Umatilla River is too shallow for a migrating salmon. The half-dozen Chinook and three steelhead trapped in the holding pen were put into a small tanker that would carry them upstream for release beyond the point where the irrigation project drains the river. The tribe is working on more water trades, a third phase to the project, which will leave enough water for salmon year-round, Croswell said.

The fish penned at Three Mile might have started their lives in a hatchery, or in the gravel of the Umatilla River, but they certainly came from hatchery stock. Because the river's salmon had vanished, only hatchery fish were available to repopulate it. So that's what the tribe used. Usually, hatchery salmon stay forever tied to hatcheries, but the Umatillas wanted fish that would spawn naturally in streams. The way salmon are counted, any hatched in the wild is considered a wild fish, even if both its parents came from a hatchery. But often, when the offspring of hatchery fish are allowed to spawn in the wild they don't survive very well, so simply turning hatchery fish loose wasn't an option.

"Wild fish are really spooky, like wild animals. They duck and hide. I wonder if hatchery fish are the same?" Minthorn said as he watched the shadows in the holding pen. The brood stock for the Columbia's first hatcheries often was taken randomly, mixed together, and moved from one river basin to another without thought. The genetic goulash often manufactured salmon that couldn't sustain themselves in the wild. Maybe the smolt migrate near the surface where they are easy prey for birds. Maybe the adults return too early to a river where they need to return late, or too late where they need to return early. Or they lay their eggs in the wrong place, or at the wrong time, or fall victim to a thousand other factors that control salmon survival but that the people who breed salmon in hatcheries can't understand.

To create wild fish from hatchery salmon, the Umatillas settled on a method called supplementation, where everything from gathering adult brood stock to releasing the young is done differently from a typical hatchery. A traditional hatchery will release smolt ready to migrate, either directly from the rearing pens or by trucking them to a release point. As adults, they will return to the hatchery or to a sorting weir placed in the river. In supplementation, juvenile salmon are released into a stretch of river before they are ready to migrate, so they imprint on that stretch of river, and return there to spawn.

It takes many years to rebuild salmon runs using supplementation, and the Umatillas still take adults from the river for hatchery stock. Again, this is done differently than at a typical hatchery. A typical hatchery collects its needed quota of healthy adults, then kills off the rest, or occasionally, if the salmon have proper genetics, allows the remainder to spawn. Sometimes unneeded fish are even hauled downriver and released so fishermen can try again to catch them. With supplementation, salmon are collected in a way that represents, in microcosm, the entire run. Most salmon come within a few weeks of the run's peak, so most of the brood stock is taken then. But a few migrate early in the season, so some early arriving fish are taken for brood stock. A few come late in the season, so some late arrivals are taken. The goal is to preserve the run's genetic diversity so that over time, natural selection will take its course, and the fish collected and the offspring they produce will be better and better suited to the river.

Supplementation is still an experiment, and even though the Umatillas' efforts often produce enough salmon so that both Indians and non-Indians can fish the river, a hatchery is still essential. "Right now we're in a place where I doubt we can get out of the hatchery business. The goal isn't just to return salmon to the river, but to provide fish for tribal members to catch, and on its own, the river can't produce enough salmon to support that," Zimmerman said. Part of the problem in the Umatilla Basin, according to Zimmerman, is habitat. Clear-cutting and mining and overgrazing have made some of the tributaries too silty or too shallow or too warm for salmon to spawn. If the habitat was in better shape, the basin could support more salmon, he said. The tribe is working to restore habitat, but it's a slow, expensive process.

I asked Zimmerman if harvest was removed from the equation, could supplementation restore self-sustaining salmon populations to the Umatilla River. He started to say something, paused for a moment, then answered, "With good ocean conditions, I think we could build the run over time."

My opinion about hatcheries vacillates. Hatcheries are as controversial as dams and many argue against them, claiming hatchery fish crowd out wild salmon, compete with them for food, spread disease, and weaken genetics. All those may be valid arguments, but they're not what trouble me. Instead, I suspect hatcheries create a false sense of abundance so we can ignore what has already happened to the river's salmon. Snake River sockeye are considered functionally extinct. All the coho above the Columbia's tidal section are either hatchery fish or the descendants of hatchery fish. And even most Chinook, the Columbia's most abundant salmon, come from hatcheries. The Columbia Basin's irrigated orchards and fields create an illusion of lushness that fades beyond their borders and threatens to vanish with drought. Hatchery salmon create the same illusion. Both the orchard and the hatchery salmon are real, but cannot exist on their own.

When my thinking leads to those conclusions, I will argue that the salmon hatcheries should close, and we should deal with the realities of the Columbia we have created. I once asked a fisheries biologist what would happen if all the hatcheries along the Columbia closed. "Salmon would disappear," he said. To let salmon vanish simply because they come from a hatchery seems as wrong as creating a false sense of abundance for ourselves.

On the ride back to town, I asked Minthorn to explain the significance of salmon to the Umatillas. "It's a big deal. When the salmon start coming in, people head down to the river to fish." Minthorn said the salmon are what allowed his ancestors to survive, and without the fish, he wouldn't be here now. "People understand the connection with their food and their ability to survive," he said.

I didn't feel he had answered my question, although I'm not certain what I expected for an answer. So I did what I often do during an interview; I re-asked the question in a slightly different way. Minthorn tried again. "Salmon are the gift of life," he said. I asked again and he responded, "Do you always ask the same question over and over? I don't know how to say it more than I said it. It's just being Indian."

My repetition had nothing to do with Minthorn. I wanted an answer to a bigger question: why do salmon matter and what is our responsibility to ensure they survive? I wanted his answer to be my answer, but that wasn't possible. That bigger question drove my entire trip, and its answer couldn't come from someone else. If it could, I could have stayed home, slept in a soft bed, eaten good meals, and helped Juliet plan our wedding.

At the marina, Minthorn and I talked some more. He looked over my kayak and asked if it held everything I needed for my trip. "Yes," I said, and he nodded as I explained that I only needed to find a town every couple of weeks to buy more groceries. Upstream from the marina, just the other side of the freeway, was McNary Dam. As he and Croswell prepared to leave, Minthorn told me his father had helped build the dam. "I see around me this manifest destiny," Minthorn said. "What's manifest destiny—it's the exploitation of the resources. It's a people that have this will to develop the resources, to exploit those resources, to help themselves, to enrich themselves. It's a short-sighted, superficial way to seeing.

"I fly over the area when I go from Pendleton to Portland for meetings. When you fly over it, that's a powerful experience. You see the power of America to use the river, to convert it from this free-flowing wild river, to tame it, and use it. But why does manifest destiny have to destroy the salmon in this process—it doesn't," Minthorn said. "America is young; the people are young. They haven't set in roots; they don't respect what they have. I guess it just comes down to respecting what the hell you've got."

Croswell interrupted, saying they had to leave to make another meeting. I hurried through my lunch once they left. The day was still, and I was anxious to get back on the river. It was June 29, the thirty-third day of the trip. I made good time and covered almost twenty miles before I camped within sight of a large winery along the Washington side of the Columbia. The high cliffs that crowded the river upstream of Umatilla were gone, and the river was so wide it looked almost like a bay. Downstream, the Blalock Islands, which before the dams had formed just one big island, hung on the horizon like low cays on a tropical ocean. Cast-off trash surrounded me: pop bottles and cans, fast food wrappers, old fishing line, cigarette butts. I hung my spray skirt and life jacket to dry on the handle bars of a decaying exercise bike, its chain and right pedal missing. Just before dusk, the mosquitoes came out. It was too hot to put on more clothes, so I escaped inside my bivy. Mosquitoes coated the bug fly and I felt like a scuba diver in a shark cage.

The night was cool enough to drive off the mosquitoes, and the next morning I made breakfast and packed the boat in peace.

It was another calm day, and I started to believe I might make it down the Columbia without facing a hard headwind. I paddled through the Blalock Islands. Deer sipped from the river and white pelicans floated by on slowly flapping wings, then turned and circled me again, as if they needed a better look before going on their way. I covered twenty miles by midafternoon before stopping at a Corps of Engineers boat ramp for a snack and to check my charts. I wanted to see if I should keep going, cover river while I could, or stop.

I pulled my sleeping pad from my kayak and stretched out on it for a nap. I told myself that after I woke up, I would paddle another five miles or so. A puff of blowing dust stirred me from my sleep, and before I could fully wake myself, that breeze had blown into a forty-knot gale, the headwind I had expected and worried over, barreling straight up the river. I decided to stay put. I told myself the wind would fall out at dusk, even though I knew it wouldn't. My days of easy paddling had ended.

10

The Swallowing Monster and the Pictograph Island

We took a pristine river and we turned it into a working river—a machine. And it is a damn fine machine. —Al Wright, Pacific Northwest Utilities Conference Committee, as quoted in Blaine Harden's A River Lost

The next morning, my bivy sack rippled like a flag in the wind. I walked around for a few minutes to wake myself up, then started to make breakfast. I filtered some water. I set up my stove and primed it. The morning's gale rattled against the stove's little aluminum windscreen. I struck a match and a hard gust blew it out. I struck another and managed to cup my hand around the flame to keep it burning. I slipped the match past the screen and ignited the stove. It hissed and whistled with the wind.

I finished breakfast, washed my pots, and started packing the kayak. The wind tossed my sleeping pad into the sagebrush, and I raced across the gravel parking lot of the Corps of Engineers's boat ramp chasing it. After that, I used large rocks to weigh gear down until I could load it in the boat.

I slid my kayak into the river and paddled toward a breakwater that sheltered the boat ramp. Gulls rested along the breakwater's top, and sometimes one would launch itself into the air and hover briefly before landing in the exact spot it had been sitting. I paused in the lee of the breakwater and took a deep breath before I pushed into the main river.

The wind had enough reach to push the water into rollers like I'd expect to find in the ocean. White capped every wave top. Foam tumbled across the water. Paddling felt like riding up a steep hill on a bicycle with a broken brake rubbing against its rear wheel. The kayak's bow dipped into the troughs and spray blew up over the deck and into my face. River water soaked my hair, spotted my sunglasses, and dripped down into my eyes. I hugged the shore trying to avoid waves and wind, but it didn't help.

I stopped for lunch after three hours of paddling and could still see the boat ramp where I had started that morning. I ate and walked the shoreline looking for a camping spot but found no place decent. I thought about staying put anyway. I rolled out my sleeping pad over the rough basalt and napped for an hour. That was enough to convince me to move on.

It was July 1, and July is the worst month for wind along that stretch of river. The wind blew forty knots, straight upriver, straight into my face, hounded me until I cursed it and called it names, as if it were a person, as if yells could make it stop. But the wind remains beyond control, eternal. David Thompson, a British fur trader who explored the Columbia River for the North West Company, passed down the river in 1811, but his comments of July 10 could have been mine. "[W]e have had a strong head Gale all day but in the eveng it increased to a Storm—the water was swept away like Snow."

Working into the wind, which is caused by the difference in pressures between the cool maritime air to the west and the warm desert air to the east, it took me seven hours to travel ten miles that day, my thirty-fifth on the river. I could have walked faster. By the time I stopped, I was too tired for anything beyond dinner and bed.

I had entered the deep gorge that constricts the Columbia as it nears the Cascade Mountains. North of the gorge, on the Washington side, the Columbia Hills roll like storm-blown swells toward the big river until they break above the confining basalt walls and tumble to the bottom in talus shards. The remains of towns that once were but are no more dot the Columbia Hills's fields of dryland wheat, and each farmhouse, with its belt of sheltering poplars or locusts, came as a surprise. To the south, the Oregon side isn't all that different from the Washington side, except it lacks even the occasional irrigated orchard or field to break the treeless monotony of July's wind-blasted landscape.

To the west, downstream, I sometimes saw the snow-covered peak of Mount Hood. With its almost symmetrical cone that tapers to a sharp point, I've always considered Hood the most attractive of the Cascade's many volcanoes. But as I fought the wind, Hood seemed almost to taunt me. More than a hundred miles away, its glaciated summit looked just as distant in the afternoon as it had in the morning, making it seem as if I traveled nowhere during a day of difficult paddling.

Instead of marking progress with the far away, I focused on the nearby—a mid-river channel marker, a ridge of rocks jutting into the water, the metal towers holding high-tension power lines. I had time to study whatever I focused on in a way I never had before. I watched ospreys and their chicks in channel marker nests. I tried to identify, from a distance, the species of plants covering rocks that at first glance seemed bare.

The ubiquitous high-tension towers that radiate out from dams and power substations became industrial-age sculptures— maybe of giant, stylized humans or enormous robots marching off to the horizon single file—crafted by some avant garde artist. The weave of metal girders became torso-less legs topped by blocky, oversized heads. The slanting insulators inside those block heads were eyes permanently squinted against bright sun and blowing dust. Still more girders, jutting out from where block heads met metal legs, became arms with insulator hands holding more power lines. Some future society, freed from the need to move electricity over hundreds of miles, might one day view the towers with the same wonder and confusion we reserve for the lines of Peru's Nazca Plain. I couldn't even guess what stories that future society might tell to explain the towers and their forgotten purpose.

In the gorge, an unchanging sameness settled over the trip with the wind. One afternoon, though, the wind fell out. I should have paddled hard to cover river in the calm, but I was already tired and instead stopped to camp on an island. Lewis and Clark had mentioned the island in their journals, had noted a small village along its banks, people spearing salmon, and a "bad rapid" just upstream, probably formed by a series of rocks that currently serve as a gull roost.

The island now is a ragged point along the river's path not quite two miles long, maybe a half-mile wide, and mostly sand but pierced by three flattopped basalt outcroppings roughly one hundred feet high. The easternmost outcropping, which forms the island's upstream tip, is sharp and narrow and reminded me of a sailing ship headed upriver, although I doubt it would look that way to anyone else. A sandy gap full of prickly pear cactus separates the sailing-ship rock from another outcropping, which is pretty much like the first except it didn't remind me of a ship. The third, and by far the largest outcropping, consists of one flow of dried lava stacked atop another like the layers of a wedding cake. It rises straight from the river as a cliff to form a plateau that fills most of the island's west end. A narrow strait splits the plateau from the Washington side of the gorge. The island's south side, the side facing Oregon, arches east to west like the outside edge of a crescent moon and the main channel bends to accept its shape.

A current, so slight I felt it only when I went for a swim, trickled its way around the island. When I ducked my head under the cool water or floated on my back, the river's potential energy pressed against my body. The way the river wanted to push me downstream, the way its bottom dropped away so quickly into what seemed unfathomable depths, made me uncomfortable. I cut my swim short. I rested on the sand and watched cows graze across the side of an old volcano, then put on my sandals and set off to find some pictographs someone had told me about. I hadn't asked for the paintings' precise location but had assumed I could find them easily.

Stiff branches of rabbit-brush and bitterbrush scraped my legs as I slowly made my way around the island and up a dune to the base of the ship rock. The basalt felt smooth and warm, and I understood why some ancient artist might have spread a palette of paints across the rock. But it was empty. (I would not have touched anything if I had found the paintings.) I walked west, crossed the cactus gap, a delicate task in sandals, and climbed the sand rampart running along the second outcropping's north side. I found only splatters of orange lichens. The cliff blocked noise from the interstate highway and Union Pacific railroad tracks that parallel the Oregon side of the river. A two-lane state highway follows the Washington shoreline as well, but plays tag with it and near the island travels high above the water. Only the Burlington Northern Santa Fe tracks, which also follow the Washington bank, intruded.

The idea crossed my mind to give up the pictograph search. An osprey circling above the narrow channel separating island from mainland folded its wings, fell into a stoop, and hit the river in a white splash. After a second or two, the bird, all flapping feathers, rose out of the water. But then the osprey, its dark back and wings blending perfectly with the green river, became invisible. For a moment, there were no wings, no beak, no talons, only a curving ripple formed by water drops falling from bird to river.

At the time, I didn't understand that I searched, in the pictographs, for a ripple to reveal what is now invisible, just as water drops had revealed the osprey. Not that long ago, the Columbia ran free. The first federal dam on the river's main stem, Bonneville, was finished in 1938, the last, John Day, in 1968. On the Snake, where dam breaching was a possibility, I rarely considered what the river had looked like without its dams, or what it could look like again. On the Columbia, I wanted to know the river as it was before the dams, wanted to know where it had swirled and boiled when compressed by its narrows and where it had turned placid and smooth when it widened. The river had changed so much that was impossible.

In October of 1805, Lewis and Clark described a stretch of the Columbia near where John Day Dam now stands. "[H]ere we halted a fiew minits to examine the rapid before we entered it which was our Constant Custom, and at all that was verry dangerous put out all who Could not Swim to walk around, after passing this rapid we proceeded on passed anoother rapid at 5 miles lower down, above this rapid maney large rocks on each Side at Some distance from Shore, a little below is a bad rapid which is bad crouded with hugh [huge] rocks scattered in every Direction which renders passage verry Difficult." Even though I passed those same places, I could not distinguish them. Nothing set them apart. No rocks jutted from the channel. Only wind disturbed the water's surface.

After the osprey became a bird of flesh and feathers again, I wandered from smooth-sided rock outcropping to smooth-sided outcropping. Searching. I spooked deer and watched them prance away. I saw a lupine, some flower spikes filled with purple blossoms, others already gone to seed. I saw the cheatgrass and knapweed that had followed the pioneers down the river, saw coyote tracks along the riverbank, but did not see the pictographs.

I didn't sleep well that night, instead tossed and turned under a full moon to the sound of cars and trucks on the freeway in Oregon and diesel locomotives on the BNSF tracks in Washington.

Before a breakfast of oatmeal the next morning, I again hiked to the cliffs determined to find the paintings. I found a lizard's tail, probably broken off during an escape from some predator, and the rotted carcass of an owl.

So I packed my kayak and prepared to move on. The wind came up, rose to a gale, blew away the calm, blew in another screaming, wind-cursing day, another day following in the path of Lewis and Clark. By then, I didn't like that the two captains always traveled with me. Whenever I ran into people along the river, somebody inevitably asked if I was retracing the Corps of Discovery's journey. Even though I have a fascination with Lewis and Clark, I became sick of the question. I had not planned my trip to copy theirs. What interests me about the men and their journey are the descriptions of places that have changed so much it might seem they never existed.

Other stories, some older than the Corps of Discovery's, some newer, cover every mile of river I traveled. Before I had ever contemplated my nine-hundred-mile journey, I worked for the newspaper in Yakima, and reported on the Yakama Nation as part of my job. (The Indian Nation and the city use different spellings.) The people who painted the pictographs I searched for did not call themselves Yakama, but they probably would be identified that way today, although people from the Warm Springs, the Umatillas, and the Nez Perce have personal and cultural ties to the area as well. The Yakamas didn't particularly want me around and hadn't always had the best experience with the newspaper I worked for, or with its reporters. Still, they tolerated me with a civility I didn't always deserve. Tribal officials, secretaries, and even people met at random shared some of their stories with me. I can't say for certain why.

To the Yakamas, who speak a language linguists call Sahaptin, the Columbia is the Nch'i-Wána, "The Big River," and it cuts through collective and individual histories as deeply as it cuts through the arid river country. Settling into a leather couch in his office, I often listened to a tribal official talk of a boyhood spent with the big river. He'd wandered the basalt islands that split a series of waterfalls and rapids stretching from the river's south bank to its north. Celilo Falls. He told me a story he'd heard many times growing up, that some rocks on one island mimicked the faces of four chiefs, that a coyote track was imbedded in another rock. He had found the track, and three of the chiefs, but the fourth forever eluded him.

People have always lived beside Celilo, for as long as people have lived along the Columbia anyway, but it exists now only in stories, only in pictures of men fishing from wooden platforms built over twenty-foot-high falls, only in memories and in desires. The rocks are still there of course. But with the completion of The Dalles Dam in 1957, they disappeared under the river's dark green water. I once asked a woman who grew up near Celilo where the falls had been. She used a set of power lines and Celilo Village, a small cluster of houses beside the interstate in Oregon, as benchmarks to describe how the falls arched from village to power lines and then on across the river. She told how tourists had come, how men had ridden in baskets suspended from steel cables to get to their fishing spots, and how her father had fished there.

For more than a year when I worked as a reporter in Washington, while Juliet and I were still dating, I made the three-hour drive from my home near Yakima to her home in Portland for weekend visits. Two or three times a month, I traveled across the Yakama reservation, over the Simcoe Mountains, and along the Columbia. Whenever I neared the village, sped by the boats and gill nets scattered in the yards, the longhouse where the residents worship, and passed the power lines, I remembered the falls. It's not right to say I felt a sense of loss since I have no real connection to Celilo. I never saw it; I didn't grow up with its stories. What struck me though was how fast it had changed. The changes touch everything: river, rocks, plants, animals, and people.

One spring day during that year of constant traveling to and from Portland, Steve Parker, a biologist friend, had driven me to the river so I could interview Yakama fishermen for a story I never wrote because, at the time, I didn't know what to write. On the downstream side of The Dalles Dam, a handful of metal camp trailers sit parked on a small piece of government land provided to members of the Columbia River treaty tribes as compensation for other lands lost to the dams. We had stopped there to talk to a man standing beside a trailer and drinking coffee from a plastic BP gas mug. The man asked Steve what he was doing. Steve pointed to me and replied, "He wanted to talk to an elder, so I thought of you." The comment was a joke about age between two friends and brought a shove and a laugh from the man with the coffee mug. At fifty-seven, Del Hoptowit had been a fisherman all his life. He had pulled gill nets from the Columbia, Puget Sound, and Alaskan rivers to provide for his family.

Del's children, two daughters and a son, had followed him into fishing even though he tried to convince them not to. There weren't enough fish left to make a decent living, he'd told them. But Del's children were trapped by the Columbia just as he was. The river captured Del as a boy fishing with his father. "The river just grabs you and holds you so that you want to see it and smell it and just live by it. There's a certain odor to this river—you just smell it and it makes you feel good," he said.

A May breeze that smelled of sagebrush and diesel exhaust popped and snapped the sides of a longhouse made from blue plastic tarps. Del's father had always said the river wouldn't last forever, but as a boy, Del never believed him. "My grandkids, they won't be able to see it," he said. Del could still remember watching his father fish at Celilo. I asked Del if he felt a sense of loss at what's happened to the river and its salmon. "The loss—there's not even a way to describe it," he said. "I have a real hurt feeling inside. I feel a real emptiness inside—like something's missing." He looked away from me as he talked. "If I couldn't see another salmon, couldn't touch another salmon . . ." His voice trailed off as if he were afraid how that sentence might end.

When the Army Corps of Engineers built The Dalles Dam, some federal biologists accepted its construction even as they opposed other dams. Ending the Indian fishery at Celilo actually was a benefit, they said, and claimed more fish would make it upriver to spawn. Those words were said to reporters and written in memos. The dam didn't end Indian fishing. Treaty fishing rights and legal battles assured that. Tribal members continue to harvest some salmon for ceremonial and subsistence purposes. Over time, however, commercial seasons for Indian and non-Indian alike vanished with the salmon. The recent increase in salmon numbers has meant brief commercial seasons for spring and summer Chinook and for sockeye, but since the 1970s, the only consistent season on the main Columbia targets a run of fall Chinook that spawn along the Hanford Reach, the fifty-mile stretch where the big river remains undammed.

The day I paddled over Celilo, a gale blew away the tops of the wind-driven whitecaps. Each time I swung my paddle forward to catch the river and start another stroke, the wind pushed against the blades. I struggled to maintain the right-left-right-left rhythm of paddling. It felt as if I was towing a bucket behind the kayak. Whenever I paused my stroke and made a quick attempt to regain my cadence, wind and waves ground the kayak to a halt. The river was no help. It didn't push me downstream.

Near the power lines, I wondered what would happen if I flipped my kayak upside-down, wondered if I could find some trace of the falls under the water, maybe see some of the rocks or hear some faint echo of falling water. I was fairly certain I could roll the boat upright. Sometimes I wish I had flipped my kayak, but even now know it would have been a dangerous gesture. I would not have seen or heard anything under all that water, would not have understood anything new about the river.

In the town of The Dalles, Oregon, just a few miles downstream from where Celilo Falls once roared, a museum dedicated to the

Columbia River houses a model complete with flowing water that shows the river's gorge before and after the dams. I had wanted to see that model and had made arrangements with my biologist friend Steve Parker to meet and visit the museum. Steve works for the Yakama Nation, and he made the hour-and-a-half drive from his home near the reservation to Horsethief Lake State Park. I had camped at the park just across the river from The Dalles so I could shower and phone family, only to find the showers non-existent and the pay phone ripped from its booth. I cleaned up as best I could in a stream of water from a campground spigot. Phone calls had to wait.

The day Steve and I visited, wind blasted down the coulees, bowed and rattled tree branches, bent blades of grass to the ground, and made me glad I wasn't on the river. Sitting at a wooden campground picnic table, I filled Steve in on my trip. He talked about salmon. Steve was forty-eight that summer, and his graying hair and beard made him look more like a sea captain than a fisheries biologist. But he has a master's from the University of Washington and researched sockeye salmon in Alaska's Bristol Bay for years.

Even though a record number of spring Chinook had returned to the river, the smolt were having a hard time making it to the sea, Steve said. "We know it's a slaughterhouse out there." The Corps of Engineers touted its plan to dump as many smolt as possible into barges and trucks so the fish could avoid the lethal river conditions, but nobody could say for certain what would happen in two or three years when those smolt were supposed to return as adults.

Part of me hoped only a few fish would show up. I reasoned a small run would show the importance of river conditions, the need to leave more water in the rivers, the pointlessness of barging, and help ease the doubts I allow myself about the dams' effects on salmon. It was a cruel and selfish hope that fish already struggling to survive would struggle some more just to provide me with certainty. Subsequent returns were smaller than they

had been, especially for coho, but it was still a banner year compared to the runs of the eighties and nineties when the salmon
suffered in a warm ocean. No doubts were eliminated.

Steve pushes against whatever doubts I have about the dams
and what they do to salmon. He reminds me the two million or
so salmon that return from the ocean in the best years are nothing compared with the eight to sixteen million that once made
their way upriver every year. He patiently explains the science of
salmon; freely admits that besides dams, poor urban development practices, poor logging and mining practices, and overfishing kill salmon; acknowledges some legitimate science
shows dams might not be the biggest reason for the decline in
salmon, but also points out other research, study after study, detailing the effects of the dams. "Science doesn't generally deliver
proof," Steve said. "There's always disagreement and the call for
more studies. We seem to think we can study this a little bit more
and find a solution. We will study it down to the last salmon."
Science cannot answer some questions.

With my doubting ways, I understand why people sing songs
about dams and drive around with "Save Our Dams" bumper
stickers on their cars, why politicians hesitate to call for change,
hesitate to let some part of the river, maybe a tributary or two, re-
vert back to the way it once was. It's true some people and powerful interest groups don't care about the river or its fish and view the
Columbia simply as an engine of economy and empire. But I think
many of us fear tearing out the dams that produce our electricity
and provide us with jobs only to discover some new study showing
it wasn't really dams killing the salmon after all. I cling to a hope
that dams mean progress and that salmon can somehow coexist
with the dammed river. That hope is never realized. Through all
the arguments about how to save the salmon, the arguments about
whether the salmon need us to save them, the fish remain.

In the slow unwinding of geologic epochs, the Columbia has
flowed across land where mountains now stand, flowed through
canyons that now sit dry. Salmon are as old as mammoths and

have somehow survived shifting channels, melting glaciers, and giant floods even as other animals were reduced to fossils. I want to claim our fate is linked with the salmon's. If that were true, doubts would vanish, choices would seem clear, but I cannot claim it's a certainty. Humans survive without thousands of other plants and animals that once shared the earth with us.

For me, salmon are a reminder. I can't see the vanished rapids and falls of the Columbia, can't feel the river's swift current, but I can see salmon, touch them, smell them, even taste and eat them. Without salmon, it might become easy to forget how the Columbia has changed, might become easy to stop thinking about what those changes mean. To do that would be to stop contemplating the future. Because salmon are so tangible, they seem more powerful than words or memories or imagination. In the Northwest, salmon are our conscience.

Before we went to the museum, Steve drove us to a traditional fishing site on the Klickitat River where we could watch salmon leap a low waterfall. People probably have fished the spot since they first started living along the Columbia. That day only one man worked the river. With the rope around his waist the only protection against a fall and certain death, he stood on a wooden platform suspended above the river and swept a long-handled dip net through the water, probing calm eddies and foaming currents for spots where a salmon might pause to rest before continuing upstream. After a few sweeps, he would stop and maybe smoke a cigarette before starting again. He didn't catch anything. We were between runs, too late for the Klickitat's spring Chinook run, too early for the fall run. A few summer Chinook spawn in the river, and sometimes one would launch itself clear of the water. Mostly silvery steelhead—the pale crimson bands running along their flanks a reminder that they are ocean-going rainbow trout—threw themselves over the falls. Whenever a fish jumped free of the river, we stopped our discussion to name the species. "Steelhead," or else "Chinook," one of us would say. The Klickitat's rapids banged like ocean breakers striking a rocky beach, and the noise flooded the edges and pauses of our conversation. Finally, Steve and I quit talking and simply watched fish.

After the waterfall, the museum was anticlimactic. We walked through displays about the river's geology and its fauna and flora, a display depicting the river as a highway for barges traveling to and from inland ports, and one depicting the river as an electricity maker. Part of the museum was given over to the river's past, to the way it looked when only pictograph makers and salmon fishermen lived along its banks. Maybe those displays are simply nostalgia for what is gone. Maybe we're trying to convince ourselves that the river is better now or that we gained more than we lost by altering it to suit our needs.

When Steve and I found the model, it was roped off, the pump that pushes water through the scaled-down gorge apparently broken. A sign read: "Temporarily out of order." Outside the museum, there was only summer sun reflecting off whitecaps, piles of crumbled talus at the base of the gorge walls, and dry hills dotted with Garry oaks. Sailboarders zigged and zagged their way across the dam pool, launched themselves from the waves, and flew into the air for a few seconds.

Before I had spent the day with Steve watching the man fish the Klickitat River and studying the contours of the broken model in The Dalles, before I had even left the pictograph island, I had made one last try to find its paintings. In the morning, after I had packed my kayak, I had prepared to leave the island but saw a circling red-tailed hawk. I had pulled out my binoculars to get a better look. I thought maybe I could use the field glasses to scan the rocks for pictographs. As I hiked around the island, the dry wind wiped away my sweat before it could even dampen my cotton shirt. It didn't keep me cool. A layer of sand formed between my sandals and the soles of my feet and worked its way in between my toes. Sometimes I stopped to brush away the sand and then resumed my search.

I didn't need the binoculars. Standing beside the river, I saw a trail as obvious as a sidewalk twisted through the bunchgrass and weeds, and as I followed that trail, I knew what I would find. On rocks I had avoided earlier because they were exposed to all the intrusions of civilization, I saw red ochre sunbursts that looked almost like asterisks; the vertical lines of tally marks that reminded me of the pencil scratches someone makes to track points scored during a game; a being with a rectangular body, square head, and stick arms and legs that I decided was a monster; and a dog, complete with curled tail. I wondered how long they had looked over the river, and stopped to contemplate each the way I might pause before a famous painting in an art museum. Already, other pictographs remained only as almost-invisible splotches of red.

I found the pictographs by simple luck, not some act of intuition, although in hindsight, the location makes sense to me. In a legend about a time before human beings existed, Coyote, Spilyay in Sahaptin, vanquishes a great monster that once lived upstream from the pictograph island and swallowed any animal that passed by. From the rocks where I found the paintings, I could see the spot where Coyote had tricked and killed the serpent-like swallowing monster, could see cars passing by on the freeway, trains on the railroad tracks, barges on the river, but I could not put the Columbia back in its old banks, could not make the Big River fit its old stories. I have no stories from a time before human beings, none even from before Lewis and Clark. I have only new stories about change and loss and memory along a river that is as much machine as river, stories so new I cannot know what they mean, cannot say what they tell about the future.

11

Watching Fish at Bonneville Dam

In the town of The Dalles, not far from the museum with the model of the Columbia River, aluminum salmon leap above a freeway, forever jumping the flow of passing cars and trucks. Metal sturgeon swim in the overpass's imaginary river with the salmon. Those sculptures are a reminder of a river that no longer exists.

Forty miles downstream from the metal fish, inside Bonneville Dam, deep in the bowels of the second powerhouse, down a set of stairs and through a door, visitors can walk onto a platform above a spinning turbine. The metal platform shakes with the force of falling water. The air is cool. It feels as if a thunderstorm has just passed. The turbine spins. Electrons flow. The Northwest and the Columbia River roll on.

Since leaving the Salmon River, I had used dams to measure my progress downriver, and after passing one, crossed its name off a list carried in my head. First came the Snake River dams—Lower Granite, Little Goose, Lower Monumental, and Ice Harbor. Then the Columbia dams—McNary, John Day, then the day after I visited with Steve, The Dalles. At McNary, the lockmaster had driven me around the dam in a pickup after I hassled him about the corps' policy of not letting kayaks in the lock. At John Day, I had again tried to argue my way into the navigation lock. When I reached the dam, I had pressed a button below a speaker near the lock, and fast-food style, a voice had echoed out asking what I wanted. "I want to lock through," I said.

"I'll be right there," the voice responded.

I was already out of my boat when the lockmaster arrived. I told him I was in a kayak and he groaned. He led me into the little glass booth that houses the lock's controls and showed me a corps memo prohibiting non-motorized vessels from using the locks. Then he began a round of phone calls.

"Don't worry," the lockmaster said holding the phone while waiting to talk to someone from the corps' Portland office, "we'll get you around the dam. If you can't use the lock, someone will drive you around in a truck." I wasn't that optimistic.

The Portland office said it would call back. When it did, the lockmaster was told not to let me use the lock. The lockmaster made arrangements for someone to drive me around the dam. Portland called again. The man on the phone talked to the lockmaster, then to me. We exchanged names, and I told the man what I wanted. He said I could portage or have a "private contractor" drive me around the dam. "Who would pay this 'private contractor'?" I asked.

"You," the man in Portland said.

"I'm not paying anyone," I said. "If my fucking kayak were painted green and had the name *Tidewater* stenciled on the side, you'd find a way to get me past this fucking dam." The lockmaster tried to stifle a laugh. It wasn't my best moment. The man from Portland responded with a calmness I could have never matched. "Through the lock, yes, but for a kayak, that's a safety issue."

"And the corps doesn't feel it has any obligation to get me around the dam even though the law says it's supposed to assist with river navigation?" I asked.

"It's a manpower issue," he said. "The corps doesn't have enough employees to drive people around the dams."

I chose to portage. I had hauled the kayak over riprap boulders onto the top of the dam and started to unload gear from the boat when a white government van pulled up next to me. A man got out, opened the back doors, and told me to load my stuff inside. "I wouldn't want to work for an organization that treats people that way," he said as we put my kayak into the van. He drove me downstream. I realized I had forgotten my paddle when we started to unload, and he drove me back to get it. Before he left, he wrote down his phone number and told me to call if I needed any help during the rest of my trip. I'm sure he meant it.

At The Dalles Dam, I ran out of good luck and helpful corps employees willing to break senseless agency rules. I faced a fifty-foot cliff on the dam's downstream side and no spot to access the river for two or three miles. There was no way to portage. I contemplated calling the man who had driven me past John Day, but didn't. Despite my vow never to pay someone, I gave a man fishing at the dam ten dollars to take me around in a pickup. It was afternoon by then, and the wind hummed up the river. Because of the wind, my goal for that day had been simply to make it past The Dalles Dam. I didn't care how far I traveled after that.

Two miles below where I put back on the river, a rock outcropping sheltered a strip of sand just wide enough to hold my bivy sack, and I stopped there for the night. It was a claustrophobic camp. Squeezed between the river and railroad tracks, there was no place to walk to and nobody to talk to. I watched BNSF freights and Amtrak passenger trains race by and inspected the bent willow frame of a sweat lodge built in the dried weeds beside the tracks. A barge pushed past my camp, crossed under the high-tension lines that span the river, and disappeared out of sight. Across the river, I could see the museum I had visited with Steve.

After The Dalles, only one dam remained. Bonneville. And I

worried over how I would get around it. I had been to Bonneville before and couldn't remember seeing any place I could portage. My charts revealed nothing. If the wind held, I might not reach the dam for three or maybe even four days, so I tried to put that potential problem out of my head so I could go to sleep.

I woke up around sunrise. The wind had dropped to maybe twenty knots. I quickly shoved camping gear into the kayak and started downriver. If the wind didn't blow up, I could cover fifteen miles and make Hood River, Oregon, by noon. Since I'd left the Snake, I'd anticipated reaching Hood River, or more precisely, anticipated sitting down in the cool air conditioning of the little bistro on Sixth Street where Juliet and I often ate, ordering a beer; a cheeseburger made from organic beef, cooked medium rare and still dripping with a little juice; and a big side of fries, fresh cut, with the skin still on, and cooked in just the right amount of oil, the kind of fries that would be ruined by ketchup. After dinner I would walk over to the ice cream shop around the block from the bistro, buy a huckleberry ice cream cone, sit on a bench, and watch the people walking and driving around town. I thought about that burger and fries when I ate my morning oatmeal, when I paused from battling the wind to eat peanut butter sandwiches for lunch, and when I ate pasta or instant couscous or Ramen noodles for dinner.

After an hour, the wind kicked up to its usual thirty or forty knots. I pushed on and made Hood River by midafternoon. Although best known for its windsurfing, not its skiing, Hood River reminds me of Jackson Hole, Wyoming. It's a place where people come to play, a rack town where some type of outdoor toy rides the roof of almost every car or truck passing through. A typical Hood River morning involves a dozen or so people standing outside a coffee shop trying to decide if they will spend the day windsurfing, rock climbing, whitewater kayaking, or mountain biking. When I was there, the town was preparing for the Gorge Games, which was something like the Yuppie Olympics for extreme sports.

Even though Hood River is on the Cascades' East Side—the conservative side—the kind of liberal culture associated with the West Side has seeped into town and taken root. Ecologists call a place where two ecosystems meet and mingle an ecotone, and the Columbia's gorge is an ecotone. Enough damp weather sneaks through the gorge so that for a few miles at least, plants from the mountains' dry and wet sides coexist. The gorge is a kind of human ecotone as well. An uncomfortably narrow metal toll bridge over the Columbia connected Hood River to Bingen (pronounced not like its sister city in Germany but Benjen, as if somebody had combined a man and woman to create a name), a Washington timber town of small houses and double-wides where raw logs line the waterfront waiting to become two-by-fours and plywood. I doubt I would like life in Bingen, but could, as embarrassed as I am to say it, live comfortably in one of the remodeled houses along Hood River's many quiet, tree-lined streets.

I thought I might spend an extra day in Hood River to do some whitewater kayaking on the White Salmon River. The White Salmon is one of my favorite rivers. Its cold, blue-green water comes off Mount Adams's ice fields and flows all summer long; it cuts through forested canyons where cedar waxwings snatch insects out of the air like swallows; and it has enough rapids and waterfalls to keep any kayaker happy. I have kayaked the White Salmon more than almost any other Washington river, and it's where I fell in love with Juliet. On our summer dates, we paddled the river just about every weekend, then drove through Bingen, over the toll bridge, and ate dinner in Hood River before saying our good-byes.

The White Salmon's rapids end in a reservoir formed by a small dam three miles from the Columbia confluence. The dam doesn't have a fish ladder, and salmon disappeared from the river early in the twentieth century. The federal government finally required the power company that owns the dam to add a fish ladder. But in 1999 the company decided the dam generates so little electricity, and adding a ladder would be so expensive, that it would be cheaper to tear down the dam. The power company, the state of Washington, the Yakama Nation, and several environmental groups crafted a plan to remove the dam in six years. The kayakers I knew speculated about what rapids might emerge with the dam gone and looked forward to watching salmon migrating up the river.

Six years later, the dam was still standing. Removing a small, privately owned dam that provides a minimal amount of electricity to free up spawning habitat for several thousand salmon should have been simple. But dams are now as much a part of the Northwest as salmon, and some people see any dam, no matter how small, as sacrosanct. Almost as soon as the removal plan was announced, residents of the two Washington counties bordering the White Salmon, Klickitat and Skamania, began looking for ways to keep the dam, while county prosecutors contemplated court action.

Some argued the silt backed up behind the dam would destroy downstream spawning habitat for the White Salmon River Chinook once the dam was removed, some argued that the sediment might contain toxic chemicals, others that dam removal would put an end to the river's rainbow trout fishery, and still others that removal would lower the property value of the houses built along the reservoir. A few people even mentioned a need for the dam's electricity. The dam will eventually come out I suspect. But in the Columbia basin, politics makes removing even a small dam a Herculean task.

From the marina in Hood River where I stashed my kayak, I could look across the Columbia and see the mouth of the White Salmon. I hiked into town and ate my cheeseburger and ice cream, then started to look for a place to sleep for the night. I knew some people in town, but they had family visiting, so I couldn't stay with them. They couldn't find anyone else for me to stay with, and there was no place nearby to camp, so I ended up sleeping behind their kayak shop for the night. I would not spend any extra time in town. By then, dealing with the headwinds had exhausted me, and all I really wanted was to get below Bonneville Dam, where the winds would let up.

In a region where dams are everywhere—there are, by some estimates, four hundred of them on the Columbia, fourteen on the U.S. and Canadian portions of the main-stem river, the rest on its tributaries—Bonneville Dam somehow remains distinct. It's the last dam on the Columbia, or the first, I suppose, depending on your point of view. The last dam. I liked that, liked the fact that after Bonneville, nothing man-made would block my path to the ocean, liked the fact that I would pass another place where I could look back on the miles traveled and look ahead to the miles left to go. I wanted to walk out over the spinning turbine and feel the metal platform shake.

At the Hood River marina, I ran into a couple, Larry and Betty Jo, who I had met upriver a few days earlier. They were bound for Canada on their sailboat the *Reality*. I told Larry about my problems getting around the dams and my concerns about Bonneville. He said that he and Betty Jo planned to stop the next night, a Sunday, in Cascade Locks, which is on the Oregon side of the river and maybe a mile or two upstream from Bonneville. They would continue downstream Monday morning. If I could make it in time, I was welcome to load my kayak onto their boat and lock through with them. Because the sailboat had a small engine, the corps allowed it in the locks. I told Larry I would think about it. Bonneville Dam, and the need to get around it, was forcing the pace of my trip.

Whitecaps already covered the Columbia when I paddled past the Hood River marina's breakwater. Windsurfers took advantage of the gale and its swells to launch themselves into wild spins and flips. I hugged the shoreline as best I could, trying to avoid the wind and waves. Nothing helped, not even the points of land that jutted into the river. Instead of offering a slight lee, the wind bent around them and continued to follow the shore. I noticed nothing but the wind. Not the views of Mount Adams's snow-covered 12,276-foot peak to my north. Not the views of Mount Hood's snow-covered 11,237-foot peak to my south. Not that I had crossed over from the Cascade Mountains's dry east side to their wet west side.

I thought about stopping when I ate lunch at a county park with a large campground. I thought about stopping when I passed the town of Stevenson, Washington, where the company that made my kayak paddle was based. I should have at least stopped for a snack, but felt that if I did, I would quit paddling for the day. And I couldn't do that.

By four in the afternoon, I had burned up all the calories from lunch. My body shook. I moved at the pace of a slow walker. Paddling took concentration. I had to think about the initial paddle plant, think about taking a stroke, and think about pulling the paddle from the river and swinging it forward again. If I let my mind drift at all, I simply flailed at the water. I wanted to give up, but realized it was worth the twelve hours of effort it took to cover twenty miles, worth spending fifteen dollars to sleep in the Cascade Locks campground, next to train tracks and a freeway, where the showers didn't work and one of the bathroom's two sinks produced water so hot it almost scalded while the other produced only cold water, worth any effort or inconvenience for a ride through the lock.

Early on Monday, July 9, we loaded my kayak onto Larry and Betty Jo's sailboat. Downstream from Cascade Locks, the river's still water held the reflections of two dozen Indian fishing platforms, unused that morning but with nets ready for the upcoming run of fall Chinook. Our conversation, the burping compression brakes of a semi on the nearby freeway, and the steady chug of the sailboat's auxiliary engine all mingled.

Larry and I both mentioned the dew that had covered everything. On the Cascades's west side, where we were, dew is common. In the dry basins east of the Cascades, heavy dew in the summer is a rarity, and only someone who lives east of the mountains would comment on it. Larry was a big and energetic man. But the night before, when I passed him as he headed to the marina's bathroom, he complained about the number of trips he was making and said: "Mike, don't ever get old." He had moved to Kennewick, Washington, from Denver twenty years earlier, and had worked at and retired from the Energy Department facility that once made plutonium for nuclear bombs. As we motored toward Bonneville that morning, I asked him what he thought about the idea of removing the lower Snake dams as a way to improve salmon runs.

"It will never happen, not in my lifetime and not in yours. The dams are too important to business and agriculture, and those groups have enough power to prevent it," he said. "The dams made this region what it is." The last comment seemed neither praise nor condemnation, just a statement of fact. "But it must have been something when the river was wild," Larry said.

"But it's beautiful now," Betty Jo said.

"Yes," he said, "but it must have really been something then."

After people come to know about it, it is often the river as it was, not as it is, that captures their imaginations. A cruise boat full of tourists, its modern hull and diesel engines hidden by an exterior imitating the old riverboats that once plied the Columbia, delayed our trip for a few minutes as it passed through Bonneville's lock. Table Mountain dominated the skyline to the north as we waited for our turn in the lock. When sternwheelers first traveled the Columbia, the river around the future dam site was a fierce rapid. Two hundred and fifty to four hundred years ago, nobody is certain exactly when this happened, a landslide sent boulders as big as office buildings tumbling down the side of Table Mountain. The slide piled rocks three times higher than Bonneville Dam, clogged the river and created a temporary lake that stretched upstream for miles. When the river finally cut through, in a great gush of water, the torrent flooded downstream, inundating the spot where Portland would one day stand. A rapid that became known as the "Cascades of the Columbia" remained, and Bonneville Dam now captures the force that once poured through tumbled-down boulders to spin its turbines.

After the tourist boat had passed and we locked through, we unloaded my kayak from the sailboat and parted company. Larry and Betty Jo went downriver, and I stopped just below the dam to eat. I was still getting used to the color green. Since paddling out of the Idaho mountains a month earlier, I'd been in dry country, a brown land where away from the river it seemed nothing grew taller than Garry oak or sagebrush. Douglas firs and cedars closed out the sky, dappling sunlight on the ground, and the smell of moss and ferns were everywhere. Months had passed since any appreciable rain had fallen, even in the country on the Cascades's west side, but the air was moist, as if the rain that had fallen during a thousand storms, over a thousand winters, had worked its way back out of the ground to fill the air. I soaked in the dampness the way someone at the beach soaks in the sun.

I took my time eating and watched a pair of ospreys circle above the tailrace searching for fish. I hiked back to the dam after lunch. Bonneville was the first large federal dam built on the Columbia River. Completed in 1938, Bonneville's goal wasn't simply to provide electricity or even river navigation and flood control, but to create Depression-era jobs and lure people to an empty part of the country. Even if the people who conceived of and constructed the dam could have known about the controversies that one day would swirl around the damming of the Columbia—how some people would blame dams for the river's declining salmon runs—I suspect they still would have built Bonneville, suspect they still would have built all the dams even if they knew the Columbia's salmon were doomed because of it. Dams then represented progress, opportunity, and were worthy of songs and accolades. They remain that way to some.

The dams are symbols, and because dams control the flow of water, that symbolism has combined with real issues over how water is used and allocated, and water, in the West, is everything. Lawsuits over water fill courts around the West. Fishermen, Indian tribes, and environmental groups sue to ensure more water stays in the rivers to help salmon migrate downstream and that some water goes over spillways instead of through turbines. Irrigators sue for the right to pump river water onto fields. I am certain that eventually, somebody will sue to force the government to tear down some big dams, although removing any of the federal dams will take an act of Congress. The conflict over the Columbia—its dams, its water, its salmon—and the inconsistent public desires that spin into litigation all seem to mirror environmental controversies around the country.

Moving water built Washington, Oregon, Idaho, and, to a lesser extent, western Montana. This is true not only of the natural world, which was sculpted by glaciers, rivers, and prehistoric floods, but of the human as well. When water flows, it works, irrigating apple orchards and hay fields, powering aluminum plants and airplane factories, running computers and cappuccino machines. Everybody in the Northwest, liberal or conservative, environmentalist or industrialist, Eastsider or Westsider, participates in a culture of the dammed. As a resident of the region, I gain from and take part in this culture—when I pay my electric bill or buy fresh fruit or do a hundred other things that are part of everyday life.

Given their significance in regional culture, it isn't surprising that dams have become tourist attractions, places for Boy Scouts, schoolchildren, and visiting relatives to tour. My first trip to Bonneville came on a late fall day that carried the hint of the coming rainy season in its dry sunshine. The looming confinement of a long, damp winter had motivated Juliet and me to hike up a nearby mountain. We went to the dam on a whim, not ready for the drive back to Portland after our climb but unable to think of anything better to do. With the summer tourist season long over, we shared Bonneville only with its employees and a group from a foreign country, although we never could figure out which country.

What I remember more than anything else from my first visit, more than whining dynamos or popping transformers or humming wires, more than standing over the spinning generator, was this: that when the dam runs at peak capacity, the force of moving water sends enough electrons flowing from generators, through high-tension lines, and out into the world to light Portland, a city of 529,000 people. From the outside, though, it's impossible to know the dam does anything except block the river. From the outside, everything looks as inert as dried concrete. Only flashing red lights topping the metal towers that hold high-tension lines—painted the red and white of a candy cane—suggest more.

We stopped early on our tour to look at a model. It held the contours not just of the river and dam but also of the land, showed how the dam fit the flood-scoured walls of the river's gorge and butted up close to the base of Table Mountain. It did not show the clear-cuts on the nearby mountains or the folds of the mountain we had just hiked where some big trees still survive, did not show how young fir trees or huckleberry bushes grew along the trunks of fallen trees taking nutrients from the dead logs, did not show the large pond on the mountain's side surrounded by ash trees, or how beavers had cut the ash for food, or how the ash had grown back from the gnawed stumps. Beyond the dam and the model were the intricate connections of the real world.

Bonneville doesn't tower like Hoover Dam, which was built around the same time. It doesn't have a monolithic face of curved concrete almost sixty stories high or art deco architecture and statues, but is functional, just under two hundred feet tall, and as the model showed, spreads across the river not as a single slab of poured concrete but as a series of structures—spillway, navigation locks, and powerhouses—with each segment separated from the next by grass-and tree-covered islands. What is now Cascade Island, the island nearest the Washington shore, was once the shore itself. In the late 1970s and early 1980s, the Corps of Engineers dug out tons of rock, made the river wider, and added the second powerhouse. Photos near the model showed backhoes and Cats moving the debris from the Table Mountain slide, working away at the task of turning dry land into river bottom.

The black divot hacked into the side of the mountain by the slide is still there for anybody to see. And evidence of other slides leads geologists to speculate another is inevitable. Part of me would like to see that, see the big river blocked by a wall of boulders that dwarfs Bonneville. I could dismiss the dam, all dams then, say either that nature can outdo anything made by man, or that man is no more chaotic and destructive than nature. But it's possible the slide will never come, or given the slow tick of geologic time, safe to assume I will not be around when it does. So I must deal with Bonneville as it is. On my first visit there, I could believe that people using engineering and science can do or build anything. A government agency can control a river, make it bigger, put it to use. I suppose that's what the Corps of Engineers wanted me to think by the end of the tour.

The dam didn't look the same when I saw it on my trip to the ocean. I walked into the cool air of the second powerhouse, looked down the row of generators, and saw the one that visitors are allowed to stand over ripped open for maintenance. I could look into the guts of it, see how everything about it was oversized. A bolt on the floor looked like a hundred-pound dumbbell. A wrench seemed made for a giant. I left the broken generator and meandered through the displays, stopping at anything that appeared interesting. To some extent, the Corps of Engineers' displays reveal a fractured view of the river and its dams, although their displays seem to me designed not so much to explain or foster thought as to promote the agency and its capabilities.

Tourist season was at its peak and people filled Bonneville's visitor center, but when I sat down in the small theater to watch a film about the building of the dam and the taming of the river, I was alone. Even that dark room vibrated with the force of falling water and hummed with moving electrons as the film rolled, showing black-and-white pictures of the dam's construction and talking about the politics of the time. Controversy surrounded the dam even then, although very little of that controversy had anything to do with the environmental issues that now make dams so controversial. Instead, the debate focused mostly on whether the federal government or private businesses should develop and run the Columbia's hydropower projects. Critics of the government plan asked, "What will a region where nobody lives do with all that electricity?" The federal government didn't listen to its critics. By 1941, Grand Coulee, located on the Columbia near the Canadian border and still the nation's largest dam, joined Bonneville in generating power. Faced with more supply than demand, the government paid two hundred seventy dollars to Woody Guthrie, who spent thirty days touring the region and wrote twenty-six songs, including "Roll On, Columbia, Roll On," for a movie encouraging people to electrify their homes. The song is now Washington's official folk song, although now nobody needs encouragement to buy the cheap hydropower. The last image I saw in that theater was a leaping salmon. It lingered on the screen before fading out as the lights came on.

The movie never mentioned the fact that when the government built Bonneville Dam, nobody could say what it—or the other dams planned for the river and its tributaries—would do to salmon runs. Nobody even knew for certain if its fish ladder would work and without a working fish ladder, salmon couldn't bypass the dam. Bonneville was built anyway. A kayaking buddy of mine once relayed what a neighbor, an orchardist from the Yakima Valley, had told him. It's the kind of hearsay that would never be allowed in court. "If only," his neighbor had said, "if only they hadn't built a fish ladder at Bonneville Dam, then we wouldn't be having all these problems." He wished that salmon would have disappeared from the Columbia River and its tributaries and wished that the controversy over dams and salmon would go away.

A story that is part myth and part truth claims that the original plans for Bonneville Dam didn't call for a fish ladder. Omitting the ladder was never a serious consideration, although Grand Coulee doesn't have a fish ladder (some people say that for three or four summers after Grand Coulee was completed, salmon returning from the ocean hurled themselves again and again at the unyielding dam, futilely trying to make it back to their natal streams), and even as late as the 1970s the federal government built dams without fish ladders on salmon rivers feeding into the Columbia. Hatcheries were built instead. Technology would compensate, make up for our overfishing, for our poor irrigation practices, for our poor logging practices, for our poor mining practices, for our poor urban development practices, and of course, for our dams.

After the movie, I drifted into a room where I could watch fish. The room, it's called the fish viewing room, has a wall of glass windows providing a glimpse inside a section of a fish ladder. People packed the room, filled the long benches arranged like indoor bleachers that face the windows, or stood touching the glass, faces pressed close so they wouldn't miss a detail. Fat Chinook salmon, aluminum bright, flashed in the tumbling water. The corps reminded everyone it was a record year for returning Chinook, posted that information, written in bold, black letters on white sheets of paper, showing the number of fish that had passed over the previous day and also that had passed over the entire year. Throughout the spring and into the summer, some people had pointed to the record run as proof that there was no problem, that the river and the fish were fine, and that the changes we had brought to the river didn't matter.

Simple numbers don't explain what is happening. Once the Columbia was one of the greatest salmon rivers in the world—although those days were over even before the first big dams were built—and once all of its fish started their lives in the gravel of streams. Even in the 1940s and 1950s, only a small percentage of the river's salmon came from hatcheries.

I watched fish swim by, big fish, some maybe thirty pounds.

Already, they were starting to die. They had stopped eating after leaving the ocean, depending only on stored fat to propel them upriver to the streams of their birth. I tried to see which fish had their adipose fins, a small fin just in front of the tail. A clipped fin means they were hatchery fish. An unclipped fin doesn't mean anything since not all hatcheries remove it, especially those run by Indian tribes, which consider the practice mutilation. I wondered which fish were headed to the Idaho mountains, where I started my trip, and which were headed to other rivers.

Most would return not to a stream but to a concrete raceway and end their lives on silver steel tables at the hands of knife-wielding technicians, their eggs and milt mixed not in flowing water, but in buckets. In a strange twist, some salmon would end up in a stream after their deaths at the hatchery. Researchers have discovered that dozens of different creatures—from insects on up the food chain to bears—depend on salmon to sustain them, and without those fish, something goes wrong in the rivers. So now, government agencies take spawned out carcasses from hatcheries and throw them in streams, sometimes even dumping them from helicopters. We do the best we can to imitate the intricate connections of the real world. It costs billions of dollars. Fisheries biologist Jim Lichatowich once told me this about the money spent on salmon: "We converted something we were getting for free into something we are paying for."

A section of the viewing room away from the windows displayed black-and-white photos of Indians fishing for salmon from wooden platforms suspended over torrents of falling water. I imagined the platforms shaking from the cascade's force, imagined the constant roar, and a thousand miniature rainbows hanging in water droplets suspended in the moist air, a storm that never ended. All around the room, I saw salmon: salmon murals on the walls, salmon mounted and displayed in glass cases, salmon posters, and salmon photographs.

The viewing room reflects the Northwest, with its salmon

place-names—the Salmon River in Idaho, the Salmon River in Oregon, the Salmon River in California, the White Salmon River and, nearby, the Little White Salmon River in Washington—and its salmon images—on t-shirts, on the sides of buildings, on a highway overpass in The Dalles—those aluminum salmon forever swimming above the freeway, forever fresh in their metallic brightness, as if new from the sea. In some ways they are the salmon we long for, not just compatible with the dammed and industrial river, but a product of it. The river rolls and a turbine turns, electrons stream out along alloy wires to fire the scalding smelters of the aluminum plants, and from the plants come salmon. A hatchery fish is as close as we can come to one crafted from refined bauxite, maybe not a product of an imitation river, but at least a product of science and technology.

Some people say a salmon born in a hatchery and a salmon born in a river are just the same, that there is no way to tell them apart, and besides, what's wrong with using hatcheries to fill the rivers. I will not argue with them, but this is what I remember most from a July afternoon spent surrounded by other people watching fish at Bonneville Dam. The salmon swam up a concrete staircase instead of a mountain stream. A piece of glass separated us from the fish. We could not touch the water, or see the green of the trees, or smell the moss; there were no water-droplet rainbows in the air, only a dimly lit room that hummed with the force of falling water becoming electricity.

12

Used Up by the Wind

With Bonneville Dam behind me, I could imagine an end to my trip. After forty-three days with the river, the ocean finally seemed real. Seawater doesn't push far into the Columbia, but the tide causes the river to rise and fall as far upstream as Bonneville Dam. I camped a few miles below the dam on a wide sandbar along the Oregon side of the river. Trees and brush screened the freeway and railroad tracks from view and muffled at least some of the noise. Across the Columbia, the eroded basalt slab of Beacon Rock towered above the river like a shark fin jutting out of the ocean.

I had the river to myself when I went to sleep, but the next morning, a flotilla of small boats had anchored in front of my camp. It was well after sunrise, and I felt a little exposed as I went about the parts of my morning routine that required some privacy. The people were sturgeon fishing, so I suspect their attention wasn't focused on me. Still, I hurried to get on the water and away from the crowd. The anglers turned the river into a slalom course. I dodged boats and fishing lines and then a tug pushing a single barge as I picked my way downstream.

I assumed I would reach Portland easily that day, and planned to stay with a friend. Lewis and Clark had covered thirty miles a day along the same stretch of river as they pushed toward the ocean in the fall of 1805, and I saw no reason why I couldn't do the same. At that pace, the ocean was only five days away. I dallied though. I spent some time talking to biologists on a Washington Department of Fish and Wildlife boat monitoring the anglers and watched a woman battle a sturgeon.

As old as dinosaurs, sturgeon look vaguely shark-like with their broad pectoral fins and high dorsal fin, but they lack the mouthful of sharp teeth. Bottom-feeders, sturgeon find food hidden in river sediments by feeling with four barbells that hang from their mouths like the oversized whiskers of a thick, white mustache. They dig out meals using their shovel-shaped snouts, and suck food off the bottom with their siphon-like mouths. Sturgeon can live for a hundred years or more and might weigh a thousand pounds, although fish of that age and size now seem more like legend than reality. Like salmon and lamprey, sturgeon are anadromous. Unlike those fish, sturgeon can cross between fresh-and salt water almost at will.

Slow to mature and slow to reproduce, overfishing decimated the Columbia's sturgeon, but strict catch limits have now stabilized the population throughout most of the river. Above Bonneville, where carefully regulated fishing is allowed, the sturgeon population languishes, neither healthy nor on the edge of extirpation. Because of their great size, adult sturgeon cannot use the dams' fish ladders. The damming of the Columbia and the Snake has trapped sturgeon within individual dam pools, and the dams keep each pool's population isolated from the others, and from the ocean. Like salmon and lamprey, sturgeon need the Columbia to function naturally, and above Bonneville, the river doesn't. Below the last dam, where the Columbia again resembles a river and sturgeon can move freely to and from the ocean, anglers crowd the river to catch them.

With half the morning gone, I finally started downstream in earnest. But by then, my enthusiasm for paddling had faded. Below Umatilla, I had started taking fifteen- to twenty-minute naps after lunch. That day I paddled two hours, slept for an hour, then paddled another hour. I beached my kayak on an island near the Washington side of the river and took another nap. I had covered only half the distance I had anticipated. Feeling guilty for not pressing on, I studied my charts trying to delude myself that I might paddle some more that evening. Instead, I slept. I could see the Portland suburbs, but the city would remain a day away.

I had beached my kayak near a picnicking family—a man, his wife, two daughters, and the boyfriend of the oldest. Between naps, the man and the boyfriend came up to me. "Where are you headed?" the father asked.

I thought about lying, claiming I was just out for an overnight trip from Portland. "The ocean," I responded, and for the first time, my destination hadn't seemed improbable.

"Where did you start?" the father asked.

"In Idaho on the Salmon River." The answer brought only more questions I didn't feel like answering.

"How long has it taken you to get here?" the boyfriend asked.

"Forty-four days." The father made some comment comparing what I was doing to that television show Survivor. I wanted to say "this is real life not some fucking TV show," but I kept my mouth shut. I must have rolled my eyes or made some other gesture because the father said, "I guess you don't like that show." I didn't respond.

The family was perfectly nice and their questions perfectly natural. My rudeness revealed my fatigue, not just a physical exhaustion from fighting the previous week's gales, but also a mental fatigue from forcing myself onto the river at times when all I really wanted to do was hide from the wind. I was, for the first time since the start of the trip, a bit depressed and would struggle in the coming days to find the motivation to keep moving. The wind had used me up.

The men kept asking about the kayak and gear. I didn't want

to answer a bunch of questions, but I did. I opened the hatches to show where I carried supplies, demonstrated how my water filter worked when asked about drinking water, pulled out my bivy sack when asked about sleeping, my stove and fuel bottles and pots when asked about cooking. Eventually, the man and the boyfriend walked back to the rest of the family.

By evening, I was alone. The island was exposed to the river, but a little ways back from the shore, a cottonwood forest offered some privacy if I needed it. The interstate in Oregon was almost a mile away, and from across the river, the cars looked small and I could barely hear them. Toward dusk, the thin bands of clouds strung out in the sky turned red. For whatever reason, I hadn't noticed many sunsets on my trip. But the one that evening caught my attention. The sky softened as light bled out of the clouds, first in the east, then the west. Completely drained, the clouds turned a bruised purple and then black as darkness finally came. Headlights moved like ghosts along the freeway in Oregon. The lights from Portland and its suburbs blurred together. Channel markers flashed red and green, and a tug and its tow moved between them headed upstream. Finally, I went to sleep.

The day had already turned warm when I set off the next morning, July 11. With a light wind at my back, I made decent time. Near Portland, the Columbia River turns into a contradiction—in some spots wild, in others industrial, and in still others, domestic. The various uses we impose on the Columbia and its tributaries always leaves them in tension with our expectations, but near Portland those contradictions are stacked one atop the other in a way they are not in other places. Houses overlooked the river. Freeways and highways were unavoidable. Creeks where salmon spawn funnel rainstorm runoff from subdivisions and strip mall parking lots, while culverts carry other creeks, where salmon once spawned, beneath city streets. The Washington Cascades backdropped smoke from mill stacks in the towns of Washougal and Camas. On the Oregon side, herons fished and geese tended their nest within sight of working tugs. Near the cottonwood backwaters of the Sandy River's delta, metallic sounds of shipyard workers repairing dry-docked barges mixed with quacking ducks and honking geese. Beyond the wall of shoreline vegetation, high levees keep the river from spilling out of its banks and into tank farms and industrial buildings during spring floods.

Along the river's backwaters and side channels, I found a flotilla of homes. The houses didn't sit on well-manicured lawns beside quiet cul-de-sacs, but instead rested on floating pads, each attached to its neighbor, so they looked like a cross between a new subdivision and boats moored in a marina. Floating docks replaced sidewalks. Potted plants replaced trees and gardens. Hen mallards and their ducklings scrounged for food the same way squirrels cruise shore-bound yards hunting for bird feeders to raid. In one of the sloughs, an old tug with huge glass doors that opened onto a stern-deck hot tub sat moored at the edge of the floating suburbia's proper homes. Next to the tug, potted plants covered the decks of a refitted houseboat that no longer sailed. Like neighborhoods everywhere, the eclectic homes always wind up somehow relegated to the fringes.

In one of the neighborhoods, not far from downtown Portland, a restaurant floated among the one-and two-story houses and reworked boats. Large umbrellas shaded outside tables where people sat drinking beer and wine. I heard the clink of silverware against plates as I paddled by. A miniature tug pushed a miniature barge loaded with construction supplies to some floating renovation project. People chatted with one another on their docks. It felt like a community. Paddling through the rows of houses, I understood why people lived there, tucked into the quiet of the river away from the noise and human worries of the city.

In one of the older floating neighborhoods, a middle-aged woman loaded household items onto a small barge the same way the owner of a terrestrial home would load a U-Haul trailer. I thought she might be moving out, but she and her husband were just remodeling and needed to clear everything from their house before the contractors started work. I asked what it was like living in a floating house. "It's very peaceful here. It's its own world," she said. Of course living anyplace brings concerns. She complained about a neighbor with a run-down house. "He's supposed to be remodeling, but it's taken him three years," she said.

I asked about the new extensions that made the high pilings that kept the houses in place even higher. The woman said they were added after floods in 1996. The water almost pushed the houses over the tops of the old pilings, so afterward, communities either sunk new, higher pilings or extended existing ones to ensure everything stayed put.

Living in one of those floating communities requires a faith in average snowpacks and in the Corps of Engineers's ability to control the river that I lack. Without the levees and the dams and the government technocrats manipulating the Columbia's water levels, those floating houses couldn't exist. But it's not just the residents of those neighborhoods that demand flood control. Portland presses itself into its rivers' floodplains. Without the river system created over the last hundred or so years, floods might regularly inundate its industrial infrastructure, its airport, even its downtown of high-rise buildings. The same floods that almost set the floating houses free from their pilings also came close to spilling into downtown Portland.

The need for flood control is just one more demand imposed on a river system already straining under demands; those in need of flood control just one more constituency. We ask a lot from our rivers, and everyone in the Northwest demands something from the Columbia and its tributaries. The long line of river users makes taking any action that alters the status quo difficult, since any change affects some already established group that then fights to protect its interests.

Because the needs of some river users conflict with the needs of others, we seem unable to find a single vision for the river. We altered the Columbia and its tributaries over and over to suit our perceived needs at the time, and now we depend on the changed river for our livelihoods, but also imagine the river can be what it once was in some distant, romanticized past. The battle over breaching the Snake River dams is, in a way, a debate about all the changes we have made to the river over the years and a symptom of our conflicted desires. I suspect it will play itself out for many years. Although I would like to see the dams removed, I make no predictions about the outcome.

Back in Idaho, when my trip was still new, the assistant manager of the Pahsimeroi hatchery had, in response to a question, told me, "Salmon aren't the only species living in an altered environment. We are too. Maybe by learning to save the salmon, we are learning to save ourselves."

Instead of focusing on the politics of dams, the economics of dams, the scientific minutia detailing the interplay of salmon and dams, maybe we should remember how little we still know about the Columbia River, remember that just as the river itself is always in flux, our expectations and desires for the river have changed over time and will continue to change. Before I started my trip, I went to a panel discussion about the future of the Columbia's salmon. That spring, as the Northwest struggled with drought and, along with California, soaring electricity prices, the Columbia's mangers had decided to maximize the river's power-producing potential, regardless of what that meant for fish. One of the panel members, a forest service biologist if I remember correctly, wondered aloud if, in thirty or forty years, when he was an old man, he would still think electricity should have taken precedent over salmon. The benefits the Columbia Basin's dams provide to the region are clear and immediate. The benefits its salmon provide are difficult to quantify and long term. The power of the immediate continually holds sway along the Columbia.

I hope we might finally pick the long-term over the immediate, but there is no right answer. If we could hold a reasoned debate free from hyperbole and unrealistic expectations, it's possible we might, as much as I dislike the possibility, leave salmon to fend for themselves in an industrial river. Such a decision would hurt many people and would mean breaking many promises, especially those made to the region's Indians, so should not be made for simple expediency.

Sometimes people will charge that those advocating for dam removal and other changes care more about fish than people. That's not true, of course. The debate has always been about people, and over the years we have simply favored some groups and their needs while ignoring others. Giving equal consideration to fisherman and farmer, urban dweller and rural resident, American Indian and recent immigrant might alter the way we look at the river and make options that now seem unlikely more realistic.

We appear unwilling to make any actual decisions though. Instead, because of simple inaction, we seem destined to let salmon disappear, or perhaps become a remnant population that depends on hatcheries and barges so it can live on as a relic. If that happens, we will have missed a chance to learn how to resolve so many of the debates now plaguing our society that flair when science, economics, and the environment intersect with politics, culture, and emotion. We will have lost a chance to learn how to save ourselves.

Around Portland, I kept to the backwater sloughs trying to avoid the city's bustle as often and for as long as I could. But the city eventually became inescapable. I ate lunch on an island across from the Portland airport. The roar of passenger jets taking off and landing drowned out the songs of nesting birds. A downed cottonwood, broad as my back, its bark peeled away by time to reveal a smooth inner trunk, invited me to nap for awhile. I woke up as two fighter jets climbed off the runway with a roar louder than any passenger plane and banked west toward the ocean. Another pair, in close formation, followed. I watched until they vanished while I tried to shake off my nap so I could again paddle.

I had made arrangements with a friend who used to work with Juliet to meet me that afternoon at a kayak shop tucked away between boatyards, marinas, floating houses, expensive condominiums, and the big box stores built on an island so people who lived across the Columbia River in Washington, which has no state income tax, can shop easily in Oregon, which has no sales tax. The kayak shop's owners let me leave my boat and gear behind the store on their floating dock. A woman who worked at the shop and had paddled the lower Columbia many times went over my charts with me. Land along the lower river is a mix of private, state, and federal property. Some spots are open to the public and available for camping, many aren't. She pointed out landmarks, and I highlighted each potential stopping point on my charts. I was about ninety miles from Astoria, Oregon, and from there it was another fifteen miles or so to the ocean.

Throughout the trip, I had always said my destination was the ocean, but really, I needed to reach Astoria. The Pacific at the mouth of the Columbia is nasty ocean, so rough that the coast guard trains its search and rescue crews there in boats specifically designed to right themselves after a capsize. Once I made Astoria, I could decide if it was safe to push on to the ocean. The woman at the kayak shop confirmed that plan was the right one.

Portland was a blur. After forty-five days with the river, I wasn't used to the traffic, the noise, the people, or the tightly packed buildings. I took my first shower in two weeks at my friend's apartment. I shaved away my scruffy beard, and then showered again just because I could. I did my laundry and ate, devouring the fresh salad she had made. After dinner, we walked to a crowded café and ate dessert while a quartet played classical music. We stayed well past eleven o'clock, which felt very late to me.

While I was in Portland, I heard a news story about four fire-fighters killed by a wildfire in central Washington. Some of the fire crew was from Yakima, and if I had stayed at the Yakima paper, I probably would have worked on that story. I was glad I was on the river. I always hated dropping myself into other people's grief, even when the intrusion was legitimate, as it was in the case of that fire, where management mistakes had contributed to the firefighters' deaths.

The next morning I showered again and ate before a friend drove me back to the kayak shop. The wind was light, the sky cloudless, and maritime air coming off the Pacific kept the day comfortable. I unlocked my kayak from the shop's floating dock and slipped into the river. A wide channel divided the Oregon mainland from the island, and the island hid the river's main channel from view. Floating houses lined both sides of the island channel at first, but eventually they gave way to a thicket of trees and vines. It was like somebody had plunked down a wilderness on the edge of a major city.

When I finally cleared the island's downstream tip, I found not more wilderness but a giant seaport. The river bustled. A huge crane plucked corrugated metal containers from a green ship flying a German flag and stacked them one atop the other on a pier like some robot child playing with blocks. Eventually, the containers would go onto trucks or trains or barges to travel inland. The ship looked the way I expected a German ship to look: orderly, freshly painted, free of the rust stains that usually stripe oceangoing vessels. More ships waited to load or unload cargo at scores of other docks on the Oregon and Washington sides of the Columbia, and near downtown Portland on the Willamette River. Everywhere, cranes moved while trucks came and went.

In my kayak, I was like a minnow moving through pods of whales. A black Panamanian ship, not quite as orderly, not quite as neat as the German freighter, swung mid-river on its anchor chain, waiting its turn to load cargo bound for distant ports. One of the Panamanian freighter's crew pointed at me as I passed by. I saw the look of surprise on one man's face before he waved. Other anchored ships filled the river, some riding high and empty like the Panamanian freighter, some sitting heavy and full. Metal crew boats moved between them ferrying sailors between the ships and shore.

Tugs pushed single barges up and down the Columbia and Willamette, and on the Washington side, row after row of the squat black tugs with white cabins sat tethered by thick rope to heavy pilings waiting for the next trip upriver. On the back of one tug, five men sat talking. When they saw me, one yelled and waved me over. They asked where I was headed, where I had started, how long I had been on the river, and when I expected to finish. My trip apparently met with their approval.

I asked questions about the tug business. I wondered why, above Bonneville, I had seen tugs pushing four barges, but below the dam had seen most tugs pushing just one barge. They explained how on the lower river, the tows get broken up. Depending on its cargo, one barge might go up the Willamette, another to a port on the Washington side, still another somewhere farther downriver, and so on. I asked them about breaching the Snake dams, and all five said "no" almost in unison. "That would be our jobs," one of them said. If tugs couldn't run all the way to Lewiston, barging wouldn't be profitable, and a lot of tugboat crews would get laid off, he explained.

"Those dams are going to be there a long time, especially because we need the electricity," another said. "They aren't going anywhere in our lifetime."

Those men needed to believe that the dams would always be there. Snake River barges carry commodities brought by train or truck from as far away as the Midwest. If the Snake's dams were removed, it's possible trains and trucks might simply travel a little farther to some Columbia River port, and from there, the goods would still go the rest of the way downriver by barge. But with the dams gone, it's also possible the economics of shipping might change ever so subtly, letting other deep-water ports siphon away product once headed overseas through the lower Columbia.

"You want a pop?" one of the men asked before I headed

downstream. My kayak bobbed slightly from the wake of a passing boat, and I took a gentle paddle stroke or two to hold my position. The cold drink would have tasted good. Taking it might have given me the chance to sit on the back of the tug and talk with those men. I might have had the chance to explore the tug. When I think back on my trip, think about what I should have done different, my focus often falls on that moment. It was a generous offer, with meaning far beyond just a drink. They must have suspected that anyone who would kayak nine hundred miles wouldn't care for dams, might want to see them gone. They offered their time anyway, despite whatever differences of opinion might have existed. But I was so intent on making time downriver, so busy, with my trip almost over, sorting through what I had seen and trying to force meaning on those images, that I had said "no." It was a mistake. If I had taken the time to sit on the tug with the men, to ask about the details of their jobs and their lives on the river, and also about their families and their homes and what they wanted from the future, I would have learned more than I could have ever learned paddling through the day.

Downstream from the moored tugs, Portland and its seaport infrastructure finally faded. Mount Saint Helens's decapitated peak stood out against a cloudless sky. Osprey nests topped channel markers, and goldfinches bunched on the banks to drink. I stopped for lunch near what looked like the decayed hull of an old steamer. My charts marked a wreck at the spot. A bald eagle floating on afternoon thermals drifted closer and closer to an osprey nest near the steamer's remains. Finally the eagle crossed some invisible line that marked the edge of the ospreys' tolerance. One of the nesting birds swooped down like a fighter jet on a strafing run. The eagle turned a half-barrel roll and extended its talons for protection. The osprey peeled off at the last minute and gained altitude for another run at the eagle. The eagle changed its course and retreated from the nest.

The ocean was almost tangible. Ships hauling containerized cargo and cars sailed inland. Others carrying grain and lumber headed to sea. The ships were an unanticipated hazard. Their speed impressed me. Their silence scared me. I stayed as close to shore as possible, but sometimes the channel hugged the shore as well.

I didn't hear the ocean-bound freighter's metallic rumblings until it was almost even with my kayak. Water peeled around its bulbous bow in a white froth. Its black hull blotted out the sky when I looked over my shoulder. If I had been in the channel, I would have died. After the ship passed, I lied to myself by saying I that I had planned to stay as close to shore as I had been, unwilling to admit the danger I had just missed. I couldn't afford an incident like the one at the confluence of the Snake and Columbia, where a tourist boat had almost run me down. A ship can't turn from the narrow dredged channel, and traveling at fifteen knots, it would take at least a couple miles for it to stop. I would be crushed if I found myself in its path. I vowed caution, promised myself I would only cross the channel at right angles and only on straight sections that offered long views upstream and down.

When I camped in the evening, I pulled my kayak high on the beach so a ship's wake wouldn't wash it away and pitched my bivy well away from the river for the same reason. The river where I camped made a gentle right turn and as a tanker, the *Chevron Colorado*, passed, I realized that if some river pilot misjudged the turn, a ship might end up on the beach with me. I tried to put that thought out of my mind.

Great thickets of Himalayan blackberries grew along the edge of the cottonwoods behind my camp. The blackberries are weeds, and along with Scotch broom, create the same types of problems west of the Cascades that cheatgrass and the knapweeds do east of the mountains. At least blackberries taste good. July 12 was a little early to pick them. Most of the fruit hadn't ripened, but as I moved cautiously around the vines so none of their thorns would puncture my feet or hands, I found enough ripe berries to half fill a cooking pot. I carried them back to camp and ate them after dinner.

When I was in Portland, I could have eaten my fill of fresh fruit, or almost any food for that matter. On the river, the black-berries were a luxury. I ate them one at a time. I chewed them slowly and let the juice linger in my mouth. While I ate, I plot-ted routes to the ocean, watched ships traveling to and from distant ports, and calculated the number of days till my trip ended. When I finished the last berry, its soft sweet taste lingered in my mouth for a while, and after it faded, I went to sleep.

13

Looking Back at Cape Disappointment

Ocian in view! O! the joy. —William Clark, November 7, 1805

I lost the sun three days after leaving Portland. A drizzle that sometimes turned to a hard rain drifted down the forested ridges of the coastal mountains. The weather surprised me. I didn't have enough warm clothes—no paddle jacket to wear while kayaking and not enough polypro to wear both on the river and around camp. I had my rain jacket but worried that if I wore it while I kayaked, water dripping from my paddle would work its way past the wrist closures and down the inside of the sleeves, and that the jacket's bottom would hang over the kayak's edge, soaking up water. Wet on the inside, the rain jacket would be worthless on or off the river. If I'd been thinking before the trip, I would have asked Juliet to leave some of my warm clothes with our friend in Portland. Instead, I paddled in a cotton t-shirt, which trapped the day's dampness next to my skin, but kept me warm as long as I kept moving. When I stopped for lunch, I would put on my rain jacket and swing my arms in giant circles.

On July 15, a wet Sunday morning, I passed the towns of Longview, Washington, and Rainier, Oregon, where the Columbia changes its course from north to west. Even at eleven o'clock, Rainier looked asleep. No cars moved. Empty streets stretched away from the river past well-kept houses. The whirligigs of a traveling carnival sat motionless and devoid of people. An osprey in its nest atop a channel marker watched me pass. On the river, a few people fished for steelhead, and a floatplane practiced take-offs and landings.

The river broke into a maze of channels braided through with islands big and small as it broadened itself into an estuary. Tidal, washed by maritime squalls that don't have the energy to push beyond the coastal mountains, the Columbia in its last miles looks more like a patch of Pacific Ocean squeezed inland than a part of some great river system flowing down from high mountains in the continent's far interior. In places, marshy shoreline bordered the river, in places, high cliffs. Everywhere, something grew. Young trees sprang from dead logs. Ferns unfurled their leaves. Moss coated rocks. Hemlock and cedar and spruce and fir weaved themselves into the canopy of a coniferous jungle. The constant dampness, from the rain and the river, brought slow decay to everything.

The remains of the salmon fishing industry collapsed into the river. Inside a rotting building built where a slough and the main river connect, gill nets sat in neat piles as if somebody had put them away at the end of last year's fishing season expecting to use them again in a few months. Nobody had touched the nets in years and nobody would. Gill-net boats, in their idleness, had grown algae on their hulls.

I could have spent a month exploring the river's sloughs, but I also wanted the trip over. I hadn't come close to making the thirty miles a day I had planned. Once, when the wind blew as hard as it had in the Columbia's gorge, I covered only five miles. The main channel, with whatever danger its ship traffic presented, was usually the fastest way from point to point. So after I passed the collapsing net shed, I took to the main channel, aiming for an island formed from dredge spoils dumped by the Corps of Engineers in its efforts to keep the river navigable for oceangoing ships. It's a common camping island. Unnamed on my charts, I later learned that locals sometimes call it Dead Wild Pig Island. The way I heard the story, which may or may not be accurate, is that some years back, a man convinced people to invest a large sum of money in his plan to turn pigs loose on an island where they could run free and fatten themselves to market weight. The pigs then would be rounded up and sold at a tidy profit.

An island next to Dead Wild Pig was the planned location for the free-range pig scheme, and according to the story, the man who hatched the scheme claimed that after being turned out, the pigs mysteriously vanished or died. Of course nobody believed him. The investors lost their money, and people speculated the pigs had never existed. At first, Dead Wild Pig Island was referred to as "the island next to the island with the dead wild pigs," but after a while, people got tired of saying all that.

The island is low, overgrown with trees and brush, and at high tide, mostly under water. The high ground is at the island's downstream tip, and three kayakers had gotten there ahead of me and were already setting up camp. Their handmade, wooden kayaks resting on shore made my plastic boat look crude. They were the first kayakers I had seen on the river since I'd left Idaho. "Do you mind if I camp here with you?" I asked. I had gone two days without talking to another person.

Somebody laughed. Somebody else said, "Not at all."

"Well ya'll were here first so it seems like I should at least ask," I said.

"Where did you come from?" one of the men asked.

"I started out this morning upstream of Longview near the mouth of the Cowlitz. But originally I started at Redfish Lake in central Idaho."

All three of the men stopped fiddling with their stoves and tents and looked at me. I didn't like the attention.

"How long has it taken for you to make it this far?" one of them asked.

"This is day forty-nine."

An open-sided shack, something like a beach cabana made of plywood, two-by-fours, and blue plastic tarps offered a dry spot to change into the few warm clothes I had. The men I shared the island with were in their fifties and on the first night of a two-night trip. I marveled at all their gear, not just the warm and waterproof clothes I wished I had, but hand-held VHF radios and GPS units. At the time it seemed a little much. I had never made a big distinction between whitewater kayaking and sea kayaking, but these men, with their elegant boats and stores of equipment made the two activities seem very different. They harassed me about my lack of equipment, but when I learned none of them could roll a kayak, I gave them a hard time right back.

Because the men were close to home and on a short trip, they carried perishable food I couldn't. They shared chocolate and fresh fruit, and made enough stir fry filled with fresh vegetables to feed me too. "What's the most interesting thing you've seen on the trip?" someone asked over dinner.

I didn't answer right away. "I went through a lock on one of the Snake River dams with a smolt barge. That was pretty cool," I said.

"So they let you use the locks?"

"No. The corps was a pain in the ass," I said, before I went on a fifteen-minute rant about the agency. That pretty much stopped the questions.

It rained hard overnight, but my bivy sack kept me dry. The next morning, I huddled in the cabana while I ate my oatmeal. As I packed up to leave, one of the men asked if I had a place to stay in Astoria. "No, but I'll figure something out," I said. I was living day to day by then, not worrying about problems until they came up. The man, Dave, wrote his phone number down in my journal and told me I was welcome to stay with him. I started the morning paddling with the three men, but left them after we passed a high cliff that jutted into the river.

I followed the Washington shoreline, passing the town of

Cathlamet just before noon. Cathlamet on Monday looked as empty as Rainier had the day before. A forklift and stacks of the plastic baskets commercial fishermen use to sort their catch rested near a crumbling dock. A sign, bright with new paint, declared "Salmon for sale." I had no idea who it was aimed at. Moored tugs and barges lined the river. A cluster of cars sat near a bar with a neon Rainier Beer sign glowing in its window. I almost stopped to see if the place served lunch, but the morning was windless, and I wanted to cover as many miles as I could that day.

I should have stopped. Just past Cathlamet, the wind started and soon worked itself into a gale. Whitecaps broke over the kayak's bow. I struggled just to keep moving forward. I looked for whatever lee I could find; only a slough offered any relief. By then, it was almost two in the afternoon, and I had burned up breakfast. I needed to stop and eat. Spruce thickets blanketed both sides of the slough, leaving no place to beach a kayak. Besides, all the land was part of a national wildlife refuge, and signs every two or three hundred yards warned potential trespassers to keep off.

I found shelter at Skamokawa, where an outfitter ran kayak tours, a little store, and a restaurant. I changed into a dry shirt and went inside to eat. I had just started in on a chicken sandwich when a woman, maybe in her early thirties, blonde, and much too tan for somebody who lived in a place of perpetual drizzle, sat down across the table. She said her name was Ginni, that she was a guide and kayak instructor, and that her boss, who I had talked to when I left my kayak on his dock, had told her about my trip. She wanted to meet me and hear about the trip. Like all the other times I'd been asked to describe my trip, I didn't know how to respond. By then, it wasn't just that I couldn't summarize nine hundred miles of river. I had always pictured myself flowing downstream from the mountains like a drop of melted snow, but in the estuary, where the Pacific Ocean held sway through tides and weather, that image didn't work. The river was different; the way people depended on and used the river was different, and so I had to look at the Columbia in a way I hadn't before.

Besides, I was a little uncomfortable with the attention. I started asking Ginni questions at some point. She said in winter she led kayak trips in Baja, Mexico, which explained the suntan. I kept eating while we talked. I needed a weather report and information on what to expect from the river in its last miles, and Ginni offered to go over charts with me in her office after I finished lunch.

She already had a chart unrolled on the carpeted office floor when I showed up. A man's voice, flat and emotionless, droned out wind speeds and wave heights from a hand-held VHF radio. I wasn't sure I had the energy to fight the wind anymore that afternoon, wasn't certain I could make it safely through the breakers exploding over a shallow bar where the main river and Skamokawa Creek collided. I wanted to know my options. There was a campground along the creek if I didn't want to get back on the river, Ginni said. I listened to the flat radio voice hoping it would tell of better weather the next day, but the loop recording instead gave conditions sixty miles out at sea.

If I put back on the river, I could camp at Jim Crow Point. "It's about six miles from here," Ginni said tracing her finger along the chart. "Cliffs drop almost straight into the river and some odd eddies form along the shore. The main channel runs right along the cliffs. The channel markers are on the cliffs," she said. So along with strange currents, I might have to contend with ships. Ginni asked if I had a VHF radio. I said no. All that equipment no longer seemed like overkill. "The thing I love about kayaking," she said, "is that you're an island. You can carry everything that you need. I mean people have crossed oceans in kayaks."

The Columbia River forecast was worthless when it came. The wind blew three or four times the ten knots predicted for that afternoon, and the following day's forecast was no different from that day's and just as likely to be wrong. I thanked Ginni for her help but hadn't reached a decision when I left her office. I had to face the ships and strange currents and maybe even the wind and breaking waves at some point, and as much as I wanted to stop for the day, I felt the need to push on and bring the trip to an end even more.

I slid my kayak into the creek. I was worried in a way I hadn't been before. Waves frothed across the shoal. They blocked my view of the main river. Even after breaking, their energy made my kayak rise and fall in time with their rhythm. I moved slowly down the creek; the paddle blades hitting water brought hesitation instead of forward progress. I bobbed briefly in the relative calm of the channel, looking for a pause between sets of waves where I could break through. I found no pause. My only option—go hard.

I twisted my body forward, stuck the right paddle blade into the water, and when I felt it bite, unwound my body. I swung the paddle forward. The left blade went in. The right blade. The left blade. A wave broke over the kayak's bow. Water drenched me. I threw paddle strokes like a boxer throws jabs. The kayak kept its momentum. It punched through one wave then another and another with a seaworthiness that impressed me. The bow dipped deep into a wave trough, river water rolled across the deck, the kayak pitched, and then I was free of the bar. It wasn't calm. The wind still ripped the water's surface, but the waves were small enough they didn't scare me.

I turned the boat west. Beyond Skamokawa, the Washington shore curves inward as if it were sucking in its stomach. I stayed close to shore, and in the concave belly of the land found not only a lee but an ebbing tide I rode to the night's campsite.

From Jim Crow Point, I saw the end of my trip. The high bridge that ties Oregon to Washington at Astoria faded in and out of view as squalls came and went. The wide spread of Cathlamet Bay and Grays Bay made the Columbia look more like ocean than river, and I understood how in November 1805, camped not far from where I was camped, William Clark might have thought he saw the Pacific.

Another blue-tarped fishing shack sheltered me from the weather that evening. I stored my pots, my water bottles and filter, and my stove on some shelves and spread my green plastic tarp on the floor so I had a sand-free spot to sit. On the shack's inside wall, imitating what Clark carved on a tree after he had actually reached the ocean, I wrote: "7/16/01 From Redfish Lake, Idaho by kayak," in pen and signed my name. It was my fiftieth day on the river.

The upriver wind collided with the jutting cliff face of Jim Crow Point to form a strong updraft. Sometimes two or three adult eagles rode the updraft, white heads constantly facing into the wind, stiff wings almost touching. Sometimes a single juvenile, plumage still a golden brown, took advantage of it. The eagles tilted their wings to dive or climb, peeled off the wind and circled around for another ride, and screeched calls that seemed half laugh, half cry. While I cooked and ate dinner, I frequently looked outside to make sure eagles still hovered above my camp.

To sleep, I tucked my bivy sack among the drifted logs scattered along the shore. Overnight, the drizzle again turned to a hard rain, waking me as it splattered on the bivy, but by morning the rain was finished, the drizzle back. A pair of eagles hovered above Jim Crow Point. A ship carrying new cars from Japan passed by on its way upriver. Another ship taking wheat to Asia passed by on its way to the ocean. A dredge sucked sand from the ship channel and spit it out of pipes onto a spoil island where yellow Cats pushed it into smooth mounds.

After a final oatmeal breakfast in the dry of the shack, I packed my kayak for the last time. The bivy sack went in wet. The clothes I had worn on the river the previous day went in wet. I kept on dry clothes I normally would have saved to wear around camp in the evening. I knew I would sleep inside somewhere that night.

An old cannery rested beside the river just downstream from Jim Crow Point. It looked like an artifact from some long-vanished culture. Like the other salmon ruins I had seen, the cannery was collapsing back into the river; windows broken out, boards rotting. Inside, I could see the old nets piled on the floor. On a sign fronting the river, the faded image of a stylized salmon jumped clear of the water above the word "Salmon" like some red aquatic ghost. The Columbia's first cannery opened in 1866, and within a few years, thirty-nine operated along the river, packing not some expensive delicacy, but food for American and English factory workers. The salmon industry collapsed because of its own waste and because of what people did to the river and its tributaries. Later, I learned the cannery is the last one standing on the Washington side of the river.

I wanted to go inside the old cannery and explore, play archeologist in its ruins, but "No Trespassing" signs stopped me. I moved on, passed a high column of basalt called Pillar Rock that looks like a miniature hoodoo dropped a thousand yards out in the Columbia, crossed the channel when I had a break in ship traffic, and set out for a channel separating two low islands.

The collision of ocean and river concentrated life. Ducks and geese came and went. Gulls and terns screeched. Cormorants dove beneath the water to fish; blue herons stalked the shallows; ospreys tended their nests; a dozen eagles perched in snags or scavenged along island beaches. The channel grew so shallow I touched bottom when I paddled. As I cleared the islands, the water again deepened, the river opened up, and I found myself a long way from any lee as a midday wind that became an annoyance, but never slowed me, started. A slight chop roiled the water. Something that looked like a glass ball bobbed between waves, and I changed course to pick it up. As I neared, I saw eyes, a nose, whiskers, and realized it was a seal. I hadn't expected seals. When I finally reached Astoria that afternoon, I paddled by the town's wharves while a dark seal shadow crossed back and forth under the kayak, keeping perfect time with me.

In what looked like a sketchy neighborhood, I beached my kayak at an old boat ramp and phoned Dave. He drove the typical kayaker's truck, an extended cab with a camper shell over the bed.

He ferried me around town in that truck for the four days I stayed with him, always introducing me to people on the street and in the town's stores and restaurants by saying, "Mike here kayaked from Redfish Lake in Idaho all the way to Astoria." Dave was a retired chemistry professor who had taught at the local community college, and everywhere we went, he ran into somebody he knew. He told me he once went through the Astoria phone book and counted up the names of all the people he knew well enough to say "hello" to. He came up with a thousand names, roughly ten percent of the town's population.

I had done nothing to deserve Dave's hospitality. One morning, he woke up ridiculously early to drive me to the town's marina where a charter boat took me and five other people out into the ocean to fish for salmon. Traveling for so long with the river and its salmon, it had become important to actually catch one after my trip ended. The day was windless and an early morning fog kept the high headlands of the Oregon coast from view. Five-and ten-pound coho hit the trolled baits with the ferocity of creatures eating a last meal before a long, and ultimately fatal, fast. Everybody quickly caught their limit of two fish.

Back at the dock in Astoria earlier than planned, I had to wait for Dave to pick me up. On a typically wet, midsummer day, the Swedish, Norwegian, Danish, and Finnish flags hung limp from their poles outside a building that housed the marina office, a local environmental group, and the river's fishermen's union. Gary Soderstrom headed the Columbia River Fishermen's Protective Union. He had white hair, a white beard, and sort of looked like a young Santa Claus, if Santa in his younger days had been strong enough to bench press a small pickup truck. "When I was a kid, this was all net racks and canneries," he said pointing with a big, open hand toward rows of sport-fishing and sailboats docked at the marina. The few gill-net boats moored on the marina's fringe were the remnants of an Astoria where salmon once ruled, of a time when instead of nice restaurants and museums for tourists, riverside buildings housed net-makers and fish-packers and twelve hundred women who worked in the canneries. "It was our lifestyle," he said, the comment an unexpected repetition of what people upriver often say about farming and ranching.

Soderstrom was forty-nine and had started commercial clamming at twelve, salmon fishing at fifteen. "In the 1980s, we were making good money, now we're down to eking out a living between my wife and myself. She works and I fish." He said his family had fished the lower Columbia since the 1870s. He often talked in the past tense, as if the fishing were over. "Fishing was a chance for people to make a good living. It was the American dream. You went out and you worked hard and you also provided good quality food," he said. Soderstrom mentioned his son briefly. "My son can't feed his family on fishing."

On the lower river, commercial fishing for summer Chinook ended in 1965 and for most spring Chinook in 1977. Sockeye fishing stopped in 1989, but there had only been five seasons between 1973 and 1988 anyway. "There are runs we haven't fished since the '60s and they're still going downhill," Soderstrom said. The salmon seasons now last at most a few weeks each year and target salmon from the Columbia's few non-threatened runs or hatchery fish released into the lower river's bays. The young salmon imprint on the bays and after leaving the ocean, return there, and instead of ascending some tributary to spawn, mill about waiting to be caught in the terminal areas. "I don't like fishing the terminal areas," Soderstrom said. Lower river towns like Astoria, Clatskanie, Cathlamet, and Ilwaco subsist now mostly on trawling for ground fish, crabbing, and tourism, he said. "Tourism is shit jobs; it's poverty jobs. We hate to be tourist attractions." There was a controlled anger in his words.

The Snake and Columbia dams ended commercial salmon fishing, Soderstrom told me. "When they built the dams, they knew the fish were dying out," he said. I didn't ask who *they* were. What the dams brought to most of the region, cheap electricity and inexpensive water access to global markets, has meant little to the communities near the mouth of the Columbia, Soderstrom said. "You killed the lower river economy. We've always been the ones first in line to take the hit, not the dams." What the people who lived inland feared losing if the Snake River dams were removed—their livelihood and way of life—the people along the lower Columbia had already lost.

Astoria is still a fishing town, but now it's a fishing town where the fishermen are disappearing. My first night there, Dave and his girlfriend served a dinner of Chinook, troll-caught from the ocean. In a fishing town, it turns out how and where a fish was caught is as important as the kind of fish. After dinner, Dave and I sat down to plan my paddle to the ocean. We looked at a weather report, which appeared good, and then at the tides. I didn't like the idea of paddling against an incoming tide, but it offered my best chance for calm seas. On the ebb, the outgoing water pushes against swells rolling across the Columbia's deadly bar, making the waves bigger, steeper, and more dangerous. Dave ran a computer program that simulated how water moved in the river with the changing tides, and it showed the eddy that would form in Youngs Bay. Just as a river's eddies flow back upstream, the tidal eddy would swirl against the incoming current and push me toward the ocean. We timed my departure the next morning so I would catch the eddy at its strongest.

The final day of my trip was an obligation. It felt like the trip had ended when I reached Astoria, but I still had to paddle those last miles to the ocean. On July 18, Dave drove me to Astoria's maritime museum. From the museum's floating dock, I slid my kayak into the Columbia River for the last time. It was six thirty in the morning. Fog obscured everything. I secured a backpacking compass beneath the kayak's front bungee cords so I could keep my heading even if I lost sight of land. I left my camping gear behind, carrying only a break-down paddle, enough food for a snack, and the EPIRB transmitter and rain jacket I had wanted to abandon in Idaho fifty-two days earlier. The kayak was light and fast and jumped forward with each paddle stroke. I cruised easily over the flooding tide, passing trawlers tied at riverside docks unloading the catch from their last trip or loading supplies for their next. Swells rolled gently under the kayak as I slipped past the high bridge that spans the Columbia at Astoria. I hoped the weather forecast was accurate and the river's mouth calm.

I crossed Youngs Bay, and as Astoria dropped into the fog, the far shoreline came into view. I felt the force of the eddy start to push me seaward. Clear of the bay, I hung close to the Oregon shore, avoiding the shipping channel and the shallow Desdemona Sands. When I finally reached the river's mouth, a white fringe of waves pressing across a shoal blocked my path to the ocean. It started to drizzle. I beached my kayak to study my charts. When I started the trip, I could only imagine the ocean; at the trip's end, watching breakers foam on a cool and overcast day, Redfish Lake and the Salmon River felt like only vague memories.

The flooding tide still had about three hours left to run. I could make it to the ocean before the tide turned without rushing, but I didn't have a lot of time to waste either. I went through my charts plotting the safest, instead of fastest, course. The crashing waves that had forced me to beach my kayak rolled over a shoal off the Clatsop Spit where in places the water was just three feet deep. The charts showed two shipwrecks on the shoal, and I didn't need any more convincing to find another path to the ocean. I needed to cross over to the river's north side.

I finished my snack, launched my kayak, pointed the bow toward the high roll of Cape Disappointment on the Washington coast, and moved cautiously toward the channel. An outbound ship crossed my path, but I saw no others. Ocean swells spun from winds far out in the Pacific surged beneath the kayak and I felt I was already in the ocean, although the charts showed the river stretched for another four miles. Even in its final miles, the Columbia is not allowed its freedom. A series of rock jetties extends into the ocean to stabilize the river's bar, and river mile zero lies past any land. The engineering has not made the river's mouth entirely safe, and rescues are frequent, deaths not uncommon.

Metal-hulled trawlers, crabbers with pots stacked on their decks, and sport fishermen bristling with rods plowed back and forth between river and ocean. An orange coast guard helicopter buzzed overhead. A small coast guard boat raced across the offshore horizon. I expected the coast guard boat to pull up beside me, ask what I was doing, and then despite the calm, warn me of the bar's dangers and tell me to go back to shore. It didn't.

The pelagic invaded the river and made it scream with life. Gulls and terns filled the air. Rafts of common murres dotted the water. Some of the duck-sized, black-and-white seabirds bobbed over the swells, some dove deep into the water, while others surfaced with beaks stuffed full with small fish. There were so many murres I couldn't avoid them, and as I passed through the rafts, murres crash dived trying to escape or skittered away, never quite taking flight. An oily slick sheened the water, and I wanted to believe that unseen below, massive Chinook and silvery coho indulged themselves in one last meal before leaving the ocean.

I paddled west into a blank horizon. After nine hundred miles in a kayak, I was at last poised between river and ocean. In that swirl of currents, the freshwater that had flowed down from the mountains mingled with salt water flooding from the ocean, salmon smolt flushed into the sea, mature Chinook and coho and maybe a straggling sockeye bound for Redfish Lake pushed into the river. I looked ahead at open ocean, then back at Cape Disappointment before I let the flooding tide carry me into the river.

Selected Sources

Allen, John E., and Marjorie Burns. *Cataclysms on the Columbia: A Layman's Guide to the Features Produced by the Catastrophic Bretz Floods in the Pacific Northwest.* Portland OR: Timber Press, 1999.

Alt, David, and Donald W. Hyndman. *Roadside Geology of Idaho.* Missoula MT: Mountain Press Publishing Company, 1989.

Ambrose, Stephen E. *Undaunted Courage: Meriwether Lewis, Thomas Jefferson, and the Opening of the American West.* New York: Touchstone, 1996.

Carrey, John, and Cort Conley. *River of No Return.* Cambridge ID: Backeddy Books, 1978.

Clark, Robert. *River of the West: A Chronicle of the Columbia.* New York: Picador, 1995.

Cone, Joseph, and Sandy Ridlington, eds. *The Northwest Salmon Crisis: A Documentary History.* Corvallis: Oregon State University Press, 1999.

Cutright, Paul R. *Lewis and Clark: Pioneering Naturalists.* Lincoln: University of Nebraska Press, 1969.

DeVoto, Bernard, ed. *The Journals of Lewis and Clark.* New York: Houghton Mifflin Co., 1981.

Horton, L. E. "Catalog of Vascular Plants of the Lower Salmon River, From North Fork, Idaho, to the Mouth (Including Notes on Abundance and Distribution)." USDA—Forest Service—Intermountain Region, Division of Range Management, September 1972.

Hunn, Eugene S. *Nch'i-Wána, "The Big River": Mid-Columbia Indians and Their Land.* Seattle: University of Washington Press, 1990.

King, Scott N. "The Effective Discharge Concept in Gravel-Bed Stream Restoration: The Twelve Mile Reach of the Salmon River at Challis." Master's thesis, University of Idaho, 2002.

Landeen, Dan, and Allen Pinkham. *Salmon and His People: Fish and Fishing in Nez Perce Culture.* Lewiston ID: Confluence Press, 1999.

Lee, Mike. "Salmon: Plight sparks activism." *Tri-City (WA) Herald.* October 1, 2000, special report, p. 16.

Leopold, Luna B. *A View of the River.* Cambridge: Harvard University Press, 1994.

Lichatowich, Jim. *Salmon Without Rivers: A History of the Pacific Salmon Crisis.* Washington DC: Island Press, 1999.

Love, Malcolm R. *The Chemical Biology of Fishes, With a Key to the Chemical Literature*. London, England: Academic Press, 1970.

Matthews, Gene M., and Robin S. Waples. "Status Review for Snake River Spring and Summer Chinook Salmon." U.S. Department of Commerce, NOAA Tech Memo. NMFS F/NWC-200, June 1991.

McClure, Michelle M., Elizabeth E. Holmes, Beth L. Sanderson, and Chris E. Jordan. "A Large-Scale, Multispecies Status Assessment: Anadromous Salmonids in the Columbia River Basin," *Ecological Applications* 13, no. 4, (August 2003): 964–89.

Peterson, Keith C. *River of Life, Channel of Death: Fish and Dams on the Lower Snake River*. Corvallis: Oregon State University Press, 1995.

Reichert, Bruce. *River of No Return: Idaho's Scenic Salmon*. VHS. Directed by Pat Metzler. Boise: Idaho Public Television, 2001.

Rieffenberger, Betsy. "Draft: Moose Creek Watershed Analysis—Current Conditions." U.S. Forest Service, Salmon-Challis National Forest, 1999.

Roberge, Earl. "Dissecting the Rand Report." *Wheat Life* 45, no. 11, (December 2002): 12–15.

Thompson, David. *Columbia Journals*. ed. Barbara Belyea. Seattle: University of Washington Press, 1994.

Waples, Robin S., et al. "Population Genetic Structure and Life History Variability in *Oncorhynchus nerka* from the Snake River Basin." Final report, DOE/BP-05326–1. Portland OR: Bonneville Power Administration, May 1997.

Waples, Robin S., and Orlay W. Johnson. "Status Review for Snake River Sockeye Salmon" U.S. Department of Commerce, NOAA Tech Memo. NMFS-F/NWC 195, April 1991.

Washington Department of Fish and Wildlife and Oregon Department of Fish and Wildlife. "Status Report: Columbia River Fish Runs and Fisheries, 1938-2000." July 2002.

Weis, Paul, and William L. Newman. *The Channeled Scablands of Eastern Washington: The Geologic Story of the Spokane Floods*, 2nd ed. Cheney: Eastern Washington University Press, 1999.

Whitson, Tom D., ed. *Weeds of the West*, 9th ed. Newark CA: Western Society of Weed Science, 2000.

Williams, J. G., S. G. Smith, R. W. Zabel, W. D. Muir, M. D. Scheuerell, B. P. Sandford, D. M. Marsh, R. A. McNatt, and S. Achord. "Effects of the federal Columbia River power system on salmonid populations." U.S. Department of Commerce, NOAA Tech Memo. NMFS-NWFSC-63, February 2005.